Your Success

Research: James Miller, Helen Sykes, Melanie Jarvis-Vaughan, Peter Guthridge, Mark Gregory and Shawn Willis

Edited By Kizzi Nkwocha (c)

Published by Mithra Publishing 2014

Sponsored by The SME Shop. Visit the shop at www.thesmeshop.com

www.mithrapublishing.com

Also by Mithra Publishing

Escape Your 9-5 And Do Something Amazing
Customer Service
SocMed: Social Media For Business
How To Start A Business With Little Or No Cash
Facebook For Business
Social Media Marketing: Write Up your Tweet
Getting Your Business LinkedIn
It's That Easy! Online Marketing 3.0
Business, Business, Business!
Mind Your Own Business
Insiders Know-how: Running A PR Agency
Insiders Know-how: Caring For Your Horse
Energy Efficiency
Social PR

Visit us at www.mithrapublishing.com

The secret of success? Don't be afraid to fail. And when you're convinced you're going through Hell, keep going.
-    Kizzi Nkwocha

"My biggest motivation? Just to keep challenging myself. I see life almost like one long University education that I never had — everyday I'm learning something new."
- Richard Branson

"Every time you state what you want or believe, you're the first to hear it. It's a message to both you and others about what you think is possible. Don't put a ceiling on yourself."
- Oprah Winfrey

"One of the huge mistakes people make is that they try to force an interest on themselves. You don't choose your passions; your passions choose you."
- Jeff Bezos

The Inspiring thought leaders who contributed to this book:

Tony Marren

Dr. Froswa' Booker-Drew

Barbara Archer

Maxine Stead

Clare Mann

Rebecca Fredericks

Simone Vincenzi

Jill McCulloch

Nick Terrone

Amanda Campbell

Corina Lorenzi

Dr Gemma Russell

Leanne Donoghue-Tamplin

Ruth King

Shani Shaker

Martine Barclay

Claire Mitchell

Marie Bean

Deborah Ogden

Alex Couley

Jennifer Martin

Sarah Cannata

Your Success is sponsored by The SME Shop. The one stop shop for entrepreneurs and business managers.
Visit the Shop At www.Thesmeshop.com

About Kizzi Nkwocha

Kizzi Nkwocha made his mark in the UK as publicist, journalist and social media pioneer.

As a widely respected and successful media consultant Nkwocha has represented a diverse range of clients including the King of Uganda, mistresses of President Clinton, Amnesty International, Pakistani cricket captain Wasim Akram, campaign group Jubilee 2000, Dragons Den businessman, Levi Roots and world record teenage sailor, Michael Perham.

Nkwocha has also become a well-known personality on both radio and television. He has been the focus of a Channel 4 documentary on publicity and has hosted his own talk show, London Line, on Sky TV.

He also co-presented a weekly current affairs program in Spain on Radio Onda Cero International and both radio and TV shows in Cyprus.

His books have included the fiction novel, Heavens Fire, the business guide books: Business, Business, Business!, Mind Your Own Business, Insiders Know-How: Public Relations and the international bestseller SocMed: Social Media For Business.

Nkwocha publishes the online marketing magazines, Social Biz Magazine (www.socialbizmagazine.com), My Logistics Magazine (www.mylogisticsmagazine.com) and Wellbeing Magazine (www.mywellbeingmagazine.com).

He also runs a successful agency called Social Biz Training which trains people to use social media for business. His agency site is at www.socialbiztraining.com

Follow Kizzi on Twitter: https://twitter.com/kizzinkwocha
Read his business blogs at: www.threeminutemasterclass.com

Foreword

Before I begin I strongly believe a vote of thanks is in order to Sonja Levy at My Well-Being Magazine.com for extending to me an opportunity to contribute to this effort.

I have spent several years of reading a myriad of secondary research on the concept of Success and what being Successful is all about. I turn 58 years old on December 13th 2014. My frame of reference runs a gamut of ideas. As such I am choosing to narrow the concepts so anyone reading this will not get lost in a wide range of issues.

I take this opportunity to dedicate this effort to Shannon Rafferty of Orem, Utah. He passed away earlier this year. Shannon was one of those individuals who inspired, motivated, and gave support to quite a few people. I am a better man for being able to sit with him while I was at Orem Assisted Care Center to recuperate from stage three moderate colon cancer surgery.

I graduated from Brigham Young University in Provo, Utah December, 1987. BYU was one of those places with many dynamics evolving at once in my life. LDS Church nuances denote that after missionary service an individual should be proactively searching for someone to marry. BYU on a temporal level was a university that had many hoops to jump. A person not skilled in "reading" the "rules of engagement" can easily get derailed. There were three professors who were easily revered as mentors; Donald Cannon of the Religion Department, Merrill Frost of the Communications Speech Rhetoric major, and John Maestas who taught many entry level classes. These three individuals were men who left impressions on me. There were other instructors who gave me a lot of "food for thought" to pursue a degree and not quit. These three mentioned above I will always remember as truly gifted scholars.

My older sister Joanne was always an amazing example in my life of "doing what it took" to attain results. When I was born Joanne assisted my Mother in raising me for the first few years of my Life. Joanne was a major reason the Marren family did not implode emotionally after my Dad died in August 1970.

I could sit here and ramble through quite a few scenarios of my Life. Frankly this would destroy the fabric that constitutes the chapter I was invited to contribute. I invite you to approach this with an open mind and regard this as a subjective oriented offering that should be viewed as part of the calculus of the equation in building a philosophy of success in your future. I endured many "speed bumps" on my Journey. I desire that you glean whatever you deem as necessary, needful, or important to get ahead honorably in Life. I never did live Life on the level of "sticking it to the Man". I figure to resort to such a level of thinking is grounds for how karma operates; "What goes around comes around". As such I choose in to "shoot straight" and let results pan out.

Enjoy this book. Take whatever is worth it to you and then pay it forward. I believe the ills of humanity WILL be alleviated as we all pitch in and proactively initiate change one day at a time and one individual at a clip. Namaste!

Tony Marren
Provo, Utah USA
November 29th, 2014

The Process Of Success

What is Success?

Success in its various forms may be one of the most desired goals or outcomes. We are constantly surrounded by representations of the meaning of success, in the media from our sporting superstars, business tycoons or the lavish lifestyles of the rich and famous. Success as a concept is difficult to define. In its application, it is difficult to determine the process to achieve success, or to be successful. For many people the idea of success can dictate how they plan and live their life, from how they define their self worth and value, role in society, future dreams, and aspirations (Frankl, 2000).

In considering the real meaning of success and the influence of differing generational, gender and socio-political expectations, let us consider the stories of three remarkable Australians.

> *Pamela is a woman from the generation of 'Baby Boomers', the prosperous decade following World War II (aged between 47 and 65). This was a generation that expected the world to improve, that challenged the definition of traditional values, with increasing access to education, consumerism and subsequent affluence (Owram, 1997). Pamela was no different, while as a child she was not aware of the implicit messages of her generation, but she saw those with affluence, the nouveau riche, as happy with social capital. She equated the meaning of success to having money, friends, and material possessions.*

> *Pamela's parents were from the 'Greatest Generation' and believed in the value and power of education. They reinforced the idea that 'if you did your best, you could succeed'. It is likely that education was viewed as a tool to advance, as many people of the Great Generation were not able to complete their education, due to the impact of the war. As such Pamela's parents made financial sacrifices to enable Pamela and her siblings the opportunity to attend private school education. Despite the increasing access to education, the traditional roles of men and women were still a large part of the social construction of identity, gender roles and society. This meant*

for Pamela that success in the professional domain entailed a career as either a nurse or a teacher. Pamela became a nurse and flourished in the medical environment, viewing continued education as a method to obtain social connections and the affluence that she connected with success and happiness. As a consequence of her professional achievement, Pamela felt good about herself, a feeling of self worth that she also equated to success. Pamela had great plans. As a young adult she was prosperous in many domains of her life, from education, career and relationships.

Pamela like many from her generation likened the idea of being successful as 'having the whole package'. This meant a career, social capital, but also marriage and children. With this came the starry-eyed idea that if Pamela could find an intelligent, good looking, well connected man, who would love her for who she was, then she could achieve anything and be successful. While success started out for Pamela as achieving a career, it became something so much more, it meant being loved and belonging.

Now many years on, Pamela reflects with wisdom about the many guises of success. She now views success as much simpler, and that rather than success a prerequisite of happiness, happiness in and of itself is success. This means every moment from a single interaction, to caring and connecting with other people, to enjoying nature, the written word, music, family, and being healthy. While Pamela may have once been concerned about whether others saw her as successful, she realizes now that success is looking beyond material things, and instead it includes accepting and challenging herself to be the very best she can be.

Don is a gentleman, facing his 91st year of life. He is part of a generation termed the 'Greatest Generation', as men and women of this era are considered to have fought and given their lives in World War II, "not for the fame and recognition but rather because it was the right thing to do" (Brokaw, 1998). In some way Don's life encapsulates the very essence of the Greatest Generation. Don was a young man who grew up through the Great Depression and joined the Australian Navy *as a seaman at barely 18 years old, serving in total 20 years for his country. He fought in WWII aboard the corvette HMAS Castlemaine and witnessed not only the loss of thousands of lives, but the atrocities of war. Don's family originated from rural Victoria and after the war Don returned to his landlocked community to work on the farm. Don outlived his late wife, but they enjoyed a long marriage of over 50 years, with 4 children, 13 grandchildren and 4 great-grandchildren. Don's connection and ability to relate to people of all ages is evident when you see him playing with his great-grandchildren.*

Don is heavily involved in the community, for which he was awarded the title of Citizen of the Year in 2003 for the Campaspe Shire of Victoria. Major Councilor John Elborough described Don's investment in the community as "tireless", where despite his busy schedule he volunteers his time generously. He is a member of various community committees and trusts, president of the R.S.L, and you will find him visiting local schools to share his experiences, to cooking three course dinners and bringing it around to the homes of those who are restricted in their independence due to their health.

Don is now a man of the minority, with people over the age of 85 making up 1.8% of the Australian population, with even fewer in this age group of men compared to women over the age of 90 (29% men vs. 71% women) (2011 Australian Census). Unlike many men of his age, Don continues to be able to drive out to the farm each day and nothing stops him from being able to complete the often long and strenuous demands of farm life. To add to Don's long list of accomplishments, he has written three books and is currently writing an autobiography of his life. Don's life provides a unique insight into what motivates or drives a person. It is difficult to identify what makes Don successful, and though his list of accomplishments are indeed honorable, he seems to be held in high regard because of his character and values. While success (however you define it) may be important, my impression from talking to those who know Don, is that it is not success that motivates Don, even though someone of his statue would be held up by many as an incredible man, if not a hero.

Gail Kelly, or perhaps more widely recognized in the corporate world, as former CEO of Westpac. Gail is a woman from the generation of "baby boomers" who epitomizes societies' ideals of success, based on socially constructed ideas of wealth, knowledge, power, and social status. However Gail's success and ability to rise as high as she did in her career is based on something much more. Originally born in South Africa, she later immigrated to Australia in 1997 with her husband. Gail began her professional career as a teacher in Johannesburg, South Africa. Upon realizing that she did not have her heart in teaching, she made a decision to pursue a job as a bank teller at Nedcor bank. Early on Gail was identified as an asset to the bank and she was fast-tracked through an accelerated training program. Within six years she had begun a Master of Business Administration whilst pregnant with her first child, graduating 1 year later with a distinction. Three years later, she was appointed head of human resources at Nedcor bank, only five months after the birth of her triplets. Despite having four children under 10, she held successfully a number of general manager positions at Nedcor before moving to Australia.

Between 1997 and 2014, Gail Kelly held general manager or CEO positions at three major Australian banks, with the Australian Banking and Finance magazine awarding her Best Financial Service Executive in 2003 and 2004. In light of her success in the banking sector and ability to increase the bank's profitability she was ranked by Forbes as one of the most powerful women in the world, holding a top ranking of 8th in the world in 2010. Gail recently remarked in her speech at the St George Foundation in August 2014 that she has not been immune to lapses in self-confidence, at times revealing the impact of the threat of failure, and not being good enough. Gail however has not let limiting beliefs hold her back and instead she sought out the support of those around her. Whilst Gail perhaps seems to have it all, a highly successful career, a supportive husband and family, this has not happened by chance. Gail first and foremost has worked extremely hard and attributes her success to seven key life lessons; (1) choose to be positive, (2) do what you love, and love what you do, (3) be courageous and embrace opportunities or challenges, (4) ensure that your team is made up of the right people, (5) nurture the ability to communicate your vision and purpose, (6) practice generosity of spirit, and (7) live a meaningful life.

The Social Construction of Success

To consider formalized definitions of success, the Oxford Dictionary defines success as "an accomplishment of an aim or purpose" or more specifically "the attainment of fame, wealth, or social status". Whereas the success of the three remarkable Australians described above is not found in their accomplishments, but in their character.

Therefore we might conclude that in simple terms, 'success' is merely the outcome of achieving a goal, but that to be 'successful', this is a far more complex state of being.

We are born into a culture and a society that is constructed by social norms and expectations. It is these unwritten, invisible rules that originally guide us during our development as to what is important and what is less important. Common examples in Westernized society include the importance of being educated, getting married, and having children as benchmarks of success. Conversely ideals in other societies are not always the same, for example traditional Aboriginal life is more focused on the family unit and wider community, about connections, wellbeing, and living one with the land.

It seems that the benchmarks of success change from culture to culture, but also generation to generation.

Despite the social construction of what is success, there is variance as to how people plan their lives, based on what they value or find to be a meaningful purpose. There however seems to be an underlying assumption that success, however you define the concept, is a prerequisite to happiness and life satisfaction. Perhaps this link between happiness and success, that is often implicitly made, is one of the most misunderstood and incorrect assumptions that we hold as humans. If success is simply the accomplishment of a goal, then how will this lead to enduring life happiness? The experience of accomplishment or mastery in the short-term can create positive feelings, but does this really represent what we are seeking? The answer is commonly no.

To understand the process of success, we need to look a little deeper at the types of goals that people choose to pursue. Underneath a goal, is something that creates meaning that is beyond the outcome of the goal. For example, a common goal that many Australians aspire to achieve is the purchase of their own home. Is success in this instance, the buying of the home, the actual acquisition of the title of the property, or the transfer the money (usually from the bank) to the seller? Maybe, but what are the reasons many people strive for this goal, from the array of possible goals that are available?

Often the buying of a house is associated with a deeper meaning or value, in that it addresses your need for security.

Research shows us that people consider that goals will provide satisfaction and happiness, however actually the association with life satisfaction is more closely related to whether our goals are aligned and address our underlying values (Hayes, Strosahl, Wilson, 1999). If we make goals that are aligned with our values, and engage in committed action towards these goals, this is when people experience a more general state of life satisfaction, contentment, or what is described as happiness (Harris, 2007).

The pursuit of success therefore could be more accurately defined, with an operationalized definition as the attempt to secure some kind of valued outcome, to create a meaningful life.

Figure 1: The pursuit of Goals or Values

1. Common method of trying to achieve "success":

Construct goals

as primarily defined by culture, social circle and gender

expectations

↓

Limited consideration of own values

↓

Empty sense of success

2.More effective way of achieving life satisfaction or

happiness:

Identify own individual values (primary goods)

↓

Construct goals aligned to values and make regular,

Pursing a Meaningful Life

Many leaders who reach the top of their chosen pursuit, whether that be sports, business or arts are sincerely and undoubtedly unhappy. The dedication and sacrificing that is often required to be the best, means that there is also a lot that is lost. These sacrifices often include their health, their friendships, their relationship with their partner, connection with their family and children, what they value, their interests or hobbies and often the best years of their life. Essentially this type of goal pursuit (that is traditionally defined as success) can leave a person with difficulty recognizing the person that they have become. In this state, it is hard for a person to explain to their often admiring community, that their pursuit to the pinnacle of their career has lead them to a place which is a long way, from where they wanted to be.

And turning back or trying to resurrect what has been lost, now seems impossible.

The message to climb the mountain to strive to be the best seems in many ways to conflict with the essence of being human. The ability to pursue outcomes (whether that be a goal, a state of mind, personal characteristics or experiences) that are personally meaningful is a natural human desire (Wilson & Murrell, 2003).

While our desires may differ from culture to culture, generation to generation, person to person, what remains true is that we all desire something.

The Good Lives Model formulated by Ward and colleagues (e.g., Ward and Brown, 2004) provides an interesting framework for considering how a person may develop their capabilities and form a life that is personally meaningful and fulfilling.

Living a whole and balanced life means seeking what the Good Lives Model terms "primary goods" that reflect your values and life priorities. Each individual will prioritize certain goals, states of mind, personality characteristics, or experiences across time and in different contexts. A person's 'way of living' may represent society's expectations or more traditional ideas success, in terms of the way they are living their life or perhaps the prioritizing certain primary goods. However, developing a 'way of living' that is meaningful does not necessarily need to represent social norms or expectations. But it is still likely to achieve the same level of life satisfaction or happiness, as an approach to life that conforms to the ideals of the "successful" person that are identified in a particular generation or culture.

Wherever you are in life right now young or old, it is possible to pursue a more meaningful life. Firstly start by looking at figure 2 and identify your current priorities (under the column 'way of living') in striving for the pursuit of primary goods. Number them in the first box 1 to 11, with 1 your first priority or of most importance most of the time and 11 your lowest priority or least important most of the time. Then, consider the second adjacent box and start to develop a 'life plan', number the primary goods 1 to 11 according to how you would like to, or plan to, live you life in the future. Now consider what it would take to be living your life now according to your life plan, what internal capacities (skills or abilities) would you need to develop? Where would you need to expand your scope to more effectively strive for all eleven primary goods? Remember the way you pursue and prioritize your primary goods is individual to you. This means, that it would be important to identify the expectations of others, or what you perceive as the socially appropriate way of living. These types of socially constructed ideas about success are likely to get in the way of you forming a way of living that matches your values and is subsequently meaningful and fulfilling.

Figure 2: Good Lives Model – Primary Goods	Your current 'way of living'	Your 'life plan'
1.Life (including healthy living and functioning)	☐	☐
2. Knowledge (how well informed one feels about things that are important to them)	☐	☐
3. Excellence in play (hobbies and recreational pursuits)	☐	☐
4. Excellence in work (including mastery experiences)	☐	☐
5. Excellence in agency (autonomy, power and self-directedness)	☐	☐
6. Inner peace (freedom from emotional turmoil and stress)	☐	☐
7. Relatedness (including intimate, romantic, and familial relationships)	☐	☐
8. Community (connection to wider social groups)	☐	☐
9. Spirituality (in the broad sense of finding meaning and purpose in life)	☐	☐
10. Pleasure (feeling good in the here and now)	☐	☐
11. Creativity (expressing oneself through alternative forms)	☐	☐

The Mindset of Success

There has been a long historical debate, that is beyond this chapter, about whether human characteristics, personality, intelligence, and ultimate potential are inherited through genes or a product of nurture and able to be cultivated. The question around human factors is not whether they are or are not a product of either nature or nurture. But rather how does your view or belief in either stand point, impact your way of operating in the world.

Success however you define it, is dependent first and foremost *on your view* of how your characteristics are formed and developed, rather than what characteristics you actually possess. A prominent researcher Dweck (2006) describes this view as a mindset in that people tend to have either, a fixed mindset or a growth mindset.

People with a fixed mindset believe that human characteristics, such as personality, intelligence, and talent are largely unchangeable. In that you were born with certain degree of these factors, whether that be low or high, and in your lifetime you have the opportunity to essentially fulfill the potential of your talents. However beyond your innate abilities, there is considered limited or no capacity to further develop these attributes. With a fixed set of characteristics your value can essentially be evaluated and compared to those around you. As such those who view their characteristics as fixed, often see little point in learning or development as they do not believe they are able to cultivate their skills. Instead their efforts tend to be directed towards proving the extent of their characteristics.

An alternative view is a growth mindset in which each individual is viewed as having a set of characteristics of differing degrees, but irrelevant of the strengths or weaknesses, there is the belief that these characteristics can be developed with enough application and experience. By holding a growth mindset, you believe in learning as a method of advancement. What is interesting about this view of characteristics is that when your performance is tested or evaluated, perhaps as is common at school or within the work place, there is no sense of failure attached to your level of performance when compared to someone else. Why? Because those with a growth mindset see an evaluation of their performance as simply a static evaluation of their characteristics at that present moment in time. This forms a basis to reflect on how to improve further, and as such an evaluation is no reflection on your worth or ability to be successful.

Now remember these mindsets are not based on whether characteristics or attributes themselves are the product of nature or nurture, but rather whether we believe that humans have the ability to develop their characteristics. In fact research shows us that genetics may create a set of pre-dispositions but it is nurture (experiences) that ultimately determines who we become (McLeod, 2007).

The mindset that we therefore endorse and the values that we hold determine how we behave in our pursuit of success. In that, irrelevant of your awareness around your motivations or desires for particular course of action (i.e., I want to buy a house), our mindset sends us on one of two paths:

1. To constantly develop and learn
In this growth mindset, success is achieved by learning and improving, you never need to prove yourself in order to be accepted as you know you can always develop further and therefore there is no failure in your current performance.

2. To prove yourself in order to feel validated
In this fixed mindset, success is considered to be related to your degree of capability.

There is a myth, or a fallacy out there, that there are some people who are simply more remarkable than others, in that they are just more intelligent, more talented, more creative and that they were born that way. There simply is no such thing as a genius or a natural talent. Gladwell (2008) remarks that there is a common thread to the tale of those we hold up as "the great" among us, in that they may have had great genetics on their side, but it was more than that, it was the opportunities they were given to develop a particular skill or expertise, the degree of support (emotional, financial, practical) they received from others who encouraged or believed in their pursuit, with their capability directly related to the number of hours that they have spent practicing and becoming proficient.

Sports: The Mind of a Champion

The ideal of a sportsman or woman as a superhero naturally possessing abilities that surpass the average human is a myth. Our sports stars, are not different from us. They are not more superior because of "natural talent", but are sporting idols because they have an exceptional willingness to improve themselves, to work harder, to put in more practice. This is what has made them the best. Interestingly children who appear to have natural talent or abilities that exceed their peers, tend to be praised and endowed with the belief that they already possess superior abilities compared to others. What often happens for those with great genetics or "naturally talented", is that they do not value the need for hard work or effort, instead believing they already have the ability or advantage, and when faced with inevitable set backs or less than perfect results, they struggle to cope or utilize such setbacks as a platform to improve.

Success for the individual (or part of a team) in the sports arena is the outcome of firstly pursuing sports as an avenue to fulfill your values (primary goods). The mind is one of the most significant components in determining performance effects. Some describe this capacity as 'mental toughness', in essence a skill that can be learnt, like any other.

The key aspects of mental toughness (Jones, Hanton, & Connaughton, 2002) include:
- learning to dedicate yourself to improvement
- to learn to cope in the face of failure, difficulties or setbacks
- reflecting on past experiences of being able to perform the skill
- to learn to, not be distracted or inhibited by less than perfect conditions -
- to believe and understand your capabilities even when the conditions may not be perfect
- to regulate emotions and keep focus under pressure
- take control by self examining the process of succeeding
- do not define yourself by a win or a loss or succumb to somebody-nobody syndrome ("if I win I'll be somebody, if I lose I'll be nobody)

Without the investment of effort and practice, success in sports is not possible. Analysis of sporting legends and in fact the acquisition of any skill to a proficient level is thought to take 10,000 hours of practice (Ericsson, Krampe, Tesch-Romer, 1993). Next time you look at someone for their spectacular abilities, admire then for their enduring effort to practice and improve, as their success is directly related to the effectiveness of their practice.

Business: Growth rather than Self Importance

A good friend of mine, Bronwyn is training to be a nurse. People frequently question her as to the reasons why she is choosing this career. Their curiosity seems driven by largely astonishment. Why would a person want to do the job of a nurse, in that the role can entail long hours, low pay, low recognition for the significant contribution that they make to people's lives? As well as having to deal with distressed or unhappy people, in often ghastly conditions. Interestingly, Bronwyn is equally confused as to why a person would not want to pursue a meaningful career. What is lost in translation here is that Bronwyn has a growth mindset and she views nursing as a way to live her life aligned with her values (primary goods). She believes that nursing is, "not about making money", but as she puts it, "I do nursing because I enjoy it, I love to learn and understand my patients. I do my best to help them recover". You will notice, that Bronwyn is not interested in pursuing a career or role, to prove herself to anyone or to get recognition or validate her self-worth. The outcome of this growth mindset is that she not only finds meaning and satisfaction in her job, but is an asset as an employee. She is personally committed to learning and improving, and thus the outcomes for the organization are, improved quality of healthcare, improved productivity, improved employee moral and ultimately a more efficient and effective organization.

In business, irrelevant of industry or size of enterprise, there are a number of factors that make the difference in productivity and effectiveness. The key is the mindset of the people who make up the culture of the organization. Organizations have been found to be most effective and successful in terms of the bottom line, when they are led by a leader and surrounded by employees that have the qualities of a growth mindset, above all else.

Four key features of operating in the work context with a growth mindset:
- belief in development and improvement of self and others as key to outcomes
- openness to feedback (giving and receiving)
- ability to face and embrace setbacks or challenges, viewing own mistakes as a platform to improve
- critical thinking rather than 'groupthink' (Turner, & Pratkanis, 1998)

Four key features for fostering a growth-minded culture within an organization:

- focus on continuous development of ability and growth in terms of employee capacity, rather than seeking the most talented prospects
- reward (i.e., bonuses) and praise given for learning or for managing a setback or challenge, rather than for an outcome (i.e., a sales target)
- invest in mentoring and employee development programs
- leaders are viewed as guides for learning that are simply more advanced in the learning process, rather that superior.

Whether you are the CEO or a junior starting your career, without the qualities of growth mindset, your qualifications and experience become largely redundant. Leaders who employ individuals with growth mindset set up an organizational culture that is dynamic, responsive and productive. Whilst employees that strive to improve, rather than prove they are superior, set themselves up to be an asset of increasing value (growth mindset), largely devoid of self-limiting fears such as the perceived threat of failure, humiliation or social judgment.

Relationships – Grow Together
Many people dream of meeting Prince Charming or Cinderella, with your eyes setting upon each other and it is love at first sight. Unfortunately there is no Prince Charming or Cinderella waiting at the ball, there is no perfect soul mate who possesses perfectly compatible characteristics, likes and dislikes, values, strengths and weakness. The belief in a soul mate or perfect partner presents relationships as easy, all you have to do is find that perfect someone. However behind this dream of Prince Charming or Cinderella, there is a mindset made up of a number of false beliefs about how relationships should work, that ultimately lead to relationship difficulties. Those who embrace a fixed mindset see and fear rejection in relationships. They believe that rejection means they are being judged with low worth or value, whereas those with a growth mindset see rejection though distressing due to loss, as ultimately an opportunity to understand, learn and grow from the experience.
Research tells us that people tend to build strong successful relationships due to their degree of emotional intelligence (Goleman, 2006) and endorsement of beliefs such as:

1. Understanding that all relationships need continuous work to evolve and

develop, working through differences.

2. Understanding that no matter how well you know your partner they cannot read your mind. It is and always will be necessary for you to clearly communicate your needs, thoughts or feelings without assumption that the other person should just know.

3. Understanding that no matter how similar your partner may seem to you, it is impossible for people to agree on everything, including expectations, rights, entitlements, or obligations.

4. That no person is perfect and without flaws

5. Relationships built on a willingness to improve one's self for the benefit of the relationship.

6. Partners are not the competition, and instead they are more effective when they are able to support each other to be their best selves.

Summary – Key Points

- The formal definition of success as the attainment of an aim or purpose, does not conceptualize the complexity or the values that underpin the meaning of success.
- Success is not a prerequisite of happiness, but perhaps the state of happiness or fulfillment is a criterion for success.
- Individual values or primary goods underpin happiness and life satisfaction, leading to success.
- Traditional ideals of success do not necessarily translate into meaningful, or productive 'ways of living'
- Growth mindset is the key mindset necessary to cultivate learning, and pursue meaningful goals to be successful
- The pursuit of success in sport, if aligned with values, is determined most significantly, not by natural talent, but by the willingness to continuously invest in effort and practice.
- Success in any level of business comes from (or cultivation of) an inner desire for improvement, rather than proving the extent of your skills or qualifications.
- Strong, successful relationships are built on the premise that there is no perfect relationship, or perfect partner, and that you are essentially an intimate team learning to work together most effectively for your joint needs or goals.

Dr Gemma Russell

References

Brokaw, T. (1998). *The Greatest Generation.* New York: Dell Publishing.

Dweck, C. (2006). *Mindset: The new psychology of success.* New York: Ballantine Books

Ericsson, K.A., Krampe, R.T., & Tesch-Romer, C. (1993). The Role of Deliberate Practice in the Acquisition of Expert Performance. *Psychological Review,* 100 (3), 363-406.

Frankl, V. (2000). *Man's Search for Meaning.* Boston: Beacon Press.
Gladwell, M. (2008). *Outliers: The story of success.* New York: Little, Brown and Company

Goleman, D. (2006). *Social Intelligence: The New Science of Human Relationships.* New York: Bantam Dell

Jones, L. (1980), *Great Expectations: America and the Baby Boom Generation.* New York: Coward, McCann and Geoghegan.

Jones, G., Hanton, S., & Connaughton, D. (2002). What Is This Thing Called Mental Toughness? An Investigation of Elite Sport Performers. *Journal of Applied Sport Psychology*, 14(3), 205-218.

Harris, R. (2007). *The Happiness Trap: Stop struggling, start living.* Wollombi: Exisle Publishing.

Hayes, S.C., Strosahl, K., & Wilson, K.G. (1999). *Acceptance and Commitment Therapy: A contextual approach to cognition and emotion in psychotherapy.* New York: Guilford.

McLeod, S. A. (2007). *Nature Nurture in Psychology.* Retrieved from http://www.simplypsychology.org/naturevsnurture.html

Owram, D. (1997). *Born at the Right Time.* Toronto: University Of Toronto Press.

Turner, M. E, & Pratkanis, A. R. (1998). Twenty-five Years of Groupthink Theory and Research: Lessons from the evaluation of a theory. *Organizational Behavior and Human Decision Processes*, 73, 105–115.

Ward, T. & Brown, M. (2004). The Good Lives Model and Conceptual Issues in Offender Rehabilitation. *Psychology, Crime & Law,* 10, 243-257.

Wilson, K.G. & Murrell, A.R. (2003). Values-Centred Interventions: Setting a Course for Behavioral Treatment. In S.C. Hayes, V.M. Follette, & M. Linehan (Eds.) (2003). *The new behavior therapies: Expanding the cognitive behavioral tradition.* New York: Guilford Press.

Dr Gemma Russell is a Clinical Psychologist and director of Clever Minds Psychology, in Melbourne, Australia. Dr Russell completed her Bachelor of Science (first class honors) and Doctorate of Clinical Psychology at the University of Auckland, New Zealand. She is a registered Clinical Psychologist with the Psychologists Board of Victoria. Dr Russell has worked within the private and public mental health sector and criminal justice system, in Australia and New Zealand. Dr Russell has been called upon to provide expert witness testimony and to complete psychological reports for the family and criminal court in Australia. Her academic career has involved publications for notable journals and the presentation of research at conferences within the disciplines of Psychology, Psychiatry and Criminal Behaviour.

Dr Russell specializes in delivering evidence-based assessment and consultation to adults interested in self-development or experiencing mental health difficulties. Dr Russell is committed to achieving outcomes according to best practice guidelines. Dr Russell is an accredited to provide interventions under Private Health, Medicare, Transport Accident Commission (TAC), Australian Defense Force (ADF) and Department of Veteran's Affairs (DVA). Her interests lie in empowering people to utilize psychological strategies to be more effective within their relationships, business or life in general. Due to Dr Russell's investment in learning, Dr Russell is an accredited Psychology Board supervisor, and holds a key role as a post-graduate supervisor at Cairnmillar Institute. In this role, Dr Russell supervises Provisional Psychologists in the Masters and Honors programs.

Relationships: The Formula for Success

"To lead people, walk beside them ...
As for the best leaders, the people do not notice their existence.
The next best, the people honor and praise.
The next, the people fear; and the next, the people hate...
When the best leader's work is done the people say,
We did it ourselves!"—Lao Tzu

My definition of success is not the typical response. Success to me is not the traditional definition of accumulating wealth. Money is a resource and although it is important, it is not the only thing of value in our lives. Relationships are critical. I believe that when I have great personal and professional relationships, I am successful. When I can pour into the lives of others using my knowledge and life experience to help them on their journey, I have been successful. Identifying your purpose and living in that space is success. Being on a path to emotional well-being, wholeness and healing can also serve as key components to success. Success is not a path that is traveled alone and in order to achieve long term success, the involvement of others will provide a foundation for your growth.

I can't say that I've always been highly relational. As a kid, I was painfully shy. It was difficult for me to talk to people and look them in the eyes. My shyness in nature got worse when I was in third grade and became the victim of a bully. The other girls in my class followed suit because they didn't want to experience her wrath. For two years of my life, I was tormented and lost trust in others. I became extremely cautious of others and did not allow anyone to get close to me. I had serious trust issues and even though I ran for office and was involved in many clubs in high school, I still did not allow others to see the real me. This pain became a part of my existence and had embedded deeply into my core. In college, I came out of my shell a bit more realizing that I could not define my future if I did not become more of an architect of my present situation.

I became more vocal, more involved and more aware of the value of relationships. I was so fortunate to have had a roommate in college who allowed me to see the multi-faceted person that she was and it helped me to accept the many dimensions that were a part of my journey. Her authenticity impacted my ability to be real. I realized that as I became more aware and accepting of my own journey, I began to attract others I could trust. I began trusting myself, paying attention to the story I told about myself which resulted in a huge difference in my relationships!

Authenticity is defined as "owning one's personal experiences, be the thoughts, emotions, needs, wants, preferences, or beliefs, processes captured by the injunction" to know oneself" and "further implies that one acts in accord with the true self, expressing oneself in ways that are consistent with inner thoughts and feelings" (Harter, 2002, p. 382). As time has progressed, I realized the value of knowing your story. I spent so much time trying to become what I thought others wanted me to be so that I could obtain their approval. I thought it was safe. It wasn't. I began to understand that my story was the key to experiencing real relationships that were mutually beneficial and fulfilling as I got older. Knowing your story is the start of authenticity.

In the book, Leadership for the Disillusioned: Moving Beyond Myths and Heroes to Leading That Liberates, author Amanda Sinclair discusses the lives of the leaders of both Enron and WorldCom. She explores their childhood and notes that they both had very difficult experiences and used their leadership to create a different story. Sinclair shares that it is important to know one's triggers in order to lead effectively. I believe that recognizing one's triggers is critical to understanding their story. I began to understand that if I didn't resolve the issues I had with being bullied—feeling less than, unheard, and not valued—I would continue to find myself in relationships that reignited those feelings until I became aware of my triggers and more so, aware of my story.

My involvement in high school as well as college has served as a foundation for my success. I am a firm believer in serving others but also building meaningful relationships. Many of the relationships I have acquired over the years I have worked hard to maintain. Relationships are a form of capital and really can serve as a resource that can be leveraged for success. Building social capital is essential—it is more than networking.

The goal is not to create solely transactional relationships but to develop transformational opportunities for all parties involved. It is the building and maintaining of true healthy and impactful relationships that in my opinion exemplify true success. This "success" is commonly known and expressed as "capital" in one form or another in our capitalistic society. More Capital can equate to More Success.

Definitions of the Forms of Capital

Before discussing social capital, it is imperative to have an understanding of what this means and how it operates in our society. In sociology, there are several concepts that discuss human potential and interactions. These concepts are referred to as human, physical, organizational and cultural capital. They are used as explanations for transactions whether financial or relational in our society. Most of these ideas are rooted in the connections that humans have with one another. Human capital, especially those in professional fields, is critical. Becker (2008) defined human capital in the Concise Encyclopedia of Economics as the values, knowledge, skills, and health held by humans different from any financial and physical assets they may have obtained. A college education is considered human capital, and "human capital can reside in the individual alone. This is not to say that human capital creation is not collective," (Robison, Schmid, & Siles, 2000, p. 3). Many businesses and organizations focus on human capital when they hire individuals.

They are seeking someone who can add to the organization's knowledge base because of their education or experiences. Yet, a college degree and the educational experiences that one gains cannot be the sole purpose in the pursuit of higher education.

The term cultural capital was coined by French sociologist Pierre Bourdieu and is a social relation within a system of exchange that includes the accumulated enlightenment and knowledge that confers power or status (Barker, 2004). An example of cultural capital includes an understanding of art. Cultural capital is primarily based on exposure. I remember taking my hair stylist to visit a coffee shop to purchase a soy Chai tea. She was unfamiliar with it and I shared with her stories of my trip to India on which I was introduced to Massala tea or Chai as it is called in the states. Without the trip to India which expanded my cultural knowledge and understanding, I would have still been unaware as well. It is important to find situations that expand one's boundaries, thinking, and opportunities to enrich and challenge their current status. It is through these experiences that include connecting to diverse ethnic groups, travel, music, art and even food that can build one's cultural capital.

A vast number of definitions explain social capital. Social capital is a resource "made up of social obligations ('connections'), which is convertible, in certain conditions, into economic capital" (Bourdieu, 2008, p.281). Putnam, Leonardi, and Nanetti (1993) gave the following definition: "Social capital includes trust, norms, and networks of a social organization, and enables improvements to the efficiency of society by facilitating coordinated actions." (p. 167)

It is important to note that in evaluating capital, there are a number of variables that exist making physical, human and social capital different. All of these forms of capital are important and are used at some point in our interactions with one another. Despite the differences, they are all interrelated and complement one another.

Many in our society focus on education heavily as the attainment of knowledge and experiences which give credibility to our resume. Although human capital is necessary in a world that emphasizes the value of a college education, without building strong relationships, a college degree could simply become a piece of parchment. It is through the establishment of relationships and networks that one is able to possibly have an opportunity presented because of knowing 'the right people'. Having financial capital is important but without having a social network that can provide inside information, guidance and advice, an investment might prove to be extremely risky.

Understanding Social Capital in Detail

The definitions of social capital are numerous but all imply the involvement of individuals and/or networks who invest in a relationship that generally creates some type of benefit in the form of knowledge, association, or financial reward. Depending upon the need or focus, various forms of capital are used in our day to day interactions to succeed. The challenge is that if you do not understand how to build the most basic relationships in order to excel both personally and professionally, you are at a disadvantage, especially in a society dependent on human interaction, whether such interaction is face to face or technological. As a result, the need for understanding the impact of social capital is critical in order to have strong business, and to accumulate resources beyond just the financial. Using social capital allows for one to initiate and generate transactions relationally, empowering one to broker for advancement and the growth/well-being for the present and even the future. Relationship building can improve your health as indicated in many studies but can also improve your wealth!

Judith Jordan, PhD and Amy Banks, MD have provided medical evidence of the value of connections. Dr. Amy Banks states that dopamine levels increase when we are in healthy, high quality relationships. Dopamine is a neurotransmitter in the brain and is responsible for the fight or flight response. This brain chemical drives a person to accomplish a goal. Often, we get this same rush through sex or eating but it also exists when we are experiencing healthy connections with others. Without becoming too scientific, I believe that some of their insights can be extremely helpful in our ability to connect in a positive way that is mutually beneficial. Dr. Jordan states, "Our entire wellbeing depends on being included, belonging and engaging in safe relationships and contributing to others." This concept is the basis of growth fostering relationships. This statement should cause reflection in our daily interactions. Are you approachable? Would someone want to connect with you deeper after they first meet you?

Keys to expanding your network of personal and professional allies to build success

So how do you build relationships that can help you both personally and professionally? Here are a few tips that can assist. These are some of the principles that I provide from the book, Rules of Engagement: Making Connections Last:

1.   Become the authentic reflection of how you want others to see you, so that you attract the right people in your life. You attract what you project. What are you projecting? What does your story say about how you see yourself? If others were asked about your story, what would they say?

2.   Knowing your purpose in life is critical to understanding how you can best create the most productive networks in your life. Your purpose will serve as your compass for the next steps that you take. Are your networks productive and what does that say about you and your purpose?

3.   To create a powerfully strong professional and personal network you have to purposely and consciously choose to live positively in attitude and actions. When things are not going well, how do you deal with it? Who do you go to? Are they positive, negative, or energy vampires? What would it look like to have a network of individuals who provided strong and positive support if that doesn't currently exist? How does your story inform the composition of your network?

Another key to note is that relationships that last are cemented in high quality connections. Think about a time when you have met with someone who drained all of your energy. You are unable to explain what happened but you walked (maybe even ran) to get away from the negative energy of the conversation. "Corrosive connections are like black holes; they absorb all the light in a system and give nothing back in return." Our goal in connecting to others is to build relationships that are mutually beneficially. We should walk away wanting to reconnect, desiring to know someone better because of the positive experience we had in the interaction. In order to have enhanced connections, Dolley and Feedele (1997), state these concepts are helpful in building stronger connections:

Empathy
Mutuality
Authenticity
Diversity

So how does this relate to building relationships? In order to build positive relationships, empathy is important. Listening to a person's story allows you to understand the position of an individual (where they are coming from). In this mode, it is more important to understand than to be understood. A colleague of mine does something that is priceless when he meets someone: He repeats their name and will ask them to tell their story. In doing so, he can find commonalities and even opportunities for synergy by listening. If we are truly honest, most of us enjoy having the floor to talk about ourselves. Allow people that space instead of jumping in first and giving your three-minute-rehearsed-in-the-mirror-elevator speech.

Mutuality is making sure that the relationship is beneficial. I hate when I meet someone for the first time and all they do is talk about themselves and what they need. They don't give me a chance to say even a word!!!! If it isn't a win-win situation for us both, why would I be interested in getting to know a person better? Mutuality is about creating a relationship based in respect. It is important to respect the other's way of thinking and their time. It doesn't mean that you must agree with everything but it is important to treat others the way you want to be treated.

I often hear people comment on encountering 'fake' individuals or people who are not who they say they are. Creating authentic relationships begins with you! How can you ensure that YOU are not projecting an image that you cannot live up to but one that is real, one that attracts other authentic individuals? In a world of so much plastic, it is refreshing to meet people who are comfortable in their skin. Become comfortable with your skills and gifts.

Lastly, but also equally important, is diversity. Examine your relationships. If everyone looks just like you, thinks like you and lives in the world the same way that you do, your network is too small. You are missing information that could be very helpful to your work. A few years ago, I conducted a research group comprised of very diverse women in age, ethnicity, and religion. Initially, when we started the group, the women introduced themselves by their titles and positions. After I asked that they reintroduce themselves again without the titles, stories were shared about their lives—the good, the bad and even the ugly. I learned through my research that in order to create relationships that last, people must have space that allows them to feel safe and comfortable. In addition, sharing one's story allows others to listen and find more commonalities than differences. Our stories often reveal psychological capital—resilience, optimism, hope, and self-efficacy.

I currently serve in the role of a Director for an international nonprofit for the US Division. My role is about cultivating and maintaining relationships. I work with a team across the United States in opening doors for them in their work but also building partnerships across the country. My team has accomplished a great deal and I believe it is due to my relational style of leadership and my strong belief in the power of authenticity. The quote at the beginning of the chapter is a reminder of the power of relationships but also the power of the story. The way we interact with others can make a difference in our trajectory. Life can be challenging but can become easier when we build relationships that last, that matter and add value to our lives. Relationships are a much needed component to our success both personally and professionally. Success is not achieved in isolation. Without people involved in a variety of roles such as advisors, mentors, or a part of our team, we are unable to fully realize and reach our goals. Without examining relationships, we limit our ability to truly measure the impact of success.

Dr. Froswa' Booker-Drew

Dr. Froswa' Booker-Drew has an extensive background in nonprofit management, partnership development, training and education. She is currently National Community Engagement Director for World Vision, serving as a catalyst, partnership broker, and builder of the capacity of local partners, facilitating the emergence and strengthening of community-led initiatives to improve and sustain the well-being of children and their families.

She supervises staff in several locations around the United States. She is a member of the Texas Nonprofit Council which provides recommendations to the legislature on policy that impacts nonprofits and faith-based organizations. She also assists a number of organizations such as the Greater Dallas Community Development Corporation, The Red Umbrella, Womanars.com, and the Texas Christian Community Development Network as a consultant, board member, trainer or adviser.

She was a part of the documentary, Friendly Captivity, a film that follows a cast of 7 women from Dallas to India. She was a semi-finalist for the SMU TED Talks in 2012, received the Girlfriends Rock Award, 2013 Recognized Alumni from the History Department of the University of Texas at Arlington, Froswa' graduated with PhD from Antioch University in Leadership and Change with a focus on relational leadership and social capital in August 2014. She attended the Jean Baker Miller Institute at Wellesley in June 2013 for training in relational cultural theory and has completed training on Immunity to Change based on the work of Kegan and Lahey of Harvard. She has also completed training through UNICEF on Equity Based Evaluations and is a member of the American Evaluation Association. She is the author of the book, Rules of Engagement: Making Connections Last. The workbook helps women build identity and psychological capital that can result in stronger social capital. Froswa' was a workshop presenter at the United Nations in June 2013 on the Access to Power and participated in the International Dialogue on Relational Learning and Leadership Conference in October 2013. She also writes for a variety of publications around the world and is an Adjunct Assistant Professor at the University of Texas at Arlington.

***Many thanks to Jonathan Mitchell who provided editing eyes to this chapter and served as a sounding board while putting this together.

BLENDING

How Women Can Succeed at their Career/Business **and** their Family

> *"The whole point of being alive is to become the person you were intended to*
> *be, to grow out of and into yourself again and again"*
> *(Oprah Winfrey, 2014)*

One of the biggest barriers for women aiming for success is the struggle to manage their family's needs or their parenting values with their career or business aspirations. This is often referred to as the "work-life balance" – this is an inaccurate term in my opinion as parenting or caring responsibilities are more significant and more challenging than having a fun or lifestyle priority outside of work. Additionally, it understates the focus and commitment required to really make the two areas work effectively concurrently. It is not about "balance" - what women really have to do to make both components work is to learn to **blend** them.

The "lean in" mentality (shaped in 2013 by Sheryl Sandberg, the CEO of Facebook) tells only one part of the story – that women must set themselves up to love what they do so that they are willing to commit to their career. But leaning one way suggests to me that you need to lean away from something else – in this case, a woman would have to lean away from their family commitments or parenting values and towards their business or career.

It is my observation from more than fifteen years as a psychologist, that many woman are not comfortable with the choice to lean away from their family to pursue their career/business goals. Women as mums or carers, constantly deal with the guilt that comes hand in hand with these roles. For example, guilt around not being a good enough parent, or forgetting something that was important to their partner, or just not being able to do everything perfectly. In many ways, to lean in will just exacerbate that guilt and this can discourage women from trying to find success outside of the home.

To <u>blend</u> is broadly defined as ***to mix or merge different parts together so that they become combined and indistinguishable from one another.***

Blending is about taking two (or more) important priorities and finding a way to mix them together so that you can successfully undertake both. Both are changed in the process of blending – they would be different if you were completing either of them on their own. But the new outcome is successful for both.

As a single parent as well as the Director of my own psychology practice, learning to blend these priorities effectively has been essential to my success (and my sanity!). I work with many women that are trying to address the same issues of finding a way to fulfill their career or business priorities while also taking care of their children or parents effectively and with love. They struggle with the feeling that they are letting their children or husband down, while also trying to demonstrate the work ethic that they feel is necessary. They report that they are uncomfortable with the choice, they feel guilty, they hate going to work, and they do not feel that they are succeeding at either role.

As a result of working with these women and applying strategies to my own life, I have identified ten critical components of successful blending that fit into three main streams:

<u>*STREAM 1: Your Thoughts*</u>

1) **Believing it is possible**

    You need to believe with every ounce of your being, that it is possible and that you deserve...**NO**, you are ENTITLED to both. This choice DOES NOT make you a terrible mother NOR a poor work asset. You need to know you are doing the right thing by yourself, your workplace, and your family.

    One of the reasons why blending is "right" is that you become a fantastic role model for your children – encouraging them to live the life of their dreams. You also become a role model for other women. Many will admire your determination and wish they were brave or strong enough to try the same thing. You will be an inspiration for many.

2) **Know and be guided by your own values**

    Your values are the beliefs that guide your life, and they are different for everyone. The following are examples of values:

- To contribute to society and make a difference in my own and other people's lives
- To always be honest and sincere with others
- To find a focus on spirituality in everything I do
- To assertively express my feelings whenever possible

If you are making choices that are not aligned with your values, then you will feel stressed or experience a kind of moral dilemma – it just won't feel right. Identify your values, know yourself and what is important to you. This will both build your self-confidence and help to align your parenting/caring with your career/business. Each day needs to increase your motivation and determination to follow this path, and that won't happen if it is contrary to your values.

3) Being true to yourself

The work you choose to do must allow you to be authentic, to fulfil your potential (or at least be working towards this), and it must be a choice. If you do something you hate or are dragging yourself to work each day, you will be stressed and frustrated and that won't be right for you or your family. Your career or business pursuits must, at some level, foster the feeling that your life has meaning and purpose. You will not be committed or determined enough to make it come together unless you feel it is authentically you.

4) Welcoming failure

See everything as dynamic and transient, nothing is permanent. We often get overwhelmed when we feel stuck or that the challenges we are experiencing won't change. This is just a thought or belief, and is not true. Change in some way is always possible. Failure is not an ending, it is a beginning of something different. It is not a label that is applied to you as a person, it describes an experience only. Failure is an important part of a quality improvement cycle and allows you to improve. Do not fear failure, welcome it, grab it with both hands and learn from it. And model this to your family and the wider community. People that succeed always describe a process of failing and trying again, then failing and trying again. The more you keep trying the more likely you will be in the right place at the right time. Adapting is an essential part of blending – learn to adapt to changing priorities, new information, failures, and feedback.

STREAM 2: Your Actions

5) Knowing it won't be perfect and that's okay

Do you remember what it was like when you brought your first new baby home? For most of us (bar the few who's babies were absolute angels) the following days, weeks, maybe even years, were filled with compromise. Beliefs you used to hold true, expectations you had of yourself and others (perhaps about levels of cleanliness or how much sleep you needed for your brain to function), had to loosen up. It was about survival...and it was okay.

We can normally accept that these compromises are part of coping with such a massive change in your life like having a baby. Being able to succeed at your career and your family is just as significant and requires the same compromises. It is okay if the house is not always clean, it is alright if your son's school shirt is not perfectly ironed, and it is fine if you are fifteen minutes late to the office more days than not. You cannot be guided by other people's expectations of you, just as you couldn't be back when your baby was first born. Focus on the big picture not the small details.

6) Getting outside the box

We are in a fabulous time in history where the definitions of "work" and "career" are no longer as clear-cut as they used to be. You can create the career or business that you want and that aligns itself with your family's needs. For example: you may not work in a full-time management position, instead you might be a consultant with flexible hours; you might run your own business to get more control rather than take an employed position; or you might combine work and part-time study to facilitate a transition to work that is more aligned with your true self. You can think completely out of the square, in fact, the most successful people usually do.

7) Reducing stress in every possible way

Always look for ways to reduce your stress – make sure you spend time with your family just having fun, being together, and having adventures together. It is these things that will make the energy needed to continue to blend family and career worthwhile. Fun and stress reducing activities are not an optional extra, they are a requirement of being able to blend successfully.

STREAM 3: Others

8) Working with your family as a team

You and your family are in this together, if you have all participated in the decision-making about your business/career or if at least everyone's views have been heard, it will be much easier to engage support. Ensure they understand how important this is to you and possibly to them (they may not be aware of any positive effects they might experience unless you spell them out). Be very clear about boundaries and rules so that everyone knows what to expect from each other. And have regular conversations with your family members to identify and address issues. Sometimes this is as simple as clarifying that you do not love them any less because you are working, in fact, it is a demonstration of how much you love them and how much you care about yourself as well. People will make their own, often incorrect, assumptions if they don't get the opportunity to talk to you about issues as they arise. So talk, listen, and work together.

9) Getting help

There are lots of business/work tasks or household chores that can be completed by someone other than you. You might use a regular cleaner, or you might get someone else to do the house renovations, or you might get your bookkeeping done by an external organisation. Whenever you get help from someone else you reduce the pressure on you or other members of your family. Blending is more successful when you accept that you do not have to do everything yourself!

10) Connecting with others

Look for opportunities to connect with like-minded souls. Avoid engaging with people that do not support your decision to blend family and work (they don't have to agree with you, but they do need to support your choices). Find people you can share your experiences with, perhaps help each other, and find opportunities to work together. Women are not always good at looking after one another – we can criticise and judge each other and try to pressure other women to do as we do. Do not fall into this trap. Rejoice in the opportunity for all women to choose our own lifestyles and encourage each other to be our best self...whatever that is.

Blending career and family is more than just a way of making life more interesting and feeling like you are fulfilling your potential. As the cost of living increases, blending is becoming essential for financial survival. The international literature indicates that the biggest predictor of poor mental and physical health outcomes is low socio-economic status or financial disadvantage. Families on one income or with an unemployed single-parent are more likely to live in financial hardship.

Many women return to work reluctantly after children, feeling they are letting their family down. But the reality is that they may be creating a much better financial future for their families, and therefore better health outcomes overall. If you can use the ten components above to blend your work and family, you may create a life you love, more financial stability, and the success that you and your family deserve.

Leanne Donoghue-Tamplin

Leanne Donoghue-Tamplin, Director of Real Success Pty Ltd, is a registered psychologist with more than fifteen years of experience working with individuals and organisations. She specialises in providing e-psychology and e-coaching services that empower women to thrive, giving them access to freedom, choice, joy, balance, success, and inner strength.

W: www.realsuccess.com.au; E: leanned@realsuccess.com.au.

How to transform your life from insanity to sane

How can one define the word Insanity? By definition insanity is doing the same thing over again expecting a different result. Can anyone relate? I know I can. That was my entire life for thirty two years. I thought I was alright, I knew something had to change when I realized what used to work no longer worked and it started to become more difficult as time went on. God had to take me through a transformation of my mind. My life was havoc and, to add insult to injury, my children were being affected by my poor choices. I knew in my heart they deserved better; God had blessed me with two wonderful children. Transformation is a process, not something that can be done overnight, but over a period of time. One must be committed to the process. Our souls are made up of three components: the mind, will, and emotions. And when we are damaged from early childhood experiences at adolescent stages of life we tend to carry those same burdens into our adult years. I know for myself that is what happened.

At the age of fourteen I was raped and almost beaten to death. I was robbed of my innocence and, that night, that little girl died. Life was never the same for me, even though I tried to get on with life but I struggled from within. I would lay awake at night. Crying so hard in an effort to push away his hands from my body and my mind. The mind is a very powerful thing and it controls every part of us. It took me thirty two years to get released from bondage. My deliverance did not happen overnight. It took so many tears and sweat but I am here today to give all women a message of hope; we cannot control what happens to us, but we can control how it affects us. Never allow the storms of life to rage on inside you. That will be the end of your sanity. So, how do you transform your life from Insanity to Sane? I will provide you with everyday life principles which are right in front of us, but we miss them every time. We often expect things to come to us in a huge way but, often times, the best gifts come in a very settled way.

If you find yourself stuck, wanting to break free, but do not know how, you have the power within you to change your perspective. Our minds are the battlefield. If you can get a hold of your mind half the battle is won. Throughout the day we have thoughts that attaches themselves to our minds and, over time, if we continue to dwell on those thoughts, our actions will begin to align themselves with those images that we perceive in our thoughts. What thoughts are telling you that it is impossible? Your life will never change? Your circumstance will never change? We all hear those thoughts at times in life, but you do not have to yield yourself to them. When those thoughts come (and they come to all of us), you must channel those thoughts with something positive that is in your life. Those thoughts of whispers are called strongholds. They come from our childhood and we begin to exercise them as pyramids in our lives. They become our compass and, when ignited, all those memories come rolling back like floods of water. Everything we do in life starts with a thought - so we have to gain control over our minds.

1.   You must deal with your past so you may embrace your future. What I mean is this: in life things happen to us just like it happened to me at the age of fourteen. I never dealt with the rape and, as a result, my life spiraled out of control. Everything I did - good or bad - was a result of the rape. What has you bound to the past? For me, I became attracted to men that were abusive. And when someone nice and decent came along I did not know how to deal with him. How many of us are in that same situation today? You have to *see* yourself coming out of your situation. So, yes, your perspective has to be changed. And that comes from having a new mindset. If you are ever going to move forward you have to take that first step. Even if nothing else feels right, eventually it will align itself.

Have a renewed mind. Surround yourself with positive people that will lift you up. You do not need others who will tear you down. Some people have been in our lives for too long. It is like having a comfortable pair of old socks. They are so comfortable - even though we know we need to throw them out, we hang on to them. Old habits die hard. But, if you are going to commit yourself to a purpose, say goodbye to those friends. This is not to say they are not good people. They are not good for you in the season that you are in. Quite recently I experienced this with a girlfriend that I had known for seventeen years. I discovered during my book promotion that she did not come out to support me. And, when the event was over, she did however call me. But at no time did she enquire about the book release party or mention anything relevant to it. At first I admit I was upset. But I remember a devotion that I have been reading for weeks and it went as follows: "Not everyone will be able to go on your journey. Dust the sand off your feet and keep moving forward." My first thought was; "not my friend of seventeen years." There are some people that we outgrow and, in order for you to excel, you must let them go. If others are not growing with you, then they cannot go with you.

You can still be friends with them. But you don't have to inform them about everything that is happening in your life. If you do they will become jealous. Now please hear me out. Perhaps they are not jealous of you, but jealous of the fact that you are moving toward your dreams and they are at a standstill. See, once again, it is our perspective. So often we think others are jealous - especially women. We struggle with this so much in life. But it is not always true. When your mind has been renewed you think differently. In my particular case, the old Barbara would have thought: "she is just jealous of you." But she is not. She's only jealous of what I am doing. Some people can only picture you doing what you have always done. My advice is to cut them out of your life today. You can pray for them, wish them well, but you go on with your life and fulfill your destiny.

2.   Find your passion. Usually whatever has caused you the most pain will help you discover your purpose. I speak with women all the time and one of the key factors I hear is how women have taken what they have struggled with and turned it into a business. Write a vision and make it plain. So often we need to write the vision down. When we do it becomes more real to us. Continue to encourage yourself, there might not be anyone around to encourage you, so you must be strong in faith and keep pushing until something happens. Study and do research in that particular industry. Find out what others have done and maybe done wrong and learn from other people's mistakes, so you do not have to repeat what does not work. Your time is precious. So you do not want to waste any more valuable time than you already have. Start connecting with a network such as LinkedIn, Facebook, and SavvySme.com.au. There are so many other sites out there and people that will help you. Do not become discouraged if the door does not open the first time. Learn from my previous section on perspective, always keep the right perspective. If the door closes just tell yourself there is a better door for you to go through. Never see it as a failure. You may go through hundreds of different doors until you find the right door. Stay encouraged.

3.   Transformation is not just in our mind and soul, but our bodies as well. We must fit in every area so we lack nothing. Join a gym, work out, exercise, take walks in the evenings change your eating habits. I know for me when God took me through a transformation I had to learn different behaviors such as eating the right foods. When we eat healthy not only do we feel better about ourselves, but we have more energy to do the work that we are called to do. So often life has a habit of weighing us down. If you are not fit how can you carry on with your purpose if you are tired?

Your mind must be fit as well. There will come many disappointments in life as you journey through your destiny. And trust me when I say at times you will feel as though all your work is in vain and you are not accomplishing anything. That is the time we generally give up. Not because we do not have what it takes, but we are tired from our unhealthy living. Too much sugar will slow your brain down. Get yourself on an eating regime that will give you what you need to produce, not just for your purpose, but your family as well. They are depending on you. As women it makes us feel good about ourselves when we dress up or get our hair and nails done. Go treat yourself to a day at the spa. When you begin to feel good about how you look it can affect the way you feel. Now don't get me wrong when I say this is only half the problem. This is the outer appearance. There is another which is the soul.

When a soul has been damaged, we feed off of it just like an animal does. You can change the outer part of your being but the inner part is still damaged. Spend time in a quiet place and think about your life and what happened to you as a child. I teach all of my clients that, if you want to know why you are messed up as an adult take a visit to your past. You may find that the answer lies in those adolescent years. I am not preaching against looking good, but, so often, we try to cover up the outer appearance because the inner being is a mess. Forgive the person that has hurt you. If you never deal with the pain of your past, you will start out in life on your path, but the very first bump in the road will spiral you back to that time and place when you were vulnerable.

Let me give you an example. Before I lost my job in 2012 I was the head person in my firm. Until one day I had a new boss and she was a woman. I thought we would get along well, but the more I tried to get to know her the more isolated I felt. Every emotion came back to that time when I was a child and I felt that my family treated me differently than the other cousins. I always believed I was not good enough. So whenever someone in my life would treat me that way the feelings always came rolling back. Yes I am talking about rejection. I had to go back and forgive the people that made me feel like a reject. But God soon revealed to me those people were hurting themselves and hurting people hurt others. So I had to learn to separate the person from what they do. And that is not always easy. But we must work toward that goal. Everything in our lives is a result of our perspective. It is the way we see life. This can make a difference in our lives. Go back to that person; ask for forgiveness. When we do not forgive, they still have us as prisoners, they are free and most of the time they had forgotten what they did to us in the first place but we are still back here holding on.

Not forgiving is a toxic poison. It filters like a cancer and, without proper treatment, it will destroy your life. So let's recap all we have learnt. The first step is renewing your mind - getting rid of all the toxins that have plagued your entire life. Forgive those who have hurt you or caused you grief or loss. Accept whatever has happened to you; it will be the same thing that will push you into your purpose. Get a new perspective in life. Deal with whatever you need to and embrace your past as a way of embracing your future. God will use the same people to bless you.

I am a living witness today. I have seen it with my own eyes. Surround yourself with positive people that will sow into your life, get rid of the wrong people that are not adding anything to your life. Write your vision and make it plain. Go after your dream and do not stop until you have reached your destiny. And even then continue on the path. Begin networking within that industry. You might not be able to build your network of friends right away, but every day make one new contact.

Treat yourself and choose to live healthy, take steps toward living a healthy lifestyle by working out and exercising. Even if money is not looking all that great for you, there are things you can do that cost absolutely nothing such as walks around the park.

What I am giving you today is what God gave me. This is what I teach women every day. Either during one-on-one sessions or on my radio platform. I tried it and I know it works. Nothing great has ever come easy. So you have to put in the work in order to reap the reward. Stay strong and encouraged. Wake up each day knowing this day will be your day of miracles. The more you speak it your life will begin to align itself. So often we want what others have. But are we willing to put in the work? Often we grow stagnant and stuck, but you no longer have to be or feel stuck.

Most women ask me this question "what can I do?" My response is, do something. If you never try, how you do you know what you can achieve in life? Get off the couch and do something and, before long, you will discover your purpose. Be blessed in what you do, be passionate. If you're not excited how do you expect others to get excited? Just a thought.

One final thought; when you have been rescued, it is up to you to go out and rescue someone else. When we do that, the cycle continues and other women will be healed as well. What you have gone through was not for you, but for someone else. And in time you will begin to see the truth.

Barbara Archer

Greetings my name is Barbara Archer. I am a women of many talents and gifts. At the moment I am using my gifts to help other women to transform their lives in mind, soul and body. I host two radio platforms which allows me to teach women.

As women we often deal with so much. A lot of times we hold our thoughts in out of fear of letting others know. But that is a danger zone for us. When we keep silent we tend to lose reality. We try so hard to look and be everything others think we should be, others see us and think we have it all together but on the inside we are screaming.

We carry that mask around for so long we even fool ourselves into believing we are alright but in reality we are suffering. It not only affects us but our children and families as well. In 2013 I went through a complete transformation. Everything that I held dear to me, including a husband, home and finally the career that I loved. Finally I found myself in a situation that millions of people find themselves in - starting over. But how do you start over after 40? These days women in their 40's are the new 20's.

There are many steps to take in the process and everything starts with a thought. So your mind must be renewed in order to gain the confidence that you need. Not only are we older but now we have to compete with a younger generation. Be confident and know you can achieve whatever you set out to accomplish. My final thought is if you can see the dream, you can achieve the dream. Change your thought perspective and finally get some new friends that will encourage you on your journey.

Your Business Financial Success

Whatever your definition of success, money is required to be successful. If success to you is living on the beach than you need a lot less a month than someone whose definition of success is living in a penthouse in New York City.

Money is best generated through a successful business. In this chapter you will learn how to understand the financial segment of your business. Don't skip this chapter. It's written in understandable English rather than accounting babble. The goal is to decipher your financial statements every month. When you understand what your financial statements are telling you, then you can make good business decisions that help you get and stay profitable and generate the money you need to be successful.

Your financial statements answer these questions:
1. Are your customers costing you more money than they generate in sales? If your customers cost you more than they generate in sales, you don't need those customers. The only way you find out if you have profitable customers is to track their revenues costs, and when they pay their bills.

2. Are your products and services profitable?
Receiving and analyzing a financial statement each month answers this question.

3. Are you running out of cash? Do you have enough cashflow to pay your bills?
The trends on your balance sheet answer this question.

4. Are your employees productive?
The trends on your profit and loss statement answer this question.

5. Do you have too much debt or are you increasing your debt load?
The trends on your balance sheet answer this question.

Financial statements are actually easy. They were developed about 1,000 years ago by the Venetian monks who had to keep track of the rich Italians' money. They <u>had</u> to make it simple. There were no adding machines, calculators, or computers. We have it so much easier today! You'll discover that financial statements are no more than addition and subtraction. You can use a calculator and a computer software program to help you.

If your experience is similar to that of most of my clients, the first few months of financial reviews are harder because you have to "look up" the analysis terms. However, each month's review becomes faster and easier. Within six months the analysis is quick and you start wondering why you ever thought financial statement reviews were hard.

Make sure your accounting is on an accrual basis.
Many CPA's report company taxes on a cash basis. Sometimes there are tax advantages for doing so. However, your operating financial statements, the statements you use to guide your daily business operations, should be set up on an accrual basis.
In cash basis accounting, you record a sale when you receive payment for that sale. You record an expense when you write the check to pay that expense. There are no accounts receivable, accounts payable or inventory on your financial statements. Your revenues don't match your costs.

In accrual based accounting, an expense is recorded even if the bill isn't paid. You know what bills need to be paid. You know what revenue should be coming in the door. You have accounts receivable, accounts payable, and inventory. You can match revenues with costs. You'll know each month, assuming your information is accurate, whether your company is really profitable.

Get your financial statements on time.

You must receive timely financial statements, an accurate balance sheet and profit and loss statement. That means they are in your hands by the 10th of the following month. January's statements are due by February 10th. Getting January's statements in April doesn't help you. Any minor issue that could have been caught and corrected in February may have caused a crisis by April.

Balance Sheets - the fundamental building block of your business.

Why is a balance sheet fundamental? It tells the story of your company from the time you started it until the day you close the doors (or sell it).

A balance sheet is simply a snapshot of the health of your business at a point in time. It shows the true profitability of your company over a long period of time. Your profit and loss statement only states profit or loss - not profitability, ie sustained profits.

Your balance sheet is literally a snapshot for one moment in time. The reason that it is a snap shot is because your balance sheet is constantly changing. It is constantly changing because your cash is constantly changing. You have a different cash balance every day which means that your balance sheet changes every day.

Calculate your balance sheet at consistent moments in time. These are usually the last day of each month and the last day of your fiscal year. This is a good time frame to make the comparisons. It is a snapshot of the health of your business at a regular point in time so you can compare and answer the question, "How is my company doing?"

The balance sheet is called the balance sheet because assets must balance liabilities plus net worth.

Figure 1 shows the balance sheet format with the major categories.

ASSETS	**LIABILITIES**
Current Assets	Current Liabilities
Cash	Accounts payable
Investments	Line of credit
Accounts receivable	Deferred income
Inventory	Warranty
Prepaid expenses	Taxes payable
Total Current Assets	Current portion of
long term debt	
	Total Current Liabilities
Long term (fixed) Assets	
Furniture	Long Term Liabilities
Tools	Notes payable
Office equipment	Owner payable
Vehicles	Total Long Term Liabilities
Buildings	
Deposits	TOTAL LIABILITIES
Less accumulated depreciation	
Total Long Term Assets	
	NET WORTH
	Capital Stock
	Retained Earnings

TOTAL NET WORTH

TOTAL ASSETS   **TOTAL LIABILITIES & NET WORTH**

Figure   1.   Balance   Sheet   Format.

Assets are things of value. Liabilities are things that you owe. Net worth (also called equity, owner's equity, stockholder's equity, or other terms) is what I call your fudge factor, i.e. if you had to close your doors tomorrow and convert all of your assets to cash and pay off all of your liabilities, what would be left is the net worth of your business.

Assets and liabilities are divided into two components - current and long term. Current assets are things that are either cash or turned in to cash within a year. Examples are cash, inventory, and accounts receivable.

Current liabilities are debts that must be paid within a year. Examples are accounts payable, taxes payable, lines of credit and deferred income.

Long term assets are the "stuff." They include furniture, fixtures, and equipment. They are not turned in to cash quickly.

Long term liabilities are not paid quickly. They are bank loan payments and owner payments.

Your Profit and Loss Statement - Short term look at how the company is doing.

Profit and loss statements are also called income statements. A Profit and Loss statement is a picture of the profit and loss of your company over a period of time. Unlike the balance sheet, which is a snapshot of the health of your business at a moment in time, a Profit and Loss (P&L) statement looks at how the company has performed over a period of time. At the end of that period of time, usually one month or one year, the P&L statement "starts over."

The Profit and Loss statement format is shown in Figure 2

Sales
- Cost of goods sold (COGS) or direct expense
= Gross profit

Gross profit
- General and administrative expenses (G&A)
= Net operating profit

Net operating profit
- Other Expense + Other Income
= Profit before taxes

Profit before taxes
- Taxes
= Net Profit

Figure 2. Profit and Loss Statement Format

The P&L equation starts with sales or revenues. Subtract the cost of sales from sales. The result is gross profit. Then subtract overhead from gross profit and the result is net operating profit. Then subtract other expense or add other income and the result is profit before taxes. Finally, subtract taxes. The result is net profit.

Sales are the monies generated from producing products or delivering services.

Cost of sales or direct cost is expenses that are incurred because something was sold. Typical direct costs include direct materials, direct labor, subcontracts, commissions, warranty, permits, and freight.

Gross profit is the result of subtracting cost of goods sold (COGS) or direct expenses from sales.

Overhead is the expense that your business incurs so that it can stay in business. Typical overhead includes rent, telephone, and utilities. You must pay these bills each month irrespective if the sales volume you generate. Even if you had zero sales, you would still have to pay your utility bill.

Overhead expenses are subtracted from gross profit to arrive at net operating profit. This is the "ordinary profit," the profit that is generated from regular sales and expenses that occur on a day-to-day basis.

Sometimes there is income or expense that is not generated from day-to-day operations. This gets added or subtracted next. Other income is usually interest received from investments or gain on sales of assets. If the company sells a fixed asset such as a vehicle, it might have a gain on the sale of that vehicle. It happens when, on the balance sheet, the value of the vehicle is $1,000 and the company sells it for $2,000. The extra $1,000 is other income to the company. Yes, you have to pay taxes on that income.

Other expenses are usually losses on sales of assets. If, the company sells that vehicle for $500 and its value on the balance sheet is $1,000, the company has a loss of $500 which it can deduct from profits.

Other income and expenses are non-operating revenues or expenses that the company receives. This part of the income statement handles extraordinary events, i.e. not usual income and not usual expenses. They are not the day-to-day operating income and expenses.

After adding other income and subtracting other expenses, the company has net profit before taxes. Then income taxes are subtracted to arrive at net income. This is the figure that is added to retained earnings on the balance sheet.

The Profit and Loss statement formula is straightforward. It is sales minus cost of goods sold equals gross profit. Subtract overhead from gross profit to arrive at net operating profit. Then add other income or subtract other expenses and the result is net profit before taxes. Subtract income taxes and the bottom line, net profit, is shown.

Monthly Financial Ratio Analysis

When you receive your financial statements each month, these ten ratios will help you analyze them. These ratios will help you operate your business on a day-to-day basis. They are not necessarily what a banker is used to seeing or expects.

They tell you instantly what is going on with your business. You'll know whether your employees are productive. You'll know if you have or may soon have a cash flow problem. You'll know if you're using your inventory properly. You'll be able to tell whether you have too much debt. The ratios are used to determine the health of your company. It is important to compute these financial ratios on a monthly basis because the trends are as important as the specific monthly figures. You can help your company avert a potential crisis by examining these ratios each month.

The ratios are divided into liquidity ratios (can you pay your bills?), debt ratios (are you carrying too much debt?), productivity ratio (are your employees productive?), and usage ratios (do you have a collection problem or too much inventory?).

Liquidity Ratios

Liquidity ratios are current ratio, acid test, and Accounts receivable to accounts payable.
Generally increasing liquidity ratios mean increasing profitability. Generally decreasing liquidity ratios mean decreasing profitability. Your company's current ratio should always be greater than one. If it isn't, your company is headed for cash flow problems.

With these ratios you have to look at the trend. A single figure won't tell you too much. Are the ratios going the right way or are the ratios going the wrong way?

The definition of the liquidity ratios are:

Current Ratio:
Current Assets
Current Liabilities

Acid Test or Quick Ratio:

$$\frac{\text{Current Assets - Inventory}}{\text{Current Liabilities}}$$

Accounts Receivable to Accounts Payable (AR/AP):

$$\frac{\text{Trade Receivables}}{\text{Trade Payables}}$$

If more than 50% of your sales are collected on a COD basis, add accounts receivables plus cash and divide that sum by accounts payable. Here is the reason: if you just divide receivables by payables and most of your business is COD, your company has almost no receivables and "normal" payables. The division would make the ratio near zero. It wouldn't be telling the right story since your company has received cash for the work that it has done well in advance of the time that it has to pay the payables for the work that was done. For COD companies when cash is included in the ratio, the ratio becomes "normal" again and realistic. COD is a great way to manage cash. However, it is not practical for some companies.

Debt Ratios.

Debt ratios are debt to equity and Long term debt to equity. Increasing debt ratios are not good. Your company is taking on debt rapidly or has too much debt. These ratios should always be greater than zero. If they are less than zero then you have a negative net worth which means you are probably running out of cash because your business has not been profitable for a long time.

For most small businesses the long term debt to equity ratio should be greater than O and less than 1.

Debt to Equity:

$$\frac{\text{Total Liabilities}}{\text{Total Equity}}$$

Long Term Debt to Equity:

$$\frac{\text{Long Term Liabilities}}{\text{Total Equity}}$$

Productivity Ratio (Percentage Compensation):
This ratio is my favorite ratio. This ratio answers the question, for each dollar in revenue that the company earns, how much is the company spending on payroll and payroll taxes? It tells you how productive your employees are.

$$\frac{\text{Total payroll plus payroll taxes}}{\text{Sales}}$$

Usage Ratios.

Usage ratios include receivable turns to get to receivable days and inventory turns to get to inventory days. They tell you how well you are using your assets and cash. If your receivable days are increasing, then you might have a collection problem. If you inventory days are increasing, then you are building up inventory - why is this happening?

Receivable Turns:

$$\frac{\text{Annualized Sales}}{\text{Trade Accounts Receivable}}$$

Receivable Days:

$$\frac{365}{\text{Receivable Turns}}$$

Inventory turns:

$$\frac{\text{Annualized Material Expense (or annualized Cost of goods sold)}}{\text{Inventory}}$$

Inventory Days:

$$\frac{365}{\text{Inventory Turns}}$$

Receivable days to Inventory days:

Look at receivable days to inventory days. Receivable days should always be greater than inventory days. For companies with no inventory, inventory days are zero so your receivable days will always be greater than your inventory days. If you have 30 days of receivables and 60 days of inventory you have twice as much inventory as you need. You can drop that down to 30 days and save a lot of cash.

Here are final thoughts on calculating monthly financial ratios:
- The more profitable your company, the better your ratios will be. The more productive your employees are, the better your ratios will be. The better you use inventory the better your ratios will be. Calculate these ratios every month when you receive your financial statements.
- You can set up a spreadsheet to automatically calculate these ratios. Or, you can do them manually. I actually prefer to do them manually because it forces me to go through the entire financial statement and look at everything. If it is done on a computer and presented to you, you are less likely to look at the individual pages on your financial statements. The ratios don't take a long time to calculate. It should take you no more than 15 minutes once a month. And it is worth going through the numbers on a case by case, line by line basis and make sure that you get the information that you need. If you find that your ratios are going the wrong way, stop and find out what's going on immediately. You'll be able to solve minor issues before they become major crises. That is the goal of financial ratios.

You must generate cash to achieve success. The best way to do it is through your own small business.   Getting and analyzing financial statements each month helps you generate profits which leads to positive cash flow.

Ruth King

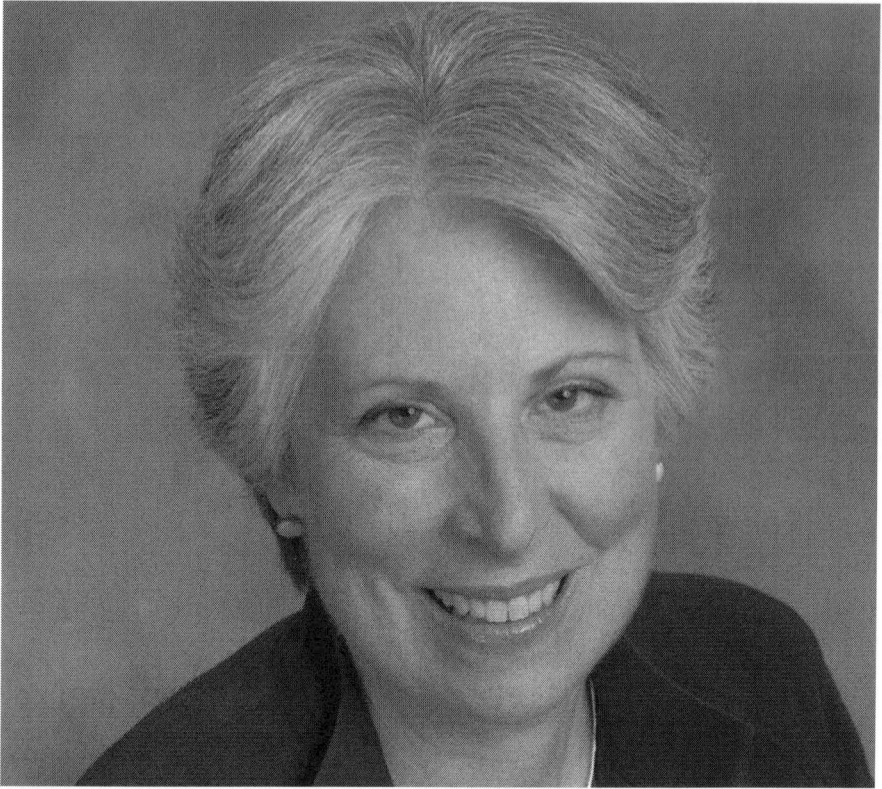

Ruth King - Chief Executive Officer of Profitability Revolution Paradigm

Profitability Master Ruth King is a serial entrepreneur having owned 7 successful businesses in the past 30 years. One of her businesses, Business Ventures Corporation, began operations in 1981. Through Business Ventures Corporation she coaches, trains, and helps small businesses achieve the business goals they want to achieve.

Ruth has been instrumental in helping small business owners understand and profitably use the information generated from the financial segment of their businesses. She has a knack for helping business owners truly understand financials.

After twelve years on the road, doing 200 flights per year, she knew there had to be a better way to reach business people who wanted to build their businesses and train their employees. She began training on the Internet in

1998 and began the first television like broadcasting in 2002. Her latest channel is www.profitabilityrevolution.com, helping small business owners run their business better, make money, live better, enjoy freedom, and give back.

She started the Decatur, Georgia branch of the Small Business Development Center in 1982. She also started the Women's Entrepreneurial Center and taught a year-long course for women who wanted to start their own businesses. This course was the foundation for one of the classes at the Women's Economic Development Authority in Atlanta, Georgia.

Ruth holds a Masters in Business Administration in Finance from Georgia State University. She also holds Bachelor's and Master's Degrees in Chemical Engineering from Tufts University and University of Pennsylvania, respectively.

Ruth was the 2006 USA Best Books Winner for Entrepreneurship and a finalist for the Independent Publisher Awards (IPPY) for The Ugly Truth About Small Business (Sourcebooks). Her second book, The Ugly Truth about Managing People, was published by Sourcebooks in 2007. Her third best selling book, The Courage to be Profitable, was published by Morgan James Publishing in March, 2013.

How I set up a successful business in the recession

Have you ever done anything against everyone's advice? Have you ever turned your back on a successful career to fulfil your dream? In 2007 that's exactly what I did! I had been working in cancer research for 15 years but was feeling disillusioned with the work and wanted to change my career. I had practiced meditation and yoga for several years and had studied for a PhD looking at quality of life in women with gynaecological cancer. My job was very stressful and my blood pressure was getting too high. In summer 2006 I went on holiday to Bali, a very spiritual place, and whilst there I used the space to think about what I could do with my career. I somehow got an idea in my head to set up a health spa and was buzzing with ideas of what the spa would look like and what services we could offer. I thought that when I got home the idea would go away, but it did not and I could not stop thinking about it. I researched health spas and did some market research and really felt that there was a market for another spa in the area. At the time, there were lots of beauty salons across the country, but not many health spas. I wanted to establish a place where people could escape the busy humdrum of everyday life, somewhere to totally relax and switch off. In 2007 I set up a brand new holistic health and well-being spa in Huddersfield, Yorkshire, UK.

Everyone in my life thought I was crazy – I knew nothing about business and nothing about health spas. None of the banks would give me any financial support. But my heart told me it was the right thing to do. I attended a business start-up training course and started putting together a business plan. It looked like it could be a profitable business. I decided to take the plunge! I was lucky enough to be able to continue working one day a week in my cancer research job which I did for a couple of years until the spa was established enough to pay me a salary. I employed two experienced therapists who helped me to set up the spa and I rented a beautiful Victorian villa with a three-year lease.

Then the recession hit the world. My business plan pretty much went out of the window! I still believed that the business could be a success and had a gut feeling that I was still doing the right thing. I linked up with some national companies, such as Lastminute.com, which meant that we were able to market the business to a wider audience with little outlay upfront.

The bookings began to come through and word of mouth, a good web site and offering very high standard of treatments and customer service saw the business begin to flourish. We worked hard to market the business locally and also established regular contact with our clients, creating enticing packages and offers to maintain their custom and keep them coming to our spa.

As the business grew, we employed more staff, including apprentice therapists, and we now employ 10 people. It was hard work during the recession and the doom and gloom constantly portrayed by the media. But people were still working hard and wanted to treat themselves and give themselves time and space to forget about the negativity. People still wanted to celebrate birthdays, Christmas, Mother's Day etc. and we worked hard to market such events throughout the year.

Despite the recession, business did grow, albeit at a slower rate than initially predicted. In summer 2013 I bought a historic property for the spa, close to the original business location, and we moved to the new premises in January 2014 after a period of renovation. This time the banks were confident with my business proposition and were willing to finance the purchase. Since we moved, business has increased by over 25%, which has been fantastic.

So why do I think the business has been so successful? The key points for me are:

I believed in my business
Despite everyone's skepticism, I knew in my heart that I was doing the right thing and although it was tough during the recession, my faith never faltered and I stayed positive. Through owning the spa, I became more spiritual and that led me to approach my life with a different attitude – a more positive one. I read many books about the law of attraction, and I truly believe that if you can imagine something, you can achieve it.

I also learnt that it's important to be authentic and not to try to be someone or something else. I had a clear vision of what I wanted my business to be. By following this vision, my customers and my staff all know the brand values and are all clear about the level and quality of service that is expected and will be delivered. It's easy to be distracted and veer off the main vision, but it's important to adhere to your brand values. For example, it has been suggested on several occasions that we should offer beauty treatments as a way of increasing customer numbers and revenue, but I wanted the focus of the business to be on how people feel on the inside rather than how they look on the outside. My perseverance on focusing on holistic therapies only has paid off, as clients know that when they visit our spa they can totally relax in the peace and quiet and they leave feeling so much better than when they arrived.

Developing and maintaining excellent customer service

Giving excellent customer service is one of our key priorities. It drives me mad when you go into a business (any business) and the people working there have no interest in you and do not care whether you have had a good experience or not. We put a lot of effort into making every single person feel valued and individual from the minute they step into the spa. We have made a lot of friends in the last 7 years and people even come and speak to us for advice about their life and their health and wellbeing.

It's easy to become blasé and forget the importance of excellent customer care but it's critically important. We have strived hard to create an environment where people have a real sense of belonging and a sense that we genuinely care. We ask every client how their treatment has been and want to ensure that every person leaves the spa feeling that they had the best treatment possible.

We also reward loyalty with a loyalty card scheme as showing our clients that we appreciate their business is vital. It also makes them stay loyal to us, so it's a win:win situation.

Employing staff who share my ethos

I've always tried to employ staff who share the same ethos of the spa and who are committed to providing the same level of service to meet the values of the business. I've found that staff who are committed to maintaining and growing the business's reputation, keen to develop their own professional and personal skills, and committed to holistic health and well-being, fit into the team the best and help to grow and develop the business. Choosing the right employees has been a key part of our success.

Caring for my staff

I always tell my staff that the spa is only as good as the people working there and that it is their spa as well as mine. People need to feel valued at work and not taken for granted. It's important to nurture and develop staff. The way you treat your staff is the way they will treat your customers. It's also important to create a harmonious team – there are bound to be occasional tensions but everyone has a collective role in creating a happy relaxed team and it's important that your staff understand this. People spend a lot of time at work and I feel that it's important that they feel happy so that they want to do a good job and they feel proud to work in your business. Feeling happy also means that the staff give out a good energy to the clients. We put a lot of effort into making our staff feel valued and investing in their continuing professional development. Often clients comment on how happy a team we have, so it does get noticed.

Providing excellent standards of treatments

People will only continue using your business if they feel that they are receiving a high quality product and it is important to maintain the standards and continually assess your products. We provide regular training for our staff, both in new treatments and also refreshing their skills in existing treatments. We strive to maintain the best standards of treatment so that we remain the best in our field in the area.

Finding a niche

If you can find a niche in the market – something that is different from your competitors – then you will attract customers. The niche that we found was to provide people an escape from their busy lives, somewhere beautiful to relax and unwind, that was not corporate, not so big that there was a hustle and bustle, and not part of a large busy hotel. We created a beautiful peaceful space that counteracts everyday busy lives. We provide a friendly, personal service that you do not always get in a larger spa and this has been a major success of our business.

Constant and varied marketing

Regular contact with clients has been key to our success. We use a range of marketing tools as different people respond to different techniques – email newsletters, social media, Trip Advisor reviews, open evenings, client events, supporting and hosting charity events, a good web site with paid search engine optimisation, networking with local businesses, and special offers and promotions. We have adapted to changing needs – for example our Facebook is very successful but we only set up a Facebook page a few years ago and we are continually adapting to other social media tools. We always have offers special promotions throughout the year – when I set up the business I was advised not to do special offers as it undervalues your business, but to be honest, the spa would have closed down had we never done any special offers. Customers in this field expect to see a special offer and our best offers are only available at very quiet times.

Customer surveys

As well as asking customers about their experience as they are leaving, we also carry out an annual survey of our customers. We've realised that it's really valuable to listen to your clients – it can be difficult to hear negative feedback but we have learnt to listen to it in a constructive way and it really has made a difference to our business. As a business owner you rarely experience what the customer experiences and so it's key to ask them for their feedback and then to implement any valid ideas. I have learnt too that you will not please everyone all of the time and that some people prefer another business – that's fine too - providing enough people do like what you are offering!

Looking after my health

I believe that it is really important as a business owner to look after your health and keep yourself balanced. In business you can work 24/7 but you will become ill or stressed or you will lose interest and so it's vital that you make time for leisure time and holidays etc. Although I work hard, I make time for exercise and short holidays and this generally keeps me fit and healthy and able to be at work every day.

So, many factors have contributed to my business success. The key factors for me have been identifying the brand values, keeping focused on these values and working hard – but also having time to relax.

Maxine Stead

I am 44, I live with my partner, and I have no children. I studied Pharmacology and Physiology at Leeds University. For 15 years after leaving University I worked in project management in cancer research, where I also carried out a part-time PhD researching the quality of life of women with ovarian cancer. Whilst the development of my career enabled me to develop a national profile within the NHS, academia and pharmaceutical industry with a good secure salary, my role moved away from cancer research and became more general and less rewarding.

I decided to make a career change in 2007 and to establish my own business helping people with busy jobs and lifestyles like my own to take time out and to develop a different approach to life.

I trained in Indian head massage and Reiki, but my main role is the running of the business which utilises my management, organisation, communication and leadership skills (and my newly acquired marketing skills) whilst employing experienced therapists to undertake treatments to a professional and high standard. I started the business with a personal loan, renting premises and initially taking on 2 full-time therapists. I now own premises for the spa and employ 10 staff. I enjoy yoga, keep fit, reading and travelling.

The importance of nutrition on physical and emotional health

How you think and feel is directly affected by what you eat. This is not a new idea. People have believed that food could influence their health and well-being for thousands of years. Hippocrates, the father of modern medicine, is known for his mantra: "Let your food be your medicine and your medicine be your food" whilst medieval medical culinary textbooks describe quince, dates and elderberries as mood enhancers, lettuce and chicory as tranquilisers, and apples, pomegranates, beef and eggs as erotic stimulants.

The last century has seen immense progress in research, primarily short-term human trials and animal studies, showing how certain foods influence brain structure, biochemistry and physiology; affecting mood and performance.

What we eat has a significant impact on our moods and how we think. Increasingly, research suggests that the root of many physical symptoms and disorders are nutritional and biochemical imbalances that either cause or intensify them. The correct diet can improve IQ, mood and emotional stability and sharpen memory whist a poor diet or not eating at regular intervals can mimic symptoms of depression, anxiety, and attention-deficit hyperactivity, as well as other behavioural issues. In addition, several mental health issues including depression, anxiety, and attention-deficit hyperactivity have been linked to deficiencies in vitamins, minerals and omega-3 fatty acids.

We live in hectic times, as we enter the 21 century, we face massive adaptive stress. Many of us use sugar, caffeine and other stimulants and generally ignore the health of our brain. Email, mobiles, instant news, designed to make our lives easier have accelerated our pace. Processed fast foods and diets high in sugar and low in nutrients are taking their toll resulting in many of us not reaching our full potential in terms of physical and mental health, alertness and clarity. Those of us struggling to adapt and rise to the challenge are living with fatigue, sleep problems, mood swings, anxiety, depression, memory and concentration difficulties and impatience, all hallmarks of our age, but often not attributed to biochemical imbalances brought on by years of poor nutrition and exposure to environmental chemicals and pollution. Those who are not able to adapt are increasingly experiencing physical and psychological illnesses. ADHD, autism, schizophrenia, depression and Alzheimer's are all on the increase. Our challenge is to find a way to stay physically well, mentally sharp and happy. The first line of defence has to be nutrition. This chapter is a brief introduction to the importance of nutrition and the effect that certain foods have on our physical health. It also explores the less recognised and understood mental health consequences of a poor nutrition and what we can do to correct this. Let's start by exploring some of the key factors that affect our nutritional status:

Biochemical Individuality

Biochemical individuality describes normal variations in the nutritional needs of individuals. Research indicates some people require more of a certain vitamin or mineral than others. If we fail to consume the correct level of nutrients it can lead to underlying nutritional deficiencies, leaving us vulnerable to developing physical, psychological and often behavioural symptoms.

Variations in biochemical individuality depend on an individual's current health, lifestyle, living and working conditions, as well as age and genetics. The concept is still not recognised by many doctors and psychiatrists; however the principal, that certain populations and special conditions require higher supplementation, is accepted for example in pregnancy, lactation, gastrointestinal disturbances, heavy exercise, alcoholism and old age.

The Gut Brain Connection

Traditionally we have assumed that all thinking is done in the brain but we now know the gut and brain are in permanent communication and that this relationship may hold the key to better brain health. Every time we eat something it signals to the brain and what we eat can alter gut bacteria which in turn affects brain function. People with high-vegetable, high fibre diets have a different gut environment to people who eat a more typical Western diet that is high in fat and carbohydrates. Studies on food-mood relationships has also found diets low in carbohydrates increase feelings of anger, depression, and tension, diets high in protein and low in carbohydrates increase anger and diets high in carbohydrates have a generally uplifting effect on mood though this is still contentious.

Recent research also reveals the gut contains over 100 million neurons, has as a many neurotransmitters as the brain and produces 75% of the body's 'happy' neurotransmitter serotonin. So as well as playing a key role in digestion, the gut plays an important role in a number of psychological conditions including depression, insomnia, memory, learning, appetite regulation, obesity and hormone function.

Blood sugar and how it affects energy and health

To function at optimum health and cope with daily stresses we need a steady source of energy. The brain uses approximately one-third of our calories and while most of the body's tissues can store sugar (glucose) and fat for fuel, the brain cannot. To function optimally the brain is completely dependent on a steady supply of glucose from food. A poor diet or not eating regularly can cause fluctuating or low energy levels which unbalances the body's biochemistry and can significantly impact on our nervous system and emotions, inhibiting behaviour and self-expression. A diet high in sugar, refined carbohydrates and stimulants leads to excessive insulin release, which in turn leads to falling blood sugar levels, or hypoglycaemia.

In this condition, the brain does not receive a steady supply of glucose and blood sugar can fall to levels so low that the brain is effectively being starved of fuel. Hypoglycaemia causes the brain to secrete glutamate a messenger molecule that serves an important function in your body. However, when excess amounts of glutamate are excreted it can wreak havoc with your brain and nervous system, causing a variety of side effects such as dizziness, irritability, palpitations, impaired memory and concentration, depression, anxiety, panic attacks and nightmares. Other common symptoms mimic a number of emotional disorders including; fatigue, confusion and in some cases, violence and psychosis. On an emotional level, when we're tired, decision-making and other mental and emotional processes become more difficult. Almost without exception, every client I see suffers from low energy levels. This often manifests as feelings of fatigue, irritability, mood swings, depression, anxiety and cravings for another sugary snack - perpetuating the cycle.

Unstable blood sugar has a profound effect on behaviour. If left uncontrolled blood sugar swings can affect calcium metabolism and deplete vital B-complex vitamins and minerals such as chromium, manganese and zinc. It can increase the risk of neurodegenerative diseases, such as Alzheimer's disease, Parkinson's and can cause violent and aggressive behaviour. In children it often leads to hyperactivity, while in older people, it can cause mental confusion. Unbalanced blood sugar also plays a role in alcoholism and drug abuse. Balancing blood sugar is quite simple with diet and food supplements and can help some people to avoid a relapse by reducing cravings for alcohol, sweets and drugs; yet it is often overlooked.

Digestion

Stabilising blood sugar is only one factor in keeping energy levels high. To effectively produce energy from our food we need a fully functioning energy pathway. This begins with the ingestion of food, continues with its digestion and ends with the absorption and transportation of nutrients to the body's cells. If any step in this pathway is blocked, whether by nutrient deficiencies, toxic chemicals or infection, a person's energy levels will drop. Often, even if people are eating a nutrient rich diet, their digestion may be compromised by chronic stress or medication which contributes to a lack of adequate enzymes needed to digest food and unlock the nutrients within it.

Once food is digested, it must be absorbed and transported into the cells. This is another area where many people have difficulty, often due to an imbalance in their ratio of fatty acids. Modern diets are often too high in omega-6 fatty acids, found in packaged and processed foods, and too low in omega-3 fatty acids, found in fish, nuts and seeds. This causes cell membranes to become less permeable and contributes to inflammation.

Once digested and absorbed, food is sent to the liver to be processed and converted to chemical substances. A diet high in sugar, carbohydrates and alcohol or exposure to chemical and environmental toxins can contribute to poor liver function, negatively impacting on digestion and compromising energy. Only after all these processes have taken place do any nutrients pass to the cells and once there they must be further processed within the mitochondria of each cell. Deficiencies of B vitamins or manganese will prevent this energy conversion and may be why many people reach for caffeinated beverages and other stimulants to keep going, putting further load on the liver, depleting more nutrients and perpetuating the cycle.

Nutritional deficiencies and excesses

Several psychological health issues including depression, anxiety and attention-deficit hyperactivity have been linked to deficiencies in vitamins, minerals and omega-3 fatty acids. But many of us never consider diet when we have difficulty with concentration, mood or memory issues. Making changes to what we eat can significantly boost psychological wellbeing, increase alertness, help manage stress and sharpen intelligence. Some people have reported improvements in fatigue, irritability, insomnia, anxiety, panic attacks, depression, obsessive-compulsive feelings, eating disorders, cravings, concentration, memory and learning disorders. It makes sense; you wouldn't expect your car to operate correctly without the necessary fuel and fluids, so why would you expect to be able to perform optimally yourself if your diet is low in nutrients and high in processed foods and stimulants? A number of nutrients are essential for physical and psychological health; these include all B-complex vitamins, calcium, zinc, iron, selenium and omega-3 to name a few:

B-complex vitamins are essential for proper nervous system functioning. Many people report more energy and less depression when they take thiamine (B1), riboflavin (B2), niacin (B3) and pyridoxine (B6). Studies show niacin can reverse psychosis. Pantothenic acid (B5) also helps energy production. B6, B12 and folic acid are the cornerstones of methylation supporting mental health. Choline and inositol, also part of the B-Complex family act as natural tranquilisers. Studies suggest insufficient amounts of thiamine (Vitamin B1) are linked with introversion, inactivity, fatigue, decreased self-confidence and generally poor mood. Improving thiamine status increases well-being, sociability, and overall energy levels. Thiamine rich foods include cereal grains, pork, yeast, potatoes, cauliflower, oranges and eggs.

Besides helping in the prevention of neural tube defects, folic acid also plays an important role in the brain. Folic acid deficiency is associated with depressed mood. Psychiatric patients are particularly at risk for developing folic acid deficiency because of possible disordered eating habits caused by a loss of appetite and anticonvulsant drugs, which inhibit folic acid absorption. Foods rich in folic acid include dark leafy green vegetables, liver and other organ meats, poultry, oranges and grapefruits, nuts, sprouts, and whole wheat breads.

Modern diets are often deficient in calcium and the nutrients needed to use calcium such as vitamin D. Calcium raises the threshold at which nerves cells fire, reducing the sensitivity of the nervous system and acting as a psychological buffer that relaxes muscles to help calm people down. Even a mild deficiency in calcium can result in irritability, anxiety, panic attacks, unexplained depression, nervousness, short tempers and violence or dementia. People on low fat diets, lactose intolerance individuals and those with irritable bowel syndrome are often advised to remove dairy from their diet, this can result in low tissue levels of calcium. Other factors that interfere with the body's calcium levels include chronic, unmanaged stress which uses up calcium much faster than it can be replenished and fizzy drinks which contain phosphoric acid which binds to calcium in the intestine and forms an insoluble product that cannot be absorbed, effectively robbing the body of calcium. Foods rich in calcium include milk, yogurt and cheese, leafy green vegetables, fruit, seafood, legumes, sardines, and dried figs.

High calcium and magnesium levels and low levels of sodium and potassium are associated with fatigue and low thyroid and adrenal activity, indicating a person is at the exhaustion stage of stress. This condition is often associated with feelings of depression but can be corrected with a nutrient rich diet high in protein and vegetables, low in sugars and fats and nutritional supplements including; thyroid and adrenal support, B-complex vitamins, a digestive aid and some calcium and magnesium to alleviate anxiety.

Zinc is also an anti-stress nutrient; a deficiency is associated with anxiety, panic attacks and emotional instability. Fortunately anxiety is one of the easiest conditions to correct using nutritional therapy. Individuals with bipolar or manic-depressive disorder often have an underlying copper imbalance. This leads to the common pattern of short periods of high energy followed by periods of low energy and depression. Copper imbalance can be corrected in most cases with nutrition in a relatively short time with relatively little difficulty. Foods rich in zinc include seafood such as oysters and crab, meats such as lean beef and poultry and dairy products including yogurt and cheese, spinach and pumpkin seeds.

Iron deficiency is one of the most common nutritional problems in both developing and developed countries. Iron deficiency anaemia can result in lethargy, low mood and problems with attention and decreased ability to exercise. Women, children, vegetarians and people who follow a diet are most at risk of Iron deficiency. Foods rich in iron include liver, vegetables such as broccoli, asparagus, and parsley, seafood, iron-fortified grains, greens, nuts, meat and dried fruits. L-Taurine and L-tryptophan have a calming effect. L-phenylalanine and L-tyrosine can enhance thyroid activity and improve energy and mood. Working with a nutritional therapist will ensure you supplement the right amounts.

Selenium is a powerful antioxidant which works inside the body to help it produce more antioxidants. Numerous studies have linked low levels of selenium in the body to poor moods, decreased cognitive function and memory loss. The brain processes selenium differently than other antioxidants, so it's important to maintain steady levels of this powerful nutrient. Fish, grass-fed and pasture-raised meats, whole grains and nuts and seeds are good sources of selenium.

Omega-3 fatty acids can influence mood, behaviour and personality. Low blood levels of polyunsaturated omega-3 fatty acids are associated with depression, pessimism and impulsivity. They can play a role in major depressive disorder, bipolar disorder, schizophrenia, substance abuse and attention deficit disorder. Our modern diet means we are consuming greater amounts of omega-6 polyunsaturated fatty acids contained in foods such as eggs, poultry, baked goods, whole-grain bread, nuts, and many oils. These fatty acids compete with omega-3 polyunsaturated fatty acids. This is especially true for docosahexaenoic acid (DHA) and eicosapentaenoic acid (EPA), both members of the omega-3 fatty acid family which contribute to the fluidity of the cell membrane which is crucial for brain development and functioning. Omega-3 fatty acids are found in fish, seafood, some plants and meat and nut oils. Many foods such as bread, yogurt, orange juice, milk, and eggs are often fortified with omega-3 fatty acids.

Food and Chemical Sensitivities
Although the precise cause-and-effect relationship between different foods and moods has yet to be fully understood, many people have found they can link eating, or not eating certain foods with how they feel. Reactions to foods can trigger psychological and behavioural problems. One explanation for these reactions is that histamine, a chemical released in response to an allergic reaction, can be released in the brain causing alterations in brain chemistry.

The foods that most often cause problems include sugar, caffeine, chocolate, wheat such as bread, biscuits, and cakes, dairy products such as cheese, fish, crustacean shellfish, tree nuts and peanuts, certain artificial colourings, flavourings, preservatives and chemicals in drinking water. Other commonly eaten foods such as yeast, corn, eggs, oranges, soya and tomatoes may also cause symptoms for some people. In addition to foods, exposure to dusts, pollen, molds and chemicals can cause aggressive behaviour and anger.

Modifying the diet to enhance physical and psychological wellness
Whilst there's still no definitive diet to enhance mood and optimise health and performance, following a well-balanced diet rich in protein, with moderate amounts of carbohydrates and healthy fats is generally supportive of physical and psychological health. Addressing the quality of food and minimising exposure to stimulants, stress, toxic chemicals and allergy provoking foods will help support blood sugar, provide a steady source of energy, minimise potential reactions on the central nervous system, boost psychological wellbeing, sharpen intelligence and help manage stress.
Although still not incorporated in the standard medical approach to health, consistently consuming the right amount of the right nutrients, and so maintaining an optimal balance of neurotransmitters and 'receptive' receptors, can sharpen your mind and memory, improve your mood and help you relax and beat stress.

Here are 5 tips for achieving optimum nutrition:

Tip 1
Balancing blood sugar will provide the brain with a steady source of fuel and help alleviate the negative effects of fluctuating blood sugar levels including; fatigue, irritability, poor concentration, depression and food cravings.

1.   Never skip breakfast and try to keep regular meal times
2.   Avoid sugar, glucose, dextrose, sucrose, malt sugar, honey, anything that contains high fructose corn syrup (HFCS), fruit juices, all artificial sweeteners, processed foods, white breads, white rice, pasta and potatoes.
3.   Never eat carbohydrates without protein, this helps slow the transit of sugar into the blood stream, keeping blood sugar levels stable. Add meat, fish, beans, eggs, nuts and seeds to rice and pasta dishes or grind and sprinkle; flax, hemp, pumpkin, sunflower and sesame seeds in soups, cereal and salads.
4.   Remember to drink six to eight glasses of filtered water per day. It's easy to overlook this, but water is vital and can quickly change how we feel, physically as well as mentally.

Tip 2

Eat a diet high in fresh vegetables, fruit, fish, nuts and seeds and low in sugar, carbohydrates, caffeine and processed foods to provide the nutrients needed to nourish mind and body.

1.   Eat a healthy diet that includes 5-7 servings of fruit and mainly vegetables per day, choose locally-grown organic if possible, including dark green leafy veg, watercress, broccoli, carrots, sweet potatoes, fish, nuts and seeds. Eat 4 or more servings of whole grains such as brown rice, oats, rye, corn, quinoa, pasta, bread (one portion equals a handful).

2.   Stop smoking.

3.   Reduce then aim to eliminate alcohol, coffee, tea and caffeinated drinks, painkillers and antibiotics which damage the digestive tract and increase nutrient losses.

4.   Avoid wheat and dairy for 2 weeks, see how you feel.

Tip 3

Essential fatty acids are vital for the healthy functioning of the body and keep the brain well oiled, particularly omega-3 found in oil-rich fish, such as mackerel and sardines, linseeds (flax), hemp seeds and their oils.

1.   Avoid processed foods and fried foods which contain hydrogenated fats and reduce saturated fat from meat and dairy.

2.   Sources of omega-3 include cold water fish, herring, mackerel and wild salmon. Eat 2-3 times a week. Limit larger fish e.g. fresh tuna, shark and Marlin to once a month as they contain mercury.

3.   Eat a heaped tablespoon of ground seeds every day or a tablespoon of special cold-pressed seed oils and/or eating oily fish such as salmon, mackerel, sardines, trout, herring and anchovies three times a week. Sunflower seeds, pumpkin seeds, Brazil nuts and walnuts also contain important 'good mood' nutrients. Try to eat a palm full 5 out of 7 days.

4.   See a nutritional therapist to get your Omega-3 to Omega-6 ratio checked.

Tip 4

Amino acids are the brain's messengers.   These messengers, when depleted, may contribute to feelings of agitation, anger, mild to severe depression and anxiety and/or sleep problems. The specific amino acids that our brains manufacture transmitters from are frequently not supplied by our modern diet or in the way our brain best utilises them. As stress further depletes supplies it is difficult, for the brain to restore necessary amounts to proper levels.

1.   Men require 3 and women require 2 servings of protein rich foods a day to ensure adequate supplies of amino acids to support mind and mood.

2.   Vegetarian sources of protein includes beans, lentils, quinoa, Tofu and peas

3.   Supplementing with tryptophan boosts mood and glutamine boosts memory, but always speak to a nutritional therapist before undertaking a supplement programme.

Tip 5

Even with the best intensions, it's sometimes difficult to get all the nutrients you need from food. A typical health supplement programme to ensure you get all the nutrients you need includes three formulations; a high potency vitamin and mineral complex, vitamin c and an essential fatty acid supplement.

1.   Start with a high potency multivitamin and mineral. Aim for one that provides the following levels of individual nutrients, or get as close to as you can; 7,500iu of A, 10mcg (400iu) of D, 100iu of E, 250mg of C, and 25mg each of B1, B2, B3, B5 and B6, 10mcg of B12, 200mcg of folic acid and 50mcg of biotin.

The mineral content should provide 300mg of calcium, 150mg of magnesium, 10mg of iron, 10mg of zinc, 2.5mg of manganese, 20mcg of chromium and 25mcg of selenium, and, ideally some molybdenum, vanadium and boron. Unfortunately you can't fit all of the above vitamins and minerals in one tablet, so opt for combined multivitamin and mineral formulas. Also, liquid drops are more easily absorbed than tablets.

2.   Vitamin C is best taken separately simply because it is unlikely that you'll find 1,800mg into a multi-vitamin.

3.   Before supplementing with fatty acids, take a fatty acids profile to evaluate your ratio of omega-3 to omega-6 and identify your individual requirements. A nutritional therapist can help with this.

Once you know what you need, supplement with a concentrated oil. For omega-3, choose either flax seed oil capsules or the more concentrated fish oil capsules providing EPA and DHA. For omega-6, supplement with

GLA found in evening primrose oil or borage oil. Even better is a combination of all three; EPA, DHA and GLA.

To meet DHA and EPA recommendations, vegetarians and vegans should aim to exceed the RDA for Omega-3 while simultaneously keeping their Omega-6 intake low. Flax, Chia and Hemp seeds have the best Omega-3 to Omega-6 ratio.

Shani Shaker

Shani Shaker BA (hons), dipION, mBANT, CNHC, is a registered nutritional therapist with a focus on regenerative and functional nutrition, mental health, disordered eating and addictions.

Before retraining at the Institute of Optimum Nutrition, Shani spent 20 years working 12 hour days in London's leading PR consultancies whilst striving to achieve a work-life balance. She founded her practice as an antidote to our non-stop, 21st century lifestyle, which she believes takes its toll on us physically, mentally and emotionally. Her philosophy is that when we balance how we eat, live and work, our body and health can be transformed, anxiety and depression can be overcome and addiction can be controlled.

Based in London she can be contacted at shani@superradiance.co.uk or visit www.superradiance.co.uk for more information.

Disclaimer: The information provided is intended for general knowledge only and is not a substitute for professional medical advice or treatment for specific medical conditions. Please consult your healthcare provider before making any changes to your medication or with any questions or concerns you may have regarding your condition. Supplementation should only be temporary. If you're eating a nutrient-rich diet, extra supplementation should only last for a month or two, just long enough to resolve the deficiency.

Success on your terms

If you ask anyone if they want to be successful, you will invariably hear a resounding, 'Of course I do!' However, if you ask what would make them feel successful, they may talk about career achievements, possessions, lifestyle or an internal sense of satisfaction in what they are doing. All too often, these choices are limited by thoughts about what they should, ought and must, have, do and be. These are myths; unquestioned assumptions. They are societal, cultural and personal, and they limit the way in which we choose the life we want to live, and narrowly define what we consider to be successful.

Much of what we desire is conditioned by our culture, which is portrayed through the media, by celebrities, and by the people around us. The things we are told we need include tangible items like clothes, homes, cars and technology. Other items are results or experiences, like holidays, promotions or being connected to (or seen in) certain places, linked with (or seen with) certain people. If we know we are influenced in this way, to a greater or lesser degree, we can stop for a moment and ask, 'Why do I want these things?'

Over the years I have posed this question to thousands of people and they respond with things like:

- I buy the latest fashions because I like to keep up with the trend.

- I need to portray a certain image if I am to be considered for promotion.

- I feel I am achieving if I have a top-of-the-range car.

- I must live in a certain area to access the best schools.

- I need to be a certain body shape or size to be considered attractive.

In each of these typical responses, people imply that attainment of the item, outcome or label is a measurable result of success. However, I believe this is only a symbol of what we really want. We are really seeking the underlying emotional state we experience, or believe we are going to experience, if we achieve such things. We are either seeking positive emotions in reaching for them, or avoiding negative emotions of feeling inadequate, embarrassed or 'less than' if we don't attain them.

Believing that we must develop a career, get on the property ladder or travel to certain destinations to be deemed socially successful, also influences us. Rarely do we ask if we really want these things or not. Instead, we ask ourselves how far we are prepared to go to acquire them. And there is a downside that we don't always consider: when we are swayed by social influences, we are setting ourselves up to be constantly dissatisfied because the social demands keep changing and we are fooled into seeking the next biggest and best thing.

If we go against the norm and seek things that maybe society frowns at, for instance deciding not to have children, or not following what others consider a successful career, we can experience anxiety. This may be in the form of self-doubt, which may increase as others question whether we are doing the right thing. We need to work through this self-doubt by trying out different things and asking whether our anxiety is caused by a lack of certain possessions or experiences, or by criticism from others, by fear that we are not doing the right thing.

Over the years, many of my clients have concluded that what they *really* want, to be successful, is freedom. Whether they seek possessions, money, fame or experiences, they believe that this will give them the freedom to choose the work they do, where they live or how they will spend their time. Therefore, it is freedom they are seeking. If this resonates with you, I encourage you to consider success in a very different way.

Success on your own terms

One way to get to the pleasure or wellbeing you believe you will attain by achieving success is to put aside all limitations on what you believe you can be, do or have. The following exercise will help you discover this.

****

Exercise 1:

Imagine you have all the money, contacts, confidence and support to do, have or be whatever you desire. There have no limitations to what this might be. What would you do if you knew you couldn't fail? Write your answer on a separate piece of paper.

****

You may find this exercise difficult if you do not allow yourself to believe that anything you want is possible. You may have answered with something that you think is likely, a reduced version of what you really desire. Maybe you have been so conditioned to think a certain way that you will not allow yourself to think big enough. The thing you can't allow yourself to imagine may be the very thing that you *should* consider.

When we allow ourselves to think about what we really want, doubts often arise and we say:

- But I am too old

- Where will the money come from?

- That's ok for other people but not me.

- What will people think?

- What if I fail?

What stands in the way?

When we dare to allow ourselves to consider what we really want to do, to think about what we believe will bring us a sense of freedom and wellbeing, things will stand in our way. These include:

- Our personal myths or beliefs about what is possible.

- Negative self-talk.

- Fear of other people's criticism.

- Fear of change

- Changing our identity

- Feeling foolish and a failure if it doesn't work out.

The rest of this chapter will take you on a journey to challenge these limited beliefs and discover success on your own terms.

The solution: embracing choice on the road to success

If you don't consider yourself to be successful at the moment, the previous exercise probably brought up some mixed feelings and reactions. You may already have achieved much of what you set out to achieve; but are you happy? What you thought was going to make you happy and feeling successful may not work any more. You may be denying the possibility of radical change, believing that it would only be possible were you able to shed your debts, your work and your commitments. You may be saying, 'If only I could win a million dollars I could make all the changes I want and become successful'.

To impose conditions on your life is to shed responsibility for your life. In many ways, it is a myth that you can't change. Even if you don't knowingly make changes, changes will inevitably occur, requiring modifications to be made. Why wait for pressures or other people's plans to initiate change in your life? You have unique abilities, talents, dreams and ideals. The problem is getting in touch with how you want to use them. You can increase your income, get out of debt, reduce your working hours or have more satisfying relationships; but, they won't just arrive one day. You are the author of your life, and if you want to change in a meaningful and informed manner, there is always a way. There is also *always* a price. Are *you* prepared to pay the price?

****

Example

On several occasions I have asked people, 'What would you do if you won a million dollars?' The answers in terms of achieving goals and realising dreams are as varied as the people answering. Here are some typical responses:

- I would immediately have more time.

- I would give up my job.

- I wouldn't feel so tired all the time because I would buy   in lots of help.

- I would travel and see the world.

- I could do anything I wanted to do—wow!

- At last I could become successful.

A million dollars wouldn't enable me to buy anything I want that I couldn't buy now. This is not because I have already acquired wealth, fame, or success, but comes from a real feeling that anything I want is available now. I would still choose to be sitting with my friends having similar conversations. I wouldn't change the partner I live with, or the direction of my life. Whilst budgeting might change, I have never been a person whose increase in income immediately matches an increase in spending. With a million dollars I might decide to live directly by the sea—or would I? If I really wanted to do that I could do it now, by making some adjustments. And however nice a place by the sea might be, I would still want the same group of friends around me to enjoy the experience.

Ask yourself the question: 'What would I do if I won a million dollars?' Your answer may provide you with valuable insight into the dreams and desires you have, and which you have suppressed in the belief that they are *not* attainable because you *don't* have a million dollars!   For example, is it really travel you want, or is it a sense of adventure? — That can be attained in other ways, without waiting for a time when you can take a big break.

****

What can you learn from this example? It is a challenge to encourage you to think *very* carefully about what you *really* want, and whether you are avoiding hearing it because you believe it is only attainable if a miracle were to happen. But that is a myth! You *can* make changes that contribute to your happiness—in the short and long term. But first you must get in touch with what it is that you truly want. The following exercises will give you an opportunity to work this out, determine how to get there, and figure out what price will be entailed in realising your dreams.

Preparing for change

When you decide what you want in the long term, it often becomes a habit to compromise and withstand the obligations you consider are necessary to achieve your goals. As time goes on, these obligations and commitments become onerous and problems exist even after the long-term goal has been achieved. This happens in many areas in our lives. Consider marriage. You may have desired a loving relationship with someone special, and marriage may have represented the means to attain it. However, within that contract other duties and expectations may have arisen which seem unrelated to your long-term goal of a loving relationship. This might be unacceptable to you, but you choose to compromise despite considerable discomfort.

The same goes for the long-term goal of a high-status job. You may have started out with a desire for a responsible, high profile job and you may have worked very hard to achieve it. However, now you have attained this goal, you are sharply aware of the duties and obligations that represent compromise in how you lead your life now.

Even in small things, you will find that routines and schedules you considered useful earlier continue without your ever appraising their usefulness or contribution to your current goals.

It is crucial that you regularly check to look at your assumptions about your life. Assumptions are those things that you hold to be true without ever questioning them. Reappraise your activities and look at your short- and long-term goals to see how much relevance they still have to your happiness. A useful way to do this is to look at what you do with your 168 hours each week, and consider how meaningfully you are spending your time.

****

Exercise 2:

Take two large sheets of A3 paper. On each of them, write the days of the week down the left-hand side. On the first sheet, create twelve headings from left to right and label them 6am, 7am etc., through to 5pm. Do the same on the second sheet, but this time from 6pm through to 5am. Create columns by drawing lines so you have space to write down how you spend each hour of each day of the week. Now write down exactly how you spend your 168 hours by filling in the columns. Write down all your activities as they are now, without any judgement.

Next, rate each activity as:

Enjoyable, Unenjoyable or Indifferent.

Rate as enjoyable those activities that you choose to do and from which you derive some happiness. Do not rate activities as enjoyable because you don't know what to do instead. Do not impose judgements on what should be enjoyable: you may swim regularly but find it more of a chore than relaxation.

Think about your work. Sub-divide your work activities and label different tasks accordingly. Activities labelled unenjoyable are those where you have to ask, 'Why am I doing this? Is it necessary? This is a chore. I feel obligated'.

Then label activities that you are indifferent about. These may include brushing your teeth or walking the dog.

Positive or negative

Next rate your activities as positive or negative. The positive ones are those you choose in order to make you happy. An example may be going for a walk when you could have chosen to do something else. The negative ones are those you do to avoid unhappiness. Visiting the family to avoid conflict with your spouse might fall into this category.

Active or reactive

Activities labelled as *active* are those that you initiate or choose to do. An example might be enrolling for a night class. However, it would be *reactive* if you enrolled to please your boss.

Are you going along with things because they are part and parcel of what you want or wanted at some time? Are you allowing others to choose for you? If you always allow others to choose for you, you will never find happiness, since what makes them happy will be different for you.

Label as *reactive* all the activities that someone else wants you to do. You may visit your parents regularly to keep them happy when you dread the conflict and fights that ensue.

****

By labelling your activities, a picture should develop of how much of your life you are actively choosing to bring about your happiness.

Reactive activities

Let us consider reactive activities for a moment. Reactive activities include things you do to preserve a relationship, even if it is unimportant to you. Ask if the time spent doing this activity is worth it. People say that compromise is necessary, but if you are with the right people—those with whom you share important values—self-sacrifice and compromise are not really necessary! Look for relationships where you don't need to tolerate unpleasant things to maintain them.

Reflect for a moment on your reactive activities. Why are you doing them?. Ask yourself if they will contribute to you achieving your long-term goals. Are they encumbrances that you haven't considered, or which you feel are necessary to achieve what you want? Are they enjoyable? Are some of them the result of earlier commitments or past mistakes? Now let's consider how productive they are in bringing about your happiness.

These *active* and *reactive* labels highlight how much choice you are exercising in your life now. The next activity goes further, and focuses you on the future and how productive your activities are in contributing to your short- and long-term goals.

****

Exercise 3:

Look at each of your activities and give them one of the following labels:

Enjoyment –activities which bring you happiness right now, e.g. watching films, cooking, tennis.

Past mistakes –activities that have arisen out of something you did in the past. This may be a financial commitment to a cause you no longer support, financial settlements on a previous marriage, or a work obligation continued because your friend got you the job and you would feel guilty if you left.

****

****

Exercise 4:

Now label your activities as:

Productive in the short term—this applies to anything you do which makes you happy now, or will do shortly. It may be aspects of your work that generate money you can spend enjoyably right away. It applies to plans and energy spent on arranging holidays or home decoration—things that give you pleasure.

Productive in the long term—activities which you believe will bring you happiness in the future apply here. You may be training to work in a new area that you believe you will enjoy. You may be working hard for a retirement home, and this is something you eagerly anticipate. The criterion to apply here is whether it contributes to your future happiness.

Unproductive—some activities appear to be done with no real hope of bringing you enjoyment. This might apply to committee meetings you attend for some cause you no longer support. It may be hours spent watching TV to avoid thinking about your life rather than for enjoyment. It may be more radical, such as a relationship that you hoped would bring happiness but only brings conflict.

****

You may find that different aspects of the same activity are labelled differently. That is why it is important to work through the activities hour by hour. You will see from the last two activities that the labels apply to different times in your life:

- Past—past mistakes and commitments

- Present—those that you enjoy

- Future—how productive they are in the short and long term

This exercise may cause you some alarm when you realise how many hours you spend on activities that simply do not make you happy. Applying labels is a way of highlighting how much you enjoy in your life, how much is duty, and how much contributes to bringing about happiness in the short and long terms. It helps you focus on seeing how frequently you do things to please others or because you never have time to appraise their value.

Ask yourself now, 'How much of my 168 hours per week is making me happy?' Try not to justify everything you do now as contributing to a long-term goal. This can be a cop-out, because the answer, 'I put up with a boring job with an aggressive boss because one day I will have earned enough to live in luxury' is a life sentence! You don't *have* to suffer now to reap benefits later. In a sense, the future is a myth anyway, since it represents hope which is experienced in the here and now.

Change involves living with anxiety. Ironically, to not change also involves living with anxiety. That is the human condition. How much better to live meaningfully in anxiety where you have better odds for happiness! So let's start with small steps.

****

Exercise 5:

Find some time every day to do something out of choice. Take some time every day to reappraise your actions now to see how they contribute to your long-term goals.

****

You may find it hard to do something out of choice every day. It may have been a long time since you really engaged with your needs. You may also say, 'I am always choosing what to do and where to go!' This may be the case—but look again. Ask yourself, 'Would I choose this if I had complete freedom?' You may find that the reply is not always 'yes'.

Life is not complicated—you make it so. Other people don't make your life difficult—you allow them to cause you difficulty. Even if you don't actively seek conflict with your boss, to live with it is collusion, for which you must take responsibility. Where you find yourself now is a result of choices you have made along the way. You have chosen to be where you are today, and you can choose not to be!

Activities, values and assumptions that exist now and no longer fit your life can be changed. This refers to bad relationships, jobs, obligations and commitments. It doesn't mean you can relinquish your responsibilities: it means you must calculate the cost of change and pay the price for it. Change begins with the decision and then action.

How do I change?

In order to change your life from what it is now to what you believe would make you happy, you must first work out what your ideal life would look like. You can then use this as the criterion against which all your activities can be judged. Those that don't contribute to your ideal life can be eliminated. The following activities enable you to take this ideal journey. By the end of it, only you can choose whether you want to take action to bring it to fruition.

****

Exercise 6:

Let's revisit our first exercise, 'What would you do if you knew you couldn't fail?' Remember, you are starting with a completely blank slate, on your own, and free of all obligations and commitments. Re-write this exercise, putting aside any worries about what is possible or how other people will react. The two paragraphs in the note below might be helpful in doing this, so refer to them first.

****

NOTE:

Be as creative as you want to be in choosing what you would do. Remember that this is your ideal. Don't be put off by thinking that it would be impossible to achieve. At this stage you can live your dream on paper. Remember that you can't change others, but you can imagine what it would be like to have people in your life you spent time with because you really wanted to. Of course you may keep people and things already in your life, in your ideal life as well. Don't include anything or anyone only because you can't imagine what it would be like without them.

Write as much detail as you can, and when you have finished, close your eyes and imagine yourself living that life. Carry this image around with you for the next few weeks and at regular times reflect on it. After a while a core image will probably emerge. It will represent the focus around which your ideal life is centred. Make a note of this—it will help you with the next step.

****

Exercise 7:

Take your list of labelled activities prepared in Exercises 2 - 4 and cross out anything that doesn't appear in your ideal life. Reflect on what is left and what proportion the remainder is of your current life. This will enable you to get more in touch with the reality of your life now.

****

You now need to consider what to do to achieve your dream life. What actions will you need to take, and how much will it cost you? If you want to train as a doctor, you will need to study, become qualified to get into medical school, find time to devote to your efforts, and pay for your studies while supporting yourself.

It is very tempting to modify your dream because it seems impossible given your present circumstances. Try to avoid this, since you will never be happy unless you have a clear picture of what you want.

****

Exercise 8:

Consider what will be entailed in achieving your dream and note this in detail:

Requirements

Time resources

Knowledge

Money

Personal costs

Emotional support

****

The next stage is to look at your current assets and liabilities, since these have implications for how and when you realise your dreams.

****

Exercise 9:

Outline in detail your current assets and liabilities. List savings, capital, money owed to you, belongings and insurances under Assets. Next, list debts, hire purchase, credit card balances, mortgages, loans and regular financial outgoings under Liabilities. Work out the total of both your assets and liabilities.

****

If your financial assets are more than your liabilities, this represents what you have to make your new life. If your financial liabilities are greater than your assets, don't be tempted to ignore your dream until you have paid off some debts. Don't procrastinate until you have enough money, since it is your current actions that have contributed to where you are now. There is no assurance that continuing as you are won't offer you more of the same rather than a path to your new life.

Making your dream a reality

The following paragraphs identify ways in which you can make your dream a reality. It is worth rehearsing this in your mind before you take action—and remember that to achieve your ideal life, action is required.

Look at your assets. If any of them are not on your dream list, get rid of them. Superfluous assets may include your car, your house and your belongings. Use the cash to pay off your liabilities. You may find at the end that you are left with no assets. However, you will have lost nothing—and you will have gained freedom. Which is better? Assets and obligations with no time to change your lot, or freedom with no encumbrances to realising your dream?

If you think you have to keep your current job to finance your move towards your dream, work out the minimum input required to meet your needs. If you want to maintain a relationship with your parents, does it really require you to visit them twice a week? Which is preferable, a son or daughter who visits willingly and enjoys the visit, or one who resents their parents and feels guilty if they don't visit frequently? You may feel they put pressure on you to visit regularly, but this might reflect part of *their* ideal—to have a child who wants nothing more in the world than to visit them. If you don't feel the same, however many times you visit you will not contribute to meeting their needs, since your actions will not match their desires. They are not missing anything by your visiting less regularly; in fact, they serve to gain only if you visit willingly and freely. Think about this! Work out what is right for you and keep your ideal life in mind at all times.

****

Exercise 10:

Look at the changes you wish to make. Write down exactly any resistance you expect, and from whom, and identify ways in which you can explain your actions to them.

****

When you begin to make changes in your life, expect to encounter resistance in the form of anger, resentment and blame. People will say you are selfish and that you are ignoring your responsibilities. Remember that a large part of this is because you are not behaving in accordance with *their* notion of happiness. It has little to do with *your* happiness.

Ask yourself, 'Are these the people I want in my life? If they are not prepared to allow me time to reflect on my life choices, do I want them in my life any more?' It is not always easy, but the cost of maintaining the status quo may be so great that you pay for it with your whole life.

Starting from scratch

It is a very seductive proposition to stay as you are once you realise the costs involved in making change, even though the costs of staying put are much higher. You may decide it is simply too hard. You may feel that the resistance from others is too great and that life is unfair to have placed you in this predicament. Remember, *you can change anything*. Work out the price you will have to pay to achieve your ideal life. Decide how much you are willing to pay for it or for certain aspects of it. Decide at what point it is not worth making the change.

Don't allow others' reactions, punishments or threats to throw you off course. Take your commitments and responsibilities seriously but don't delay paying the costs of making changes to your life.. Here are some reminders of what you can do on the way:

- Take responsibility for your choices and don't blame other people, society or social norms for not exercising them.

- Recognise that you can change almost everything in your life as long as you are prepared to pay the price involved.

- Identify things in your life that you would prefer *not* to do now but continue with because of previous investment. Remember that the *only* way to gain the equivalence of resources wasted so far is to use your time, money and efforts now exactly how you want to.

You must now decide either to pay the price or don't: to face a short, sharp, sudden pain or opt for a life of quiet desperation. You cannot avoid the price owed for your choices but if you don't choose to pay it for the things you want, you may have to pay for the things you don't want—every day you have left. And the price will have increased, because you now know the ideal life you have abandoned.

Now is the time to test the foundations of your friendships. Would you prefer to be with people, not knowing whether they would support your quest for happiness? Alternatively, you can challenge their friendship, knowing that you will have lost nothing if they reject you once you reveal you want to be true to yourself.

Recognise what it is that you want from your relationships and decide what you are getting, and at what price. If the equation doesn't balance, decide how you might be able to get a better deal somewhere else. Remember that when you make changes, expect to feel withdrawal symptoms, since we do make strong attachments to others.

The film *Life as a House* portrayed Kevin Kline who, learning that he had cancer and four months to live, quickly refocused his life and became more honest in his interactions with and expectations of others. Don't leave it until circumstances—health, fate or old age—pressurises you to change. Embrace your life now and make changes you, and ultimately others, will benefit from. By working through the exercises in this chapter you can truly get in touch with what it is you want and, set out on the path to success on your own terms.

The secret of success

Success is about knowing what is important to you and creating a life that allows you to bring these things into your life. It requires you to challenge personal, social and cultural myths and unquestioned assumptions, and to live on your terms. Change is challenging, especially when other people discourage you or criticise your choices because they don't fit the norm or their expectations. Many of your earlier commitments and obligations can be relinquished, and you *can* carve out the successful life you want to live.

What can you do to facilitate change in your life, when the immensity of change seems too great to face? You can:

- Identify your worthy ideal.

- Recognise that you are the author of your life and that you can make informed and meaningful choices.

- Accept that embracing your freedom will bring you anxiety but that the rewards will be enormous.

- Accept that you can change and achieve success on your own terms.

- Examine the assumptions by which you live your life and change them if they no longer work for you.

- Reappraise your daily life and consider how your actions

contribute to your short- and long-term goals.

- Identify how you spend your time *now* and focus on things that are enjoyable and positive, and catalysts in bringing about your happiness.

- Look for ways to eliminate those activities that are unenjoyable, negative or reactive, for they will only block your path to freedom and happiness.

- Consider your short-term activities and their contribution to your long-term happiness. Do not compromise your time now to achieve some promise of happiness in the future.

- Begin change now by doing something out of choice every day. Be ruthless in making it *your* choice, not something chosen from a range of choices you believe are available and socially acceptable.

- Appreciate that the rewards of having people in your life who want you to be happy are priceless.

- Plan your dream life now and imagine paying the cost of getting it.

The late Earl Nightingale in the recording of 'The Strangest Secret' in the 1940s said, 'Success is the progressive realisation of a worthy ideal'. Make it your quest to identify what your worthy ideal is, and use the exercises here to move progressively towards that goal.

Good luck!

Clare Mann

COMMUNICATE 31

CONNECT • COMMUNICATE • COLLABORATE

Clare Mann is Sydney-based psychologist, existential psychotherapist and trainer who helps people become successful by improving their communication and interactions with others. She believes that the quality of a person's results is directly linked to the quality of their communication – with themselves and others. Throughout her creative workshops, she helps people identify and remove the blocks that limit their success and wellbeing. She then provides them with proven tools and strategies to get the results they want and live their lives 'on purpose'.

She is the author of numerous books including, *The Myths of Life and the Choices We Have,* and *Communicate: HOW to say WHAT needs to be said, WHEN it needs to be said and in the WAY it needs to be said.* She believes that much of the anxiety and stress people experience is because they lack the skills to make necessary changes to create success on their own terms. Her FREE audio program, 'Overcoming Stress and Anxiety' addresses existential concerns as well as providing immediate strategies to help people get unstuck. Join her webinar series, *Take Back Your Power to be Heard*, and acquire empowering tools and techniques to have difficult conversations with ease. For more details: http://claremann.com

Success is what you make it

Everyone is looking to be successful and honestly who wouldn't want to be successful? For most of my adult life I found myself chasing success; whether that be the nice house, good car, happy family or job others wanted. Then about five years ago it dawned on me that I was interpreting my success by other people's standards and it was exhausting. After my second child, I experienced some health issues and it really forced me to consider who I wanted to be and what legacy I wanted to leave for my family, friends and the broader community.

Through my reflections at that time I realised that success is relative to who you are and what you want to do with your life. And much of that is determined by your heritage, family, friends, life experiences, values you hold dear and where you are in life. As a student at school, success is very much about your grades, whether you're in the cool group and get invited to parties. As a young adult, your parent's view of success might be whether you have a job, how much you're earning and whether you job has prospects for the future. At that stage I was more concerned with what money I had to spend on clothes and whether I had any going out money. I wasn't too concerned about job prospects as I was studying a post graduate course part-time. I also didn't know what job prospects I wanted as I didn't have a clear vision for my career like others I knew. As I got towards my late twenties, my parents became concerned about my level of savings and my grandmother became concerned I hadn't met anyone yet. Fortunately none of those things bothered me and was completely normal according to lifespan development where my need for success was met through work consistent with my personality and abilities.

Perhaps I was a late bloomer but I was perfectly happy being single, going out with friends and earning enough to pay my way. Fortunately I did meet a wonderful man and we got married. And as many of you know once you're married the pressure for grandchildren starts soon after. Fortunately because I had earned the reputation as a workaholic people soon gave up wondering if we would or not. Right after getting married we emigrated to Australia and success at that point meant finding somewhere to live, jobs and making friends. Children came much later which surprised those who had given up on us. And so it goes on. The older worker may consider success as still having a job, spending quality time with grandchildren and having enough savings to retire or it may be spending the next five years as a 'grey nomad'. There comes a time when you have to decide whether the expectations on you from others are going to manage you, or if you are going to manage them.

Through my work I have been fortunate to work with some highly successful people running significant business that other people are dependent on. What I have observed with these people is that they share a similar approach to life. They have a clear view on what success would look and feel like for them and they pursue this vision relentlessly with discipline. Their vision embraces all areas of their life and it plays to their strengths. Interestingly while they hold a personal vision, they also hold themselves accountable to a higher purpose that is in the interests of the broader community and enables them to serve others.

The purpose that propels successful people forward is also responsible for helping them develop deep specialist knowledge and networks in their field. This over time coupled with their strengths gives them 'expert' status and later for some, 'guru' status.
Due to this clarity they are highly motivated and able to focus their efforts, eliminate time wasters and take decisive action. This clarity and focus enables them to come across as real and others are attracted to it and want to be a part of it, whether they be clients, co-workers or aspiring juniors. Interestingly their purpose is so strong that setbacks only provide more resolve to achieve it, and they manage to find a way.

Successful people find ways to look after themselves both physically and mentally understanding the importance of downtime and physical exercise. I was always surprised the see the busiest people managing to find time for a run or swim in their day. After commenting on it to one of them, they remarked how important exercise was to them and how it helped them do their work.

Successful people demonstrate a genuine interest in others and show high emotional intelligence. Rarely will you see a successful person 'lose it'. They are able to effectively manage their emotions so that they are able to influence others. They live in the moment and tend to have an optimistic outlook on opportunities and life.

Successful people are lifelong learners, they have a strong sense of self worth and show humility when praised by others. They recognise anything they do reflects the way they do everything and consistently look to give their best efforts to activities.

In my experience working with highly successful people their mindset is what gives them their edge as much as their skill set, which is an extension of their purpose. Through my work with high performers in high stress roles I realised that I was helping them become more of who they wanted to be and realised it was time for me to do the same. Since that time I have revisited my thoughts on success which now extends beyond the possessions I own, people I know and the status I derive from them.

At a high level, success to me means being who I am in all situations and feeling confident that that is enough. It means I can wake up every morning feeling good about myself and I have a healthy self-esteem. It means I have the courage to ask for what I want and expect it's possible. My version of success now takes into account all that I am and want from life. It considers my livelihood and lifestyle; my body and wellness; creativity and learning; my relationships; romantic, friendships, work collaborators, colleagues and clients; and, my contribution and spirituality.

As a result of this reflection I have made some choices that would be at odds with the previous Martine. In relation to my livelihood and lifestyle, I have given up the secure full-time career job and started my own business. Which I realise after holding off for so long I should have done years ago. I recognise building your own business is not for everyone however I have found it has provided me with the way to achieve the lifestyle I currently view as successful. I wanted a way I could spend more quality time with my children while still feeling like I had a meaningful career.

I know my earning capacity has taken a dive while I build the business however I get to spend more time with my children and support them in the way I want to, which I wasn't always able to do before. And I am able to be the parent I want to be rather than the one I had time for. Now I find my children and I are having more meaningful conversations and connecting with each other in a deeper way. I am getting to know a whole new side of them, as I am sure they are of me. Career wise, I am building a practice I love and have the opportunity to work with more people who are like-minded. I still get to go on holiday even if it is more local than before. I have realised that it isn't where you go that makes the difference as much as who you're with and what you do. Of course I would love to go overseas again and experience what a foreign place has to offer. However I currently don't feel like I am missing out. I know a time will come when I will want to travel overseas and I am planning for my business to be ready for that. With regards to clothes I have decided that success means you get to wear what you want, when you want. As a result I have found myself dressing for me rather than others. What this has meant is that I can appreciate the beauty in fashion and not feel like I would like to own and wear all that I see. I still buy clothes and shoes, what woman doesn't? I am more choiceful about whether I would really wear it and whether it would do me justice.

When I was ill, it was difficult to exercise and run around with my children without feeling tired. Fortunately I was able to recover with the help of a naturopath and my doctor. It took nearly three years for me to recover my physical health during which time I couldn't really exercise. It was during this time that I realised how important our bodies and our wellbeing was. Up until I got ill I had always taken it for granted that I would be healthy, fit and able to do whatever I wanted physically. During that time I learnt all about the properties of food, herbs and stress and how it affects our chemistry. The body truly is amazing. While I was recovering I promised myself I would exercise regularly, in the form of yoga, when I was well. I am pleased to say I now manage to practice yoga regularly. Prior to my illness, I was introduced to meditation by a colleague and have been working on integrating that into my life as well. Now that both activities are firmly integrated into my routine, I miss them when I don't do them. For me, body and wellness means looking after myself so that I can care for others. This means eating well, exercising and finding time to relax.

Fortunately in my line of work, I have been able to combine my love of learning and creativity to build great content and experiences for clients. I consider this the easiest area in my life to satisfy because I am naturally curious and keen to understand the world around me. It is also the area I have most control over. For many years I thought there may be something wrong with me because I didn't have an all encompassing interest that took up my spare time like gardening or Star Trek. And then I realised that my hobby is learning about people. When my first child was born I took up photography so that I could photograph the milestones. While I still photograph the milestones I have also combined it with my fascination with nature. It is not unusual for me to go into the bush and take pictures of flowers and plants. I find it gives me a lot of joy and reminds me how beautiful the world around us is.

In the area of relationships, I consider myself successful when we can both be ourselves, enjoy each other's company, be comfortable to challenge each other, and show the other how we really feel. I don't have many girlfriends so the ones I have I really appreciate and treasure. The other measure I use for success with relationships is that we contact each other spontaneously to let the other know we care. One of my girlfriends is particularly good at this and I aspire to be as thoughtful as her. What I have noticed is that as you go through each stage in life the number of friends you have, may expand or contract, and there remains a core of friends who stick by you irrespective of what stage you're in. Now that we, as a family, have stopped moving around, I hope to have the same core of friends when I am much older so that we can reminisce about the 'old' days together.

With regard to relationships with work collaborators, colleagues and clients, success to me means building and delivering solutions that move people and organisations forward. It also means respecting each other's contributions and being able to challenge in the interest of creating a better outcome. I struggle to work with people who are unable to provide open and honest feedback and who take robust conversation personally. I know I have been successful at building strong working relationships when we are able to have those conversations and still share a giggle together afterwards.

I was raised in an agnostic bordering on atheist household. My parents believed that you were the master of your own destiny and religion didn't really come into it. As a result for many years I struggled with the concept of religion and what it meant for others and for me. However I am very clear about my spiritual practice which has become more important as the years go by. To be successful in my spirituality, I need to continually demonstrate love, kindness and compassion to myself and others; regularly meditate and follow my truth. This may sound easy but as a reformed perfectionist being kind to myself is no small task. I have had to work on unrelenting standards and learn to forgive myself for mistakes I make. After all, I am only human. Initially I learnt to meditate because I wanted to acquire a skill that I knew would serve me well. Now after five years of meditating I see it as an integral part of how I connect with myself and let go of those things that hold me back from participating in the world around me.

After twenty years of building skills in others, working in three continents, being happily married for sixteen years with two beautiful children and a supportive group of friends and colleagues, I think I am right where I need to be. What I have learnt about success is that ii is about being brave enough to stand up for what you believe in and relentlessly follow it because those who matter will support you. Inevitably my view on what success is for me will change as I develop, and the needs of those close to me change. Good luck with determining what success means for you – have some fun with it!

Martine Barclay

Martine runs a consulting, training and coaching business that specialises in helping professionals manage stress, prevent burnout, identify their areas of specialty and achieve their career goals. Martine consults to organisations on identifying and developing their high performers and providing career development opportunities for their staff. Martine has a psychology and corporate learning background with over 20 years experience developing professionals to achieve career success. For more information please visit www.redefineyouredge.com.au

REINTERPRETING SUCCESS

Success. We all want it don't we? We all want to feel like we're successful people and that we're leading a 'successful' life.

But what does 'success' actually mean?
Is the definition of 'success' different for men and women?
What does it mean for people living in the 21st Century?
What does it mean for women living in the 21st Century?
And, more importantly, what does it mean to you?

These are all excellent questions, yet questions very few of us have actually asked ourselves any of them.

But, without knowing exactly what success is, how can we create it in our lives? How can we live a 'successful' life according to our own, authentic, metrics if we don't really know what it means to us?

So, that's what this chapter is all about. It's about helping you to redefine what success means to you, for you, and your life.

This chapter also includes some exercises. These exercises will help you to put this information into practise in your life. So, please complete each exercise as you go along. I know you have the best intentions, but something will come up and the exercises will get forgotten. So, prioritise yourself. Prioritise your success. Prioritise your happiness, and complete the exercises as you go.

WHAT IS SUCCESS?

It is both an amazing and a difficult time to be a woman. On the one hand we have every opportunity and possibility open to us and therefore the ability to create the ever-coveted 'successful life'.
But, on the other hand, with these endless opportunities, comes the burden of the woman.

The ideal to do it all and do it all perfectly. The pressure of being all things to all people – a perfect wife, mother, and careerist. The strong independent type and yet the supportive dutiful partner. The size zero gym sculpted sexual goddess, who also has time to iron their partner's socks and change nappies at 4am. The promotion-chasing executive, who knows how to rustle up a picture-perfect goats cheese soufflé.

And, when we inevitably come up short – the disappointment of what we think is failure.

Because it's all supposedly possible – we expect it of ourselves. We expect to be able to do it all, to be it all and to excel. And, when we don't measure up to this ideal self – our self-esteem comes crashing down. We feel like we're not good enough, like we're not successful.

The celebrities can do it all. Why can't we? They manage to lose all their baby weight whilst still eating McDonalds. They manage to be all made-up without a hair out of place at the school gates at 7.30am in the morning. They are able to launch and manage multi-million pound businesses, whilst being the perfect wife, mother, friend and daughter.

They are successful.

We are not.

But, other than the fact we only see what they want us to see, the fact is, that if you honestly speak to any busy woman, be she a stay at home mother, a career woman, or a celebrity, what you will discover is that no one lives, or even think they live, a perfectly successful life.

The trick is to understand what success looks like to us, as an individual, and then to forge ahead, ignoring the potential disapproval, funny looks and 'should's, 'ought-to's and 'musts' prescribed by our parents, friends or society.

Because 'Success' means something different to each one of us. For me it might be a happy and healthy family, to you it might be the ability to afford 2 holidays a year and private schooling for your children.

And there is no right or wrong. There is only right or wrong for you.

But before we look at what success might be for you, let's turn to what might be preventing you from understanding what might be holding you back:

THE AUTHENTICITY ROBBERS

When we're young we are highly susceptible to the beliefs, judgments and ideas of the people around us. This means that sub-consciously we absorb and accept a mixed set of 'should's', 'ought to's', 'musts' and 'have to's' before we are old enough to understand, question or process them properly. These are simply the expectations and beliefs of other people and the society in which we live.

However, many of us still live our lives in accordance with them. And, worryingly, many of us have no idea that we're doing this. We don't know that we are making decisions and judgments based on beliefs and ideals that we haven't even rationally decided for ourselves. This means that we are working towards fulfilling the goals and ambitions that are *imposed upon us*, rather than the ones we really want for ourselves.

Let's take a look at this in practice. Karen is an accountant. She got great A-Levels, went to university, studied accountancy and became an accountant. But she's not happy, and she doesn't feel like she's leading a successful life. She doesn't mind being an accountant – but it's not what she really wants to do. What she really wants to do is become an artist. That's what she's always wanted to do. But, from as young as she can remember, her parents, friends and career advisors have always told her to 'get a proper job', do something that is secure, reliable and that will pay the bills. So she does. She does, because she was always told she 'should', and that she 'ought to'. But following this path, a path society has told her is safer and better and more successful, has led to an unfulfilled life which is making Karen feel like she's a failure, and that's she's unsuccessful.

And this is why many of us are living unhappy, unfulfilled and inauthentic lives. We are living in accordance with a set of rules and expectations of ourselves that we didn't decide upon, and that we don't even necessarily even agree with. We are making decisions for our futures according to a fixed set of views and beliefs about how our lives *should* be and not necessarily how *we want them* to be.

So, what can we do about this?

Let's look at a strategy I have put together to analyse just this:

I call it the:

Breaking Down the Expectations Strategy™

1. Thoroughly analyse and assess your life as it is. What are the things that you do, think and believe because you think you 'should', 'must' or 'need to' or that are 'right' for the sort of person that you think you are?

2. Where did this idea or belief come from?

3. Does it still work for you in your life now?

4. If not – what belief or ideal would serve and support your life and your Ideal Self, better?

5. What are you going to do to make this new belief or ideal your new reality?

So let's work through this strategy now. Turn to your Exercise Blueprints, at the end of the chapter, and write down a list of 5 – 10 things that you do or think because you believe you ought to, should, or must.

What are the things that you are doing with your life because you have been led to believe that they are right and expected and will lead to a successful life?

Now these could be far reaching, surprising and painful. Some common examples are:

- that I *need* to get married
- that I *must* have children
- that I *ought* to put my children through private school because 'it's better'
- that I *have* to get a well paid desk job
- that I *need* to cook dinner every night in order to be a 'good' wife and mother
- that I *must* work a 5 day week

And then beside each of these write down where these ideas or beliefs came from.

Who told you these things?
Why do you believe them?
What is the logical rationale?
Are they really the right beliefs for you?
Do you actually agree with them?
Do they work for the person you are and the person you want to become?

And, if not – what belief or ideal would work better for you and what are you going to do to bring this into your life going forwards from today?

Spend some time now working your way through this strategy. Really put these expectations under the microscope and work out where they came from and whether they really are right for you. Only by knowing the answers will you ever truly be able to live an authentic life, as the authentic you.

Pause to do Exercise 1

HOW TO FIND AUTHENTIC SUCCESS

Now we know that we need to determine what success actually means for us, as an individual, let's look at how to do this in practice.

The process, as with most things, is to understand what really matters in our world, what's important to us and the person we want to be.

Let's go back to the example we used before of Karen. As you'll remember Karen was an accountant who felt like she was living an unsuccessful life. And the reason that she felt that she was living an unsuccessful life was because she was doing something that she didn't want to be doing; accountancy rather than art.

Now let's look at Lauren. Lauren left school at 16, when she moved to London to live with her then boyfriend. She spent a few years waiting tables and temping to make money. At the age of 21 she decided that she wanted to go to University and study to become an accountant. Lauren is now 32 and she's working, full time, as a qualified accountant. Lauren has fulfilled her goal and believes that, in her career, she is successful.

Karen doesn't want to be an accountant – and, therefore, she feels unsuccessful. Lauren, on the other hand, really does want to be an accountant and, therefore, feels like she is leading a successful life.

What these fictitious examples are illustrating is that, in order to feel successful, we need to be doing the things that we want to be doing, things that are important to us, that give us purpose, meaning and pleasure.

Unfortunately we don't all know what these things are, so, in our next set of exercises, we're going to start asking ourselves some questions that will help get to the route of what we, authentically, want for ourselves and our lives.

So now I want you to answer the following questions to help you to understand yourself, your passions and your values more clearly.

Question 1: What would I like to spend my time doing, if money were no object?

For example, would you be working in a homeless shelter? Would you be teaching, or would you start up your own business? What have you always wanted to do but have lacked the confidence to do, or worried that it was more of a hobby and wouldn't allow you to pay the bills? This is not a time for realism by the way – this is a time for idealism.

Because, what we're interested in is what you really want to do – however crazy or unrealistic it might sound now. Bear in mind, that behind every piece of reality, there was an original idea – an ideal even – and what we're after here is to see what those original and authentic ideals are, however buried they may feel, under the weight of every day pressures and restrictions.

Pause now to do Exercise 2

- **Question 2: What specifically do I want to look back on and be proud of in my life?**
(what we're interested in here is something that is completely about you, and does *not* involve your connection with somebody else – e.g. don't include pride about your children or your relationship with your partner – it needs to be something you can look back on as being only about you)

Maybe you want to have reached a senior managerial position within a company? Maybe you want to have helped people or animals? Maybe you want have written a book?

We all want to be proud of ourselves and achieve something with our lives, whatever that may be. So, what do you want to achieve with your life? This is an important question, so if you don't know the answer immediately, really spend some time thinking about what it could be.

Pause now to do Exercise 3

- **Question 3: What am I passionate about and why?**

What do you find yourself thinking about? What do you love to do? What do you wish there was more time in the day to do? Is it writing music? Painting pictures? Singing? Exercising? Reading? What are your passions?

Be as specific as you can be here and try to describe it/them, as vividly and fully as you can.

And, to answer the second part of the question, the why, try to identify what the passion gives you that makes it so important to you – is it intellectual stimulation that you don't get elsewhere, an adrenalin rush that makes you feel alive, or perhaps an artistic expression that really allows you to feel connected with yourself? Try to keep asking yourself the 'why' question until you're absolutely clear on exactly what this/these passion(s) bring(s) to your life that makes it/them so important to you.

Pause now to do Exercise 4

- **Question 4: What do I think my message to the world is, if I had to pick just one?**

Now this may seem a little airy fairy for some of you – but it's a great idea to strongly believe that you have a message to share. It might be something very simple and day to day. It might be something very blue sky and all encompassing.

My message is that I want to encourage women to take control of their lives and to take action to make their wishes, their reality.

But your message could be anything you strongly believe and want to share with others.

A great way to find your message is – to ask yourself what you'd go back in time to tell your 14 year old self. What lesson would you give her if you had the chance?

Pause now to do Exercise 5

- **Question 5: What are my values?**

Your values are the unconscious principles that you live your life by. Your values are the things that you hold most important in your life. They determine your priorities and help you to make decisions.

At the deepest level, values are responsible for our behavior. Values are the way we judge what is good and bad, right and wrong.

The values we live our lives by were, in the most part, installed into our brains when we were very young. We weren't born with these values and the values we have are often shared by the society in which we live.

Now many of our values are sub-conscious. This means that we don't necessarily know what they are – or where they sit in our values hierarchy.

But, knowing your values is a really important part of knowing who you are, and what's most important to you.

Values should be the ultimate filter to help you decide what you devote your life to.

If you don't know what your values are, think about what it is that you consider to be important and valuable in your life.

These can be values like:

- love
- freedom
- family
- success
- creativity
- service
- sincerity
- generosity
- courage
- persistence
- honesty

- loyalty
- excitement
- variety

In order to really understand yourself, and what success is to you, you need to be absolutely clear about the values that make up your own personal code,
your own personal philosophy.

So, stop reading, and write out the 5 most important values or virtues in your life today. Write down the 5 qualities that are most important to you in your Exercise Blueprints now. Really think about what your values are. If you're struggling, have a look at the decisions that you have made in life – if you were happy with them – they are likely to reflect your core values.

Pause to do Exercise 6

Now, with your list of values – look through them and select the one value that is more important to you than anything else. This is the value
that will take precedence over all other values if you are ever forced to choose.

And this is a terribly important point. A higher-order value always takes precedence over a lower-order value. Once you have picked your first value, pick your second, and then your third.

This means that the value numbered 1 is more important to you than the value numbered 2 and your decisions will be based to run inline with value 1 if their was a choice between the two.
So, for example, if 'Love' was your value number 1 and 'Financial Security' was value number 2 then, when you were given the choice to be promoted where you got a 20% increase in salary but had to work 10 hours more per week which meant your relationship was likely to suffer, you would turn the promotion down. You would value 'love' more than the 'financial security' you would get from accepting the promotion.
So let's take another example of what I mean by this:
Let's take two different people. Let's call one Suzy and one Helen. Both ladies have the same 3 top values. These include: Family, Health, Career. However the order of their values is different.
Suzy's values are prioritized like this:

1. Family
2. Health
3. Career

So this means that when coming to make a decision, Suzy will always choose her family over her health or her career, and she would choose her health over her career.

Helen's values, as we know, are the same as Suzy's – Family, Health and Career. However her values are prioritised into a different order, so her values hierarchy looks like this:

1. Career
2. Family
3. Health

So this means that Helen would choose to make a decision in favour of her career over her family or her health. And she would choose her family over her own health. Same values, different resulting choices.

So, really think about the order of your values and create your values hierarchy in the Exercise Blueprints now.

Pause to do Exercise 7

Excellent. You now have your core values, these values represent who you are today and will help you to realise the decisions that you need to make in order to create a successful life that's authentic to you.

It's really important that you understand your priorities in life, and who you are today, and knowing your values will really help you to do this.

Having answered all these questions and created your values hierarchy you will have a good idea about what a successful life looks like: You know what is important to you, you know what you are passionate about and you know what you need to be doing for success.

Create an Avatar of the Successful You

We're now going to create an Avatar of this successful you. An avatar is simply a representation, of you. And no, it doesn't have to be green and speak with an American accent!

So, I want you to turn to the Exercise Blueprint at the back of the chapter, and create a mini successful you on the page. Do this however feels best, you can draw a picture, rip up some old magazines or write a paragraph out describing yourself. This represents who you want to become.

Give yourself 10-15 minutes to do this.

Pause to do Exercise 8

Accept

Now let's look at the final part of this process, and this is to simply accept what success means to you.

We all need to learn to accept who we are, and what we really want. Your ideal of success may not be conventional, it may go against what your parents want for you, it may be the exact opposite of what you are doing now. And that's ok.

If we remember that there is no right and wrong, that there is generic interpretation of success, that success means something different to us all, that success is knowing ourselves and knowing what we want for our lives and then living authentically to that, then we can accept our decisions and we can accept ourselves.

But this isn't easy. If you've been brought up to believe that a successful women is married, with 2.4 children and you decide that actually becoming the CEO of the company and never having children is actually what success means to you, then this is going to be hard. But you do need to accept yourself and what success means for you, before you can ever feel truly successful.

I have put together a strategy to help you to accept yourself. This is the aptly named:

The Self Acceptance Strategy™
    i)   Realise that success means something different for each one of us.
    ii)   Accept that there is no one-size fits all, generic definition of 'success'
    iii) Accept your own definition of success as valid, important and authentic to who you are

iv) Say it.

> Every morning say to yourself in the mirror ' I accept myself, unconditionally, right now'. Cheesy? Yes. But if it works for Arianna Huffington it'll work for you too.

Stop reading now and work through The Self Acceptance StrategyTM.

Pause to do Exercise 9

CONCLUSION

Congratulations! You've reached the end of the chapter and, you will now have a clear understanding of what success really means to you.

And, whatever 'success' means in practice, the result that we all want is happiness.

Happiness is what we want for those we love, for our children, and for ourselves. Leading a happy life is leading a successful life.

It is a difficult time to be a woman, but when hasn't it been? You owe it to yourself to take the time and do the work and create the life that you want to live. It will take courage, it will take persistence, it will take hard work. But you know all that, and when has that ever stopped you from doing anything before? Don't let it stop you now.

Now go out there and make your life the success you want and deserve it to be.

Be successful. Be happy.

Good luck, I'm rooting for you.

Rebecca Fredericks

YOUR EXERCISES

EXERCISE 1

BREAKING DOWN THE EXPECTATIONS STRATEGY[TM]

Idea / Belief	Where it Came From	Why do you believe it?	Does it Work in My Life?	What new one would work better?	What I'm going to do to Make this New Belief / Ideal my new Reality

EXERCISE 2

Question 1: What would I like to spend my time doing, if money were no object?

_____
_____
_____
_____
_____
_____
_____

EXERCISE 3

Question 2: What specifically do I want to look back on and be proud of in my life? (what we're interested in here is something that is completely about you, and does _not_ involve your connection with somebody else – e.g. don't include pride about your children or your relationship with your partner – it needs to be something you can look back on as being only about you)

_____
_____
_____
_____
_____
_____
_____
_____
_____
_____
_____

_____
_____
_____

EXERCISE 4

Question 3: What am I passionate about and why?

_____
_____
_____
_____
_____
_____
_____
_____
_____
_____
_____
_____
_____

EXERCISE 5

Question 4: What do I think my message to the world is, if I had to pick just one?

_____
_____
_____
_____
_____
_____

EXERCISE 6

Question 5: What are my values?

_____
_____
_____
_____
_____
_____
_____
_____

EXERCISE 7

Create a Values Hierarchy, with the most important value at the top, and the least important values at the bottom.

1. _____
2. _____
3. _____
4. _____
5. _____
6. _____
7. _____
8. _____

EXERCISE 8

MY IDEAL SELF AVATAR

- If you're writing, use the paper below, if you're creating a pictorial avatar get a new sheet of paper.
- Create an avatar of your Ideal Self. This avatar, or model, is who you want to become.
- You can do this with pictures, you can rip up some magazines or you can do it with words.

My Ideal Self Is: _____

_____

_____

_____

EXERCISE 9

Complete the Self Acceptance Strategy:

The Self Acceptance Strategy™
i) Realise that success means something different for each one of us.
ii) Accept that there is no one-size fits all, generic definition of 'success'
iii) Accept your own definition of success as valid, important and authentic to who you are
iv) Say it.

Every morning say to yourself in the mirror ' I accept myself, unconditionally, right now'. Cheesy? Yes. But if it works for Arianna Huffington it'll work for you too.

Rebecca is an advanced Certified Personal Trainer, Nutritionist, Life Coach, Fabletics Sponsored Athlete, Neuro-Linguistic Programming Practitioner, Presenter, and Entrepreneur with a degree in Psychology.

Rebecca combines her fitness, nutrition, and business credentials with NLP, neuroscience, and positive and behavioral psychology to give fitness, weight loss, business, relationship and life advice that empowers women to create the success they dream of.

Rebecca is the founder of www.rebeccafredericks.com and www.rfweightlossbootcamps.co.uk and she works both online and one on one with women all over the world.

She is passionate about arming women with the confidence, belief, knowledge and the tools and strategies to help them create the lives, and bodies they want, and deserve.

Having started 3 businesses by the time she was 23, Rebecca is a true entrepreneur. For several years Rebecca ran her own successful fashion business and then went on to become Brand Director for a leading lifestyle brand. Throughout this period, she continued her studies into Psychology, Self Development, Coaching, Neuroscience and Business Training theories, specifically focusing on their applications for women.

Rebecca decided it was time to take all her knowledge and experience to help other women to fulfill their true potentials and live their best lives.

Rebecca is also a leading health and fitness writer, having written articles on wellbeing and fitness for a number of national and international magazines.

That Eureka Moment

So we all have them, don't we? I'm talking about 'Eureka!' moments. You know when you say, why hasn't anyone invented one of them? Why don't they do it this way? If only they'd designed it to do that, it would be so much better! Most of us, then forget about our moments of genius and carry on with our lives as normal, but what happens when you can't get the idea out of your mind.

Well that is what happened to me. We were new, first time parents, who one Sunday had a family gathering arranged an hour's drive away to show off our beautiful daughter. Just as we were leaving the house, a little late, I picked my daughter up and found the inevitable had happened and we had a nappy change to deal with. Great! So quick change and we eventually found ourselves in the car, buckled up and on our way, now really late.

I'd driven 2 minutes and suddenly remembered the clean sterilised bottle I'd prepared was still on the kitchen table. I asked my husband if he'd picked it up, as I couldn't remember getting it. He said 'oh you will have done'. 'No!' Manic new mother in me arose and I asked him to check the baby bag, because I would have to go back if it was still at home, as he clambered over the seats and rummaged through the bag, I ranted 'Why hasn't anyone invented a teat that can directly attach to the carton of ready-made formula!' Good news, I had picked up the clean bottle and we carried on to the party. About 6 hours later, we set off home and I casually said 'I wonder if anyone has invented it?' 'Invented what?' typical man, he'd already forgotten. 'I wonder if anyone has invented a teat that directly attaches to the carton?' We spent the next hour discussing the idea and researched the internet once we got home, after all we were new parents and didn't know if the product already existed. We wrote reams that night on the idea and didn't have a clue what to do next, so emailed Peter Jones from the Dragons Den telling him we had the next BIG thing and to call us. We immediately received an automated email response thanking us for our enquiry, and saying if you have patented your idea please fill in this form, if not, this is how you patent... and that is how our journey began.

So what do you do after you have the idea, you dream of course! You dream of sipping cocktails in warmer climates, of selling your company for millions in a few months' time and of living the highlife. Hello, this is the real world!! So, with my dreams in tow, I followed the advice and organised a free half hour meeting with a patent attorney and this is where all products journeys should start. I want to explain to you that everyone you go and see will tell you what you want to know, and you will only hear what you are interested in, when actually you need to delve deeper and listen to everything that is being said, because you are about to step on a rollercoaster ride of a lifetime, it will be exciting, terrifying, have the hugest highs and the lowest lows and twists and turns that will make you scream in delight and absolute horror! Be warned, once you're seated and the ride begins, you can scream as much as you like for the ride to stop, but you can't get off until it is over.

Now I've warned you and you are still determined to go ahead. OK, so let's do it together, you've had your 'EUREKA!' moment, it is SO exciting isn't it! You are full of adrenalin and questions and taking over the world. STOP! Breathe and count to ten. There are some things you need to think about first.

If I knew at the start what I know now, would I have ever started? That is a huge question and the answer is probably no. However, if I started again, knowing what I know now, I would definitely do it but with the knowledge that I knew exactly what I was getting myself into. You see the biggest issue with many things we do, is we make and take uncalculated risks, what I mean by that is, we were going to be in the shops in 6 months and so putting all costs on 0% credit cards was a great idea... the reality was it took 4.5 years to get to market! GULP!

The first thing to do is to KEEP YOUR IDEA TO YOURSELF, don't go telling everyone down the pub. This has to be your little secret for the time being because if you plan on protecting it, this is essential.

Then, I want you to learn from my mistakes and practise 'Poka-yoke' a Japanese term that means 'mistake-proofing', getting it right first time, with two things in mind every step of the way 'COST & TIMESCALES'.

WHAT IS YOUR IDEA AND IS IT ANY GOOD

Time to brain storm the idea and make it bigger and better than your original thoughts, think outside the box. In my case, don't think just formula milk, think water or any flow able matter. In the case of tissues for elephants, elephants don't use tissues, bin that idea! Do some research, if it's a new product, search patents online. If it's a new / improved service, research what's already out there.

WHAT MAKES YOUR IDEA SO SPECIAL

Time to make your product / service better than what is out there. To open another pub in an area already inundated with struggling pubs is a little crazy until you add your magic ingredient, which will make you fabulous and unique.

IS THERE A MARKET FOR YOUR PRODUCT

Sometimes things aren't available to buy because simply there is no market for them, just because you want one, does not mean anybody else does. However go to the trade shows in your industry, sign up to trade publications and get facts and figures behind you and your idea.

PROTECTING YOUR IDEA

Do you even need to or want to? This is a rollercoaster ride on its own, if you choose to step on, I want you to make sure you know exactly what you are letting yourself in for. Get a free half hour meeting with a patent attorney that preferably has some experience in your field. Prepare for the meeting, so you understand the difference between a patent, design registration, trademark, copyright etc. Don't waste your half hour being told 'A Patent is...' Turn up with a sketch of your idea and any supporting information you have found, these attorneys are bound by professional confidentiality, so you need to trust them and explain what your idea is, then listen to their response and feedback. If you decide to consider any form of protection (it is not always necessary but when it is, it is vital you get it right), then question

COST & TIMESCALES!

Ask for a simplistic project timeline including costs of ALL, yes ALL the stages of the IP protection you are considering and even those that you are not. Then once you step on that rollercoaster, the bill you will receive each month for the IP, that will be larger than your mortgage, will not be a shock!

CREATE A BRILLIANT BUSINESS PRESENCE

If you are going ahead, you need to be serious about things and show a professional and responsible business. Decide on a business name, buy the domain name   and use a business email address. Fluffybunny@anything.whatever is really not good. You may laugh but I have seen it! Create a professional website, start developing your presence (Good is good enough, now crack on, we can all strive for perfection, but that is why we have versions, so that you can make some money, tweak it and release a new one.) Start thinking of social media and which ones you will be using and register on them with your company name. Obviously it goes without saying you need a good quality business card, bank account and to consider what kind of company you wish to be, sole trader, limited company, etc and understand the benefits of VAT registration.

BRAND CREATION

All I can say here is stand out from the crowd, don't blend in, STAND OUT (in a good way of course).

THE PRODUCT / SERVICE

The time has come to nail it down, what is required to get to market. It may sound obvious, but do you know what standards / regulations you have to adhere to? You need to find out what these are. They can be found from a number of sources including Trading Standards and any regulatory bodies in your industry, for example ours is the Baby Products Association. If it is a product, a test house can do a risk assessment which will highlight the standards required. This is essential to complete at the outset, because once you've started designing it is costing you money and no-one wants a re-design. Don't rely on your designer to give you this information, designers are great at designing and creativity but make sure they know what they are doing with your project management. Beware that designers need to be reined back in sometimes, the fancy one with wings is over complicated with eleven parts and costs too much to manufacture and has priced you out of the market, whereas the simpler 4 part design without wings is the answer, so please KEEP IT SIMPLE.

Once you know what you want to do, then you need someone to help you create it. Find someone that has experience in designing products in your industry. Find someone local to you, that you can sit round a table with. Quiz them, see what they know already about the standards you have to adhere to. If they don't know anything, consider finding someone that does, otherwise you will be paying them to learn on your job. Ask them how they work, the words you are looking for is PROJECT MANAGEMENT AND PLANNING, once they say those words, ask what that involves exactly. You want to hear that they will plan your project from start to end, they will include **COSTS & TIMESCALES** for every project stage. See where they put the standards and regulations in that process, if it's at the beginning, ask why and make sure they haven't just read this. If they put it anywhere later in the project, run for the hills or at least to the next design company. You normally need to include a manufacturer prior to prototypes being made, as they will come back and say that something is un-manufacturable and again we don't want a re-design, so better to include them as early as possible.

PRODUCT TESTING

You don't have to prototype all aspects of the product to start with, just the critical bits, because you'll be doing these a few times to get them to work. However you do need to test the final product to ensure that it adheres to the standards. It is plain foolish to take a product to market without the correct certificates in place. Make sure you understand the certification.

KNOW YOUR HURDLES

Every company has things lying in wait for them, get to know them before they trip you up.

Whilst all this is going on, be thinking about packaging, marketing, launching, selling it and exporting if appropriate (and if it is a product, social media nowadays forces you to export)

FINALLY, COSTS AND TIMESCALES

So you now know the costs and timescales of your complete project add 100% contingency to both, as it will cost more and take longer than you plan. Then go and find grants and funding, get them in place before you start (many will only pay out if you have haven't started when applying). Remember it's a crazy roller coaster ride and once you're seated and the ride begins, you can scream as much as you like for the ride to stop, but you can't get off until it is over.

HOLD ON TIGHT AND ENJOY THE RIDE!

Claire Mitchell

Claire Mitchell, Inventor of the multi-award winning innovative Chillipeeps adapter that allows a teat and spout to be attached directly to cartons and bottles of ready-made formula milk and bottled water, allowing babies to be fed and rehydrated easily when out and about.

Chillipeeps came from a real 'Eureka' moment and is now selling in 14 countries and Claire is still sat aboard her roller coaster ride and hopes it ends in her realising her vision of making a difference.

Claire loves random acts of kindness and is currently working on a new Chillipeeps innovation in childrens books.

Find your life purpose in 60 minutes

"The two most important days in your life are the day you are born and the day you find out why." Mark Twain

I pondered long on this quote of Mark Twain and I could not really see its meaning until one day.
That day something happened that changed my life forever.

Today your life can transform too, if you allow these words to sink into your consciousness.

My name is Simone Vincenzi and I am the co-founder of GTeX (Growing Together eXponentially). We are the leading personal development community in London. Our goal is to help people live a confident and purposeful life, so they can become wealthier while making a positive impact in the world.

In the following pages I am going to share with you the exact step-by-step process hundreds of people have now used successfully to connect with their true purpose in Life.
You are going to experience the results of more than 4 years of research and studies on the topic that stole my heart, my mind and my sleep.
What you will learn has been proven and tested, giving me predictable results every time I share it with my clients and during my transformational workshop *Purpose to Abundance ™, Awakening your aligned self.*

My intention is to get you really excited to embark on what may become one of the biggest revelations of your life - or simply a silent confirmation that you are on the right track.

During this chapter you will learn:
- Why it is vital for you to connect with your purpose in life.
- What happens if you don't live in alignment with your true source.
- The 7 Keys to awaken your true purpose in life.
- How to make a sustainable transition from where you are, to living your purpose every day.

It is estimated that 80% of the people on this planet (following the Pareto principle) are not living their true purpose in life and they are just drifting, day after day, they are washed over by the waves of an ocean that is not of their making. Living dreams that are not their dreams. Living a life pleasing their partner, colleagues, family and friends. Ultimately, living a life just to pay their bills, which is the death of every passion, desire and ultimately , the death of our soul.

Today you are going to embark on a journey of discovery that will put you in the driving seat of your life. Today you will be in that place where 80% of the global population would love to be.

There are four simple questions you need to ask yourself before we start;

Are you ready?
Are you ready to let go of what is not serving you anymore?
Are you ready to embrace your true purpose?
Are you ready to put 100% of your concentration in this chapter of the book?

If you are, let's start the music!

But before we start there is something you need to know about me.

Before starting GTeX my life was very different. I am going to tell you a bit more about me and my background in the following paragraph so you can understand how this simple and effective tool I am going to share with you, changed my life. And how you can use it in the most effective way to change yours.

I grew up in a loving and caring family in Maranello, Italy. A small village made world famous for being the motherland of the car Ferrari. I grew up there; fascinated by the speed and the beauty of that car that, everyday, was roaring past my house.
Everything was fine until the day my grandfather died. I was six years old at the time and I did not realise that that day would be a real turning point in my life.
You might be thinking now that it was my pain that would be a catalyst in that moment.
Not at all. I was too little to remember and feel that pain, but my father, a recovering drug addict, decided to bury his pain with a bottle of red wine.

The years were passing and the bottles were passing too. The wine became liquors and, year after year, my father fell into the deadly trap of the sweet nectar.

My mum was really strong at the time and she did everything she could to protect me and my little brother from the reality of our family. She has always been the shield between us and the issue of my father. She always did her best to help us live in a "normal" family and not feel the pressure and the pain she was feeling inside.
However there are few things in life that can remain hidden forever.
I was 14 at the time and I still remember that evening when two police officers came to our home and took my drunken father down the stairs. Through my mothers tears I could finally see her pain and what had been boiling under the surface.

In that moment I decided that I had to take charge of my life. In that moment I decided that I could only count on my own strengths.
I managed to find myself a job in a restaurant where I discovered my passion for food, wine and the catering industry.
That passion, with the help of my friends (and a lot of marijuana) helped distract me from what was happening at home.
I started focusing relentlessly on my career and I met mentors who, over the course of just a few years, helped me become one of the highest paid waiters for my age in my region.
I was earning more than my father and mother put together and I was living a very opulent lifestyle; going to night clubs, strip clubs and playing poker every other night.
At the age of 19 I managed my first Michelin Star restaurant and at the age of 20 I was managing a restaurant, pub, disco which catered for over 300 people.

In the meanwhile I was studying philosophy at university (not with any great success as I rarely attended my classes) and passing the few exams I signed up for.

But I was happy. I was happy being a waiter and I was happy working in a restaurant. An expression of satisfaction from a customer made my day worthwhile.

Now I want you to pause for a minute and consider what you have learnt so far from reading my story.

Ask yourself: What is the message that is in this story for me?

It might be that is time for you to take action. To stop pleasing other people and stand up for yourself (yes you are a grown up now!). It might be that this is a challenging period in your life and that everything will pass. That everything has a meaning we might not be aware of yet, to do what makes you really happy in life and don't settle for less...
What have you learnt?

Getting back to my story, at the age of 21 I was recruited as a head waiter for one of the most prestigious Michelin Star restaurants in London. I decided to leave my family in Italy and move to London, riding the horse of this new adventure.
My life in London was incredible and the never-ending party was getting heavier than ever before.
My job allowed me to travel around Europe quite frequently and the quality of my life was outstanding.

However, after two years in London I found myself lost and depressed. I was no longer enjoying what I was doing. I wasn't enjoying the company of my friends. I wasn't enjoying the lifestyle I was living.
I started locking myself in my room and spending a lot of time hiding from other people. I was not happy anymore and I started developing an extremely self-destructive relationship with myself – progressing from anorexia to bulimia and, then, eventually, to massive overeating.
I gained over 10kg and found it painful to look at myself in the mirror.

It was at this point that, one foggy November day, the owner of the restaurant, Pietro Fraccari (the man who became one of my first mentor in life), took me aside and told me: "Simone, I really think you are wasted here. I firmly believe you can do much more with your life than serving food in my restaurant."

I still can hear those words echoing in my mind to this very day.

Those words touched a responsive chord in me that still resonates every time I think about that moment.

That was the first moment in my life that I questioned myself with what became my obsession for the next 4 years: what is my purpose in life?

In that moment I did not know at all about coaching, NLP, personal development and all that funky jazz.

Not knowing what to look for I took my first hesitant step on a cold December night. The rain was pouring outside my window and I was high on sugar from my last binge.

I decided to turn to my only mentor and guru at the moment. Google!

I started with typing, "How to be happy." After that day, my life changed forever. A whole new world opened up for me and brought me to where I am today.

In every book I was reading there was a constant reminder that "All successful people know their true purpose in life". So I started looking for it everywhere.

But after years of attending countless seminars and reading books I still could not find anything that could help me, in a clear, simple and effective way, to understand my purpose.

What you are going to learn now is the culmination of thousands of hours of painstaking research, studying and coaching over a number of years.

Please have ready a paper and a pen because I will guide you through a workshop that will change your life forever.

To get the most out of this lesson, it is essential that you pay close attention and follow the process step by step, as described here.

What you will need:
- A nice pen
- A blank sheet of paper
- 60 minutes of quiet time, not disturbed by anyone else (you might want to move to a private space in your house, in a coffee shop or at the library)

How it works:
- I will guide you through seven questions you will need to answer in this specific order.
- You will have a maximum of two minutes to write down the answers.

- At the end of the seven questions I will give you the key to solve the puzzle of the answers and understand how they all work together.

Are you ready?

Let's start the music.

1. What has been your biggest challenge in life that you have already overcome and what did you learn from that?
2. What is your biggest challenge at the moment and what are you learning from it?
3. What is the #1 thing that upsets you the most in life? And Why?
4. What is the #1 thing that makes you happy the most in life? And Why?
5. What are your 3 main values in life?
6. What is the most important message you would pass on to your grandchildren, to make their life better?
7. If there was one thing you'd like to be remembered for after you die, what would that be?

Welcome back.

Now pause for a moment and take a closer look at the answers.

How did you find the 7 Keys?

What have you learnt about yourself that you did not know before?

What are the elements that have been reconfirmed?

This process is part of my main seminar *Purpose to Abundance™, Awakening your aligned self* . When one of my clients, Patrick, did this exercise for the first time, he was astonished at what he found out. He couldn't believe that he was already living his purpose without even knowing it. During the seminar he stood still for a while and, with wet eyes, gently said: "I know why I am here!" The entire room stood up and gave him a huge round of applause. Now Patrick is the founder of *Bad Boys Chocolate Factory.* He uses his delicious healthy chocolates to give people a second chance in life. (You can find more about Bad Boys Chocolate Factory and his amazing work here http://www.badboys.org.uk).

On the other hand, when Mark did it, he felt frustrated because he realised how far off from his purpose he was. The gap felt huge. But now, after months of inner work and taking action, the overall quality of his life has increased massively and he is making daily choices that are in alignment with who he really is.

Now you might feel like Patrick, or you might feel frustrated like Mark. Wherever you are is perfect.
Yes… wherever you are is perfect.
We often forget that there is no other moment than the present moment. In the search for our purpose or a higher, better and updated version of ourselves, we tend to live in the future. And we often neglect the beauty and the perfection of every moment we live in. Every breath we take is perfect. Every step we make is perfect. Every screw up we have is perfect.

I am perfect, you are perfect and we are perfect.

Just starting from this assumption, really appreciating where you are at the moment, not wanting or desiring to be anywhere else, you will be able to connect with your true purpose.

Otherwise you will feel like a hamster on a wheel. Running, running and running but never feeling satisfied.

Now ask yourself:
Are you feeling more like Patrick or Mark?

Stay with that feeling and take a breath. There is nowhere to go.

In the next few paragraphs I am going to explain what every question really means and how they all work together to give you a conscious clarity of what, on a deeper level, you already know, but for a number of different reasons, you are not following.

Question 1:
What has been your biggest challenge in life that you have already overcome and what did you learn from that?

We start from the past. A past experience, which has been somehow traumatic for you, or very challenging. Something that maybe led you to an emotional, physical or financial breakdown. We call these "awakening experiences".

When talking about life purpose, a key aspect is to understand our challenges. In our challenges sit our greatest lessons and gifts. It might not seem like this at the moment. Well... It does not seem like this at all! But the more you focus on the learning and the growth you are experiencing as a result of this challenge, you will experience inner growth and expansion more and more.

The first question reveals an important phase of your purpose called the *sharing phase*.

What is the *sharing phase*?

The sharing phase happens when you have fully overcome a challenge. When you possess the learning you were meant to learn in your life, you are ready to share it with other people. In fact it is your ultimate duty to share it with the people around you. Because some people will resonate with that message and are just waiting to hear it from you.

Let me give you an example.

My biggest challenge in the past few years was a self-destructive relationship with myself coming from the absence of self-love and purpose in my life.

I used to spend my nights binging bags of food, destroying my body. Passing days locked up in my room under my duvet, without a shower and human contact. I used to smoke marijuana because I could not sleep at night. All because I was not living my purpose.

But despite all of that I was determined to find a way out and get my life back. This is why I embarked on a journey to seek the true purpose of my life. And the more I was learning and aligning my life to who I really am, the more I was sharing my message with other people. The more I felt a loving and appreciative relationship with myself started arise, like the first sunlight of a morning spring.

This is why I help people live their purpose. Because I went through it successfully and now I am ready to share. I made it my mission to use my life as a mirror for my teachings. Yes, sometimes it is not easy and it is a hell of a lot of work! But it is extremely rewarding and fulfilling as I would not trade what I feel now for anything in the world. I am not saying this to impress you, but to give you a benchmark to set for yourself. Do not settle for less than who you truly are and what you truly want.

This is how the first question helps you understand what you are supposed to share in this moment in time with your fellow human beings. The more you do, the more you will find unlimited doors opening for you to so that you can move along the path of your purpose.

Question 2:
What is your biggest challenge at the moment and what are you learning from it?

With this question we tap into what I call the *building phase* of your purpose. As explained earlier, a part of our purpose in life is the *sharing phase*. The sharing phase is the message that we are ready to share with others because it is something we have successfully completed. But before every *sharing* phase we have the *building phase*. The *building phase* is the moment where the challenge is actively at its peak. The moment where everything seems to go wrong. The moment where we are asking why this is happening to us? The moment where we are asking what is the meaning of all of this? The moment where we are left wondering whether it's even worth living. This is the *building phase*. The *building phase* is there for teaching you, for helping you expand and grow. The *building phase* is your greatest master. It is the training you need in order to go out and share with the world what you have learnt.
I believe there is an infinite cycle of *building and sharing phases* during the course of our life.
They can be on a smaller scale or on a much larger scale. The truth is that no message is too small to be passed on.
For someone teaching others how to ride a bicycle the challenge might seems like a small sharing. However it is something we have learnt, done and failed at multiple times before getting it right.

The final message here is: "Go through your challenges with an open and curious mind." One day you will share and inspire people with what you do and what you have learnt.

Before moving to question 4

In the graph below you can see the cycle of *building phase* and *sharing phase* as it happens in our reality.

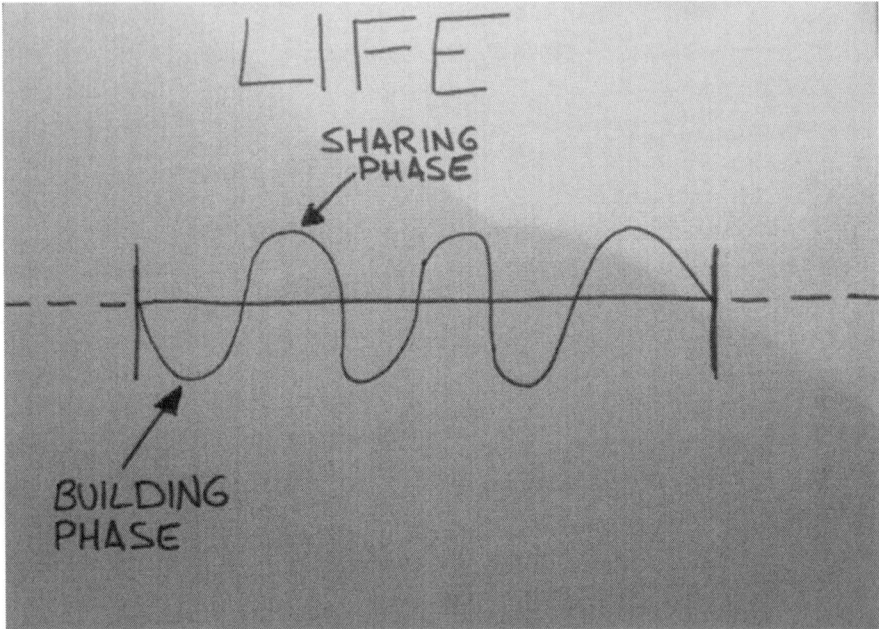

As you can see here, our life purpose follows a waved-shape that constantly moves from *building phase* to *sharing phase*. As you might know the primal structure of our subtle reality is composed by waves of energy vibrating at different levels.

As life is formed by waves of energy, it makes sense that our life purpose too, follows the pattern of a wave.

The constant alternating of *building phase* and *sharing phase* is, as far as my understanding goes, the ultimate truth of the reality we live in.

Question 3
What is the #1 thing that upsets you the most in life? And Why?

This question is fundamental because it explores a part of our reality, some of us, often neglect. If you are reading this book, it means that you might have been involved in personal development and positive thinking for a while. If it is so, you know already what I am talking about. Unfortunately there is a growing trend to judge and demonize what we labelled as "negative" emotions. I am deliberately using the word "label" because the only reason why we call them this is because we have been trained (and we are subconsciously wired) to move away from feelings and emotions we find uncomfortable. What is great about that is that this force allow us to take action in situations we find challenging and we want to avoid in the present and the future. So what is the downside of this? The downside is that neglecting any kind of emotion, positive or negative, doesn't allow us to understand them deeper.

What do I mean by this?

I start from the assumption that every emotion is there to be explored, understood and questioned. If we move away from every negative emotion, we deny ourselves the privilege of understanding our deepest nature.

And through this understanding we can really understand what our true calling is.

Let me give you an example.

When I was a teenager I was heavily bullied. I still remember the felling of dread every morning before taking the bus for school. I remember how hard it was for me to look forward to a great day at school when I knew what was waiting for me. I still remember that day very vividly. I was 11 years old and I went to spend the afternoon with two of my "friends". One of them was really wealthy and we were playing in the garden of his big house, jumping on the trampoline. Everything was going smoothly and we were all having fun. But something happened I was not expecting at all. It all happened in a heartbeat. I saw them looking at each other with a cheeky smile. Suddenly one of them got me from the back and locked my head between his knees. The other guy blocked my legs so I could not kick. I was trapped and I could not move. From that position both of them started hitting me in my face and my stomach with punches and kicks. Shouting at me that I was worth nothing and this is what I deserved. They shouted that I should stop messing about with them because this is what would happen.

I still don't know why they did it, or what caused them to change so drastically towards me in few seconds. But that day changed my life forever.

I secretly promised myself that one day I would be strong enough to stop bullying. At the moment I meant physically strong, but that intention was so powerful that it is now part of my purpose in life.

What got me into coaching in the first place was the desire to help the younger generations learn mutual respect and overcome bullying. That intention was so strong that I became mentally and spiritually fit to live this part of my purpose. This is why I now work with a number of youth organisations in the UK as a team leader or course director. So I can offer help to the ones that are bullied and be an inspiration for change to the pupil on the other side of the spectrum.

The message here is that, by following what upsets you the most and really understanding the reason why, you can use and channel all of that powerful energy that is boiling beneath the surface. You can learn how to use that energy to fulfil your calling and live your purpose every day.

The question now is: What upsets you the most?
And remember to write down the why, as in the why is contained the meaning of this part of your purpose.

Question 4
What is the #1 thing that makes you happy the most in life? And Why?

Let's shift into the realm of positive energy now. This question is crucial because your main purpose is to be happy and fulfilled. The practicalities of this are just to find out "how" you are going to achieve this state of happiness.

Some 80% of people are working and striving for a future happiness that will never come. They usually repeat to themselves: "If I have_____, I will be happy".

The truth is that happiness is nowhere. If you are the kind of person that is looking for your happiness outside your self and in your achievements, you will have a very tough life.

Why?

Because you are never going to be satisfied with what you will have in the future too. This mind-set creates a habit of dissatisfaction and unfulfilment. And you don't want to be dissatisfied, do you?

If we said that the purpose of our life is to be happy, it makes sense that doing more of what makes us happy is the key to feeling this state of happiness right now.

And you might be asking yourself. What are the benefits of feeling a natural state of happiness? The answer is that the universe responds to your vibrational energy and current feeling. What I mean by that is that your next moment is created by the way you feel in this moment.

I will give you CJ's example. One day CJ was coming to one of our advanced courses of Live Your Purpose, Live Your Life™. He started his day disorganized and unprepared. That disorganization put him in a state of stress.   The more he was stressed the more stressful events were happening. He lost the camera charger he was supposed to bring to the course and he missed two trains. Nothing seemed to be going his way. He knew that this was the reason why the reality he was experiencing was not in flow with him. So he took some time off and decided to clear his mind and energy.

After that moment things started to flow much better for him for the rest of the day.

The message in this is to take some time out when you feel stressed and frustrated and do what makes you really happy. Clear your energy and get back into flow because your purpose is to be happy now.

It might sound uncommon, but this is what happened one night to me.

I did something to my girlfriend which upset her deeply. Something which I am not proud of at all. She was considering ending the relationship and I felt like spears were passing through my heart that night. It was my birthday celebration and we were supposed to meet for a bowling night with some friends.

She did not turn up. I stayed there with my friend and a bunch of white lilies that I had bought for her.

In that moment I felt devastated. But I instantly knew that those feelings were not going to help and support me in the long term. If I wanted to have a healthy conversation with my girlfriend I needed to come from a place of gratitude and happiness, not from a needy or frustrated one.

So I decided to really rock the bowling night and I ended up having one of the funniest and most exhilarating nights I'd had in a while. We started break dancing in the lane, doing moonwalks and launching ourselves with the bowling balls. Then from that state, I felt much more relaxed, positive and ready to love again.

In the end my girlfriend and I decided to go through the challenge together and we felt closer than ever.

Now the question is, what makes you really happy?

What is that you would do every single day of your life if money was not a factor?

What is it that makes your heart sing?

What is it that you do that makes you feel in flow and in peace with who you really are?

Is it playing an instrument? Reading? Volunteering in a particular sector? Changing people's lives? Dancing? Listening to some damn good music? Painting? Software creation?

For me music and dance is fundamental to my health and wellbeing. I often do break dancing and Parkour and I play 5 different musical instrument, my main one being the didgeridoo.

I started playing the didgeridoo for fun two years ago. And in just two years, following my flow and a couple of YouTube videos, I had the opportunity to perform with some of the best didgeridoo players in UK at the stage of the didgeridoo festival in Wales.

And this is just because I found what I loved and I kept doing it for myself. Not for any other reason.

Now find out what the one thing is that makes you the happiest- and commit to do it!

Question 5
What are your 3 main values in life?

Your values are your subconscious drive that keeps you on track for your purpose. They are part of your ego and they provide you the emotional check to know if you are in alignment with your higher self or not. In Live Your Purpose, Live Your Life, my students learn to live the train of life. Imagine your life like a train. You are that **train**. The **destination** of the train is your purpose (a train without a destination does not go anywhere and does not get any passenger on board). The **railways** are your values, the solid track that take the train safely to the destination. Like a train follows its railways to get to the destination, you can get to your purpose just following your railways. The **driver** is your belief system, which allows the train to go slower, faster or at the right speed.

For the purpose of this chapter of the book I am going to focus just on our railways, our values.

When you connect with what you value the most, you satisfy the needs of your ego. When you meet these needs in a healthy way, you are able to align with your higher purpose, through your ego and be in the flow.

Let me give you an example. My three core values are, in order of hierarchy, Growth, Fun and Social Responsibility. If I don't fulfil them at any time, I feel lost and not in tune with my purpose. My life becomes very hectic and ultimately I am not happy. But knowing what my true values are, I can make conscious choices in my life to make sure I take just what fully resonates with me.

My core values are also the core values of my company as GTeX is an extension of me and my purpose in life. I have created an environment for growth where people can learn and experience with fun, becoming socially responsible beings.

In this way you can distinguish between *distractions* and *attractions*. Distractions are all the fake opportunities that come to you, to test how fully you are prepared to live in your core. They are often appealing and mouth-watering but are not your main meal. If you choose to follow your *distractions* you will end up like a train out of your railways. Stuck.

If you follow your *attractions*, however, you will feel in flow and every opportunity will be the door of another incredible opportunity aligned to your purpose.

The only way to distinguish if what you have in front of you is a *distraction* or an *attraction* is to check if the opportunity meets your 3 core values in full.

Now ask yourself.

What are your 3 core values? What are the 3 things that you value the most in life? Why do you value them?

Once you find your 3 most important values, arrange them in order of importance. If you feel stuck and you don't know how to order them, ask yourself: Would "value X" give me "value Y"?.

If the answer is yes it means that "value X" is more important for you than "value Y".

Once you have them in order, write them down on a small piece of paper you can always carry with you and put in your purse, wallet or clip. Every time you are presented with a decision, check if that decision meets your values or not and take action accordingly.

Question 6:
What is the most important message you would pass on to your grandchildren, to make their life better?

With this question we move our timeline from the present to the future. Visualizing yourself in the future helps you disassociate from what you believe your current capabilities are and makes you connect with the unlimited possibilities of the Universe. Also when you think about a child you love, like a grandchild, you connect with the energy of purity and innocence that there is in you. From this energy you can be connected with a caring and loving message. This same work in consciousness follows the same rules of Inner Child Healing that is core in Live Your Purpose, Live Your Life™ and is extremely powerful as a way of connecting with your emotions. When focusing on the message you would like to share to a grandchild, your consciousness immediately associates the message of your purpose in life, to the purity of the child energy, resulting in an incredibly powerful emotional message, streaming directly from the heart.

When I answered this question the first time, the first answer that came to my mind was: "Live your purpose, because only when you fully live your purpose, you live your life". From this message Live Your Purpose, Live Your Life ™ was born.

Now think about what your message would be. What is the part of your purpose that, if you share it, will make the life of your grandchildren, the future generations of this planet, much better?

Question 7
If there were one thing you'd like to be remembered for after you die, what would that be?

Thinking about yourself and your accomplishment just a few seconds before you die is an incredibly powerful exercise. In this moment you are ready to let go of everything you have done and take a final breath. Before this final breath you think about your life and all the amazing adventures you have accomplished. Between all of these incredible achievements, you can focus on one in particular. The one that fulfils you the most. The one you are the most proud of. For example, my mission is to give every human being on this planet the opportunity to connect with their purpose in life and enable them with the tools to live it fully with confidence.

What I want to be remembered for is for having created a global organisation, GTeX, that allows their clients and employees to live their purpose fully with fun and joy. Hence why all my present actions are designed to support me in creating this vision I have for GTeX and the world.

What is your accomplishment you'd like to be remembered for?

It does not have to be something massive. It can be being a really loving and caring mother or father. Or being a supporting brother. Or creating a small impact in your local community. But if you, like me, are a visionary leader, why not dream big? Why not allow your mind to create the massive change you want to see in the world because of the work you do?

Now explore this question and jot down the answer. After this task you are going to understand how those answers are all part of your current purpose in life.

Now that you have the answer to all the questions let me explain to you how they work together.

Question #1, #3: *Sharing Phase*

Question #2: *Building Phase*

Question #6, #7: If the message is something you personally own and it is part of your daily life they belong to the *Sharing Phase*. If you still have to work to make your life a reflection of those messages, they belong to the *building phase.*

Question #5: Always check if you are on track with your values.

Question #4: Do more of what makes you truly happy!

This is how your life purpose works in all its parts. Now you have the keys to crack the code of your life purpose it is time for you to take action.

Make small changes, day after day, that will allow you to live your purpose fully, so you can fully live your life.

If you are wondering: Will my life purpose always be the same?

The answer is no. As you grow and evolve, your life purpose will grow and evolve with you. The way you can allow and follow the evolution of your purpose is to live your current purpose in every single aspect, and the next door will open up for you.

What I have just shared with you is not a tool that you can use once in a while, it is a way of life.

The more you get used to this way of living, the faster the next step of your purpose will open up for you.

When I started my work, my purpose was to *"support other human beings to connect with their purpose in life".*

By following that calling, I unlocked different cycles of my purpose and now in this point in my life my purpose is: *"To support other human being to connect with their purpose in life, so they can live it fully with inner-confidence and make positive changes in the world, through their life and their business and become wealthy as a result."*

Just the Universe knows what my purpose is going to be in few years time. I have the feeling that it will settle for a while as I have been expanding greatly in the past few years. But I don't know and I am not interested in knowing. I am interested in following the process and enjoying it fully, day after day.

To recap, in this chapter you have learnt:
1. The truth of living a life of purpose.
2. What the purpose of life is.
3. The 7 keys to connect with your life purpose.
4. How you and your life purpose are constantly expanding through the alternation of *building phase and sharing phase*.
5. How to focus on the process instead of the end result.

If you want to know more - and for free resources - feel free to visit www.gtex.org.uk or contact me at simone@gtex.org.uk and I will make sure I will personally respond to your enquiries.

I am looking forward to seeing you growing and glowing the light of your purpose on this planet and remember to always:
LIVE WITH PURPOSE!

Simone Vincenzi
Co-founder GTeX, Life Purpose Expert, Transformational Speaker, Author.

Simone Vincenzi is an award winning author, speaker, Inner Confidence Catalyst and a co- founder of GTeX. He co-founded GTeX after spending years trying to make his own business of success, which is when he realised the importance of a strong community that provides the right support and information to encourage young entrepreneurs like him.

Since founding GTeX, Simone has been delivering the 'Awaken Your Inner Confidence' workshops in the UK and Italy to over 2,000 people. Following great reviews and demand for personal development program, Simone has built an online community to help him reach out and support more people.

The 'Lazy' Way to Success

'No one will pay you to run'
That's what many business people told me when I first suggested making a business out of running. Luckily, I have proved them wrong and over the past ten years thousands of people have paid me to *run!*
However, when I started my business I wasn't just asking people to give me money to run. Running is easy, anyone can do it. It's just a matter of putting one foot in front of the other and keep doing it over and over again. I didn't ask for people to pay me for that.

My very first advertisement in our local newspaper announcing my new business asked these questions:
Would you like to learn how to run?
Do you want to improve your running and fitness?
Have you always wanted to run a fun run, or the biggie, a marathon?
Are you a runner, but would like to improve your running efficiency?

My phone rang hot all week.
I was asking people to give me money for more than just the act of running; I was asking them to give me money to help with their running—there is a difference between the two.
As I got more into the business of running I found that people will pay for other things as well— enthusiasm, expertise, motivation—all of these things I offered as part of my business and I was paid for each of them. Did they pay me bucket loads of money? Did these things make me an instant millionaire? No. But the bottom line in business is that you need to be paid to keep that business alive and successful—and people will pay for anything they feel they need, even running!
Most businesses measure success by the money they generate, so how do you get that money to turn in to bucket loads?
I have made up a list of things that I apply to my everyday business dealings and workings. Doing these things has made my business the success it is today.
- Do what you do well.
- Be passionate and enthusiastic about what you do.
- Be the best at what you do.
- Do more of what you do.
- Add extra things to what you already do.
- Get people to tell others about what you do.

- Train others to do what you do.
- Last, but never least, be happy and enjoy what you do.

Will this guarantee that you will make bucket loads of money at what you do? No. But you are far more likely to be successful if you are doing the things on this list. What I can guarantee is that if you don't do these things, your business will not be successful and, most likely, will not last long. I have this list printed up each year and pasted in my new diary—and yes, I check it and tick the things off regularly.

When I talk about successful businesses, I am not just talking about rich, multi-million dollar business; I mean businesses that are operating well, are growing and expanding, have lots of customers and, yes, are making good profits. It may not have been done consciously, but if the owners of those businesses had a look at the list and compared it to the way they operate their business, I bet all of those boxes have been checked.

You may say, Oh yes, that's easier said than done, but you would be wrong; all of those things are easily done. I do those things in my business every day without even thinking about them.

In the beginning it was not as easy as following my list and becoming automatically successful at what I do. Let's just say there were plenty of speed bumps along the way.

Let me take you on my business journey – my lazy way

My idea to start a running club as a business and charge people to come along was not born out of a lifelong dream or a blinding passion—I needed a job. I was a personal trainer at a local gym, the gym went out of business and I was out of work. At that time there wasn't a lot of work in my area of expertise, fitness and personal training—and bottom line, I needed money to live on.

One of the clients at the gym I was working at mentioned to me that she would like to join a running club. She had never been a runner and would love to learn how to run properly. She quipped, 'You are a runner, you should start a running club. I could be your first member'. That simple sentence planted my business seed.

I did start that running club, I called it Lazy Runner after me! And as I mentioned above, people were intrigued and interested and wanted to come along. I soon got lots of calls from far and wide. A number of people suggested that I start one of my Lazy Runner clubs in their town, so I did. A year in, I had seven running clubs, all of which I was coaching. Yes, hundreds of people paying me to run.

Now, you are probably thinking, What a great success story. One year in and she has set up a successful, profitable business, bringing in bucket loads of money. Mmmmm...keep reading!

Yes, people were paying me money to run, but not hundreds or thousands of dollars. They paid me ten dollars a session per person—you need thousands of people to come along if you want that bucket filled. I did have hundreds, but not thousands—not yet anyway.

Being a one person show meant I could only be in one place at the one time. The money generator, the running, was mostly early morning, before people went to work. It was an hour-long session—that meant, at most, I could work between seven and ten hours a week. You cannot make bucket loads of money on those sorts of hours, well, I couldn't anyway, not at ten bucks a session.

This was a business, not a job, so a lot of the money that came in was eaten up by the cost of setting up and running the business. My potential buckets of money were being gobbled up by my ever expanding little business.

When I was a year into my business, I was offered another job back in a gym. It was to be fulltime and I would get a good income, enough for me to live on. I was told that I would have to give up my little Lazy Runner business if I were to take on the new job as it would be a clash of interests! My first thought was to give up the business. I needed an income and as much as I loved running my Lazy Runner clubs I could never seem to get a reasonable income out of it.

Whilst I was agonising over what to do—I had one week to decide—I was having coffee with some of my runners (most runners run for coffee!) after a coaching session and one of them said to me, 'Wow, you must be so happy with how successful your business has become'. When I revealed to her that I was actually thinking of getting out of it, she looked horrified and asked why. I told her that I just wasn't very good at it. What she said next changed everything. 'Are you serious? You are the best at it. You have inspired and motivated so many people to run and be healthy and you have changed people's lives. How can you say you are not good at it?'

I guess that's what many people refer to as their 'aha' or 'light bulb' moment. It made me rethink everything I thought I knew and how I approached this business of running. I was very good at what I did, excellent, in fact. I was passionate and enthusiastic and people loved it. I was getting emails daily about how wonderful I was and even how I had changed people's lives, and there I was, thinking I should stop doing the thing I was best at—just throw in the towel.

It was then that I said to myself, *start putting some of the amazing passion and motivation you have for your running and coaching into the actual business and see what happens.* I'm ten years on and what happened over that time was success. I am still in my business, and now I am making my bucket loads of money.

Did that happen just from a light bulb moment, a well-placed compliment, or the passion I had for coaching runners? No, it didn't, but those things helped and put me on the right path.

The success and money came from hard work (sorry, but it needs to be said), new inventive ideas for my business, enthusiasm, expansion, listening to what my clients want, doing the things I wanted to do and basically doing what I do best, coaching running.

My light bulb moment, made me question and re-think everything I thought about being in a business and what was required to keep it going.

I realised from the start that all I was focused on was the money coming in, and then of course, seeing money going out. I know I am not alone with those thoughts. Over recent years I have spoken to many people in all levels of business through my public speaking engagements and I have heard my story played back to me many times. I thought that was what being in business was all about, you know, that bottom line thing. However, when you focus on the money, and it doesn't flow the way you want it to, you feel bad, you feel like your business is failing, you think you are not good at it.

In those early days that was the way I felt all of the time. *I am not good at this.* But the thing was, I was very good at what I did—attracting customers, keeping customers, getting customers to spread the word about how fantastic I was. That was my business, I needed people to come along and pay me, and they were. I *was* good at it.

Now when I am called on to give advice to business owners or I am speaking in the corporate world, I try to get my audience to focus on certain elements of their business and ask themselves a few home truths, and of course, they need to find the answers and solutions to these before they can progress and earn their success.

Lazy Home Truths
Always ask yourself, Why did I get into this business in the first place?
When I am having struggles or a bad day in my business (don't worry, I still do; all business owners do), that is the question I ask myself, even ten years in.

My reasons for starting were those I mentioned earlier. I created a business so that I could give myself a job in an industry I was very passionate about. When I ask myself if that is still the case, the answer is always yes. I do have a job, and I am getting paid to work in an area that I am incredibly passionate about.

Never lose sight of why you started your business in the first place. Often, when we are working hard, we get caught up in other aspects of our businesses and we forget the reasons we started. Many businesses start from passion, excitement, enthusiasm and a love for what we do. If that still applies to you then give yourself two big thumbs up.

I started my first Lazy Runner club because I was out of work, I loved running and I knew I could impart that love onto others. Ten years later that still applies. Sure, there are lots of other streams that come from that original concept, but I still have a good job and I am very passionate about –getting people running.

Do the things you do best. Then do the other things.

There will always be the main part of your business that you are good at. It's often the original idea, the reason you started your business, the thing you knew lots about it and how to do. Great, that is what you need to do, keep doing it. But, as we know, a business requires lots more than that.

I loved the coaching, but as I have already mentioned, that only took ten hours of my week. That left lots of time for, what? Doing other things in the business. If it took ten hours to do the easy work, then surely I could add in ten hours for the not so easy bits.

Things like marketing, budgeting, timetabling, recruiting—these things were not my areas of expertise but still needed doing. I broke my day into work roles. My business only had one staff member, me. But the staff member had lots of roles to fill. I set up a roster for the running coach, accountant, marketing department, human resource manager, receptionist, cleaner and even the tea person, yes, all me. Each job began at a certain time and when they clocked off, a new job started. I filled all the shoes over the day and I found so much more got done on the other things if I set up a roster and stuck to it. Some jobs were easier than others, more fun than others, and more demanding—but it didn't matter, they all needed to be done and they got done over the day.

Do what is right for you.

This can be hard, as money can often be the bottom line in business. But if you are not happy or enjoying what you are doing, then money will not improve anything in your life. The need to make money is strong and relevant in this world, but you also need to look after number one—yes, that is you. Even now, my profits and cash flow still go up and down. My priority is that I am still enjoying what I do and living my dream.

That's a very clichéd term now, 'I'm living the dream'. Many people think the dream in business is to make lots of money and that happiness and good things will flow on. I don't believe that. If you are happy and enjoying what you are doing, this is when good things come.

If your dream is to make lots of money, then yes, you should follow that dream, and of course, work very hard. My dream is to have a good life, and that is more than just money. I want to be happy, healthy and be able to achieve all the goals I set for myself—that is my dream and I am living it. Every dream is different (thank goodness). Find out what yours is (that part is important— you don't want to be living someone else's dream) and then follow it. And no, I don't mean trot along behind it, chasing it like a puppy dog—you get in front of it, work hard and make it come to you.

Growth for you and the business

Grow something in your life, every day. Most businesses, and even your dreams, shrivel and die if they are not encouraged to grow. Every day I work on growing myself and my business.

What I mean by growing myself is making sure I am up to date and have my finger on the pulse of what is going on, not just in my business, but everyone else's. I research many different things associated with my industry. I like to see what is happening out there, not so I can steal an idea and replicate it for the benefit of my own business—it's more for keeping on trend with this fast paced world we live in. Some of the information I garner is a load of nonsense, but usually once a day, I find a little gem, and I use it. It could be a great quote to put on Facebook; a new idea in my industry I want to find out more about and incorporate into my business; or it could be something amusing I send out to my trainers and licensees so that we can have a good laugh.

Many people may see this as a time waster, but listen to me—it's not, its growth. Many business owners have their heads down and bums up, working so hard on their business that they become oblivious to what is going on around them. Once you start to grow yourself, things open up for you in life—this is what you need to be successful.

You have probably guessed by now that I am a runner. I have been for over twenty-six years and I have done some amazing things with my running. I've run marathons, ultra-marathons and crazy off-road adventure races all over the world. You would think that I could hang up my running shoes by now, kick back and relax. No way! I am very fit from my job, and don't need to run for that part of my health, but now I run for my soul. My running gives me great joy and it motivates me in many ways; this creates a flow on effect in my business. People from all over the world read my books and blogs just to hear what crazy running adventures I get up to. So by growing myself, I am also growing my business. Win/win!

The other growth aspect, in addition to growing yourself, should be directed towards your business—daily. This can be harder, as often what our business needs isn't in line with our own interests. I was speaking at a large national conference in Sydney recently about easy ways to grow your business. I mentioned Facebook and very quickly a lady in the audience shouted 'I'm not on Facebook, I hate it'. To which I replied, 'You may not like it, but your business loves it. Do something nice for your business for a change'. What I am saying is suck it up. Facebook is a powerful social medium that really works to attract interest, and in turn, business connections. Your business thrives on those things. You don't need to like something to do it.

If there is an aspect of my business that I don't want to do, I ask myself, Would my business like it? If the answer is yes, then I suck it up and just do it. Or pay someone to do it. Often we need to separate our own wants and needs from our business's.

I have always treated my business like a human, in fact I refer to it as 'he'! I have four children (all adults now) but over the years that I have been in business they have often said that Lazy Runner is my fifth child, and they joke they have an extra sibling. They could be right—yes, I love 'him'. I feed and sustain 'him'. I worry about 'him'. I would get up in the middle of the night for 'him'. All of those things I would do for my children!

If I continue with the human analogy, in the early stages the business is a baby that needs lots of attention and care. The toddler stage is when things really get going and you are busy, busy, busy. My business is ten now, but that is still a child that cannot be left to fend for itself and needs care and attention on a daily basis. God help me when the teenage years kick in! However, the message is, the business has its own wants and needs and they cannot be denied, but need to be catered for daily.

Embrace Competition

If you are looking to be successful, you need to be competitive, but you also need to accept and celebrate competition in your industry. Many of the people who work for me send me stressed messages about new health and fitness businesses starting up in our Lazy Runner areas. I say, bring it on.

Business owners who worry about competition or try to meet their new competitor's deals and prices, send themselves crazy. I had many instances over the years of businesses like mine starting up and offering amazing, free opening specials that I couldn't match, and in reality had no interest in matching. If I follow the 'success' list above, and I do, I know that no amount of hype and buzz or number of freebies will create success. Passion, hard work, and a good work ethic are things that make businesses last and sustain them—not a 'first week free' or '50% off everything' offer.

The best thing about competition is that it motivates you to work harder—come up with some new inventive ideas to improve your business; ramp up your marketing; etc.

I started out in the fitness industry working with top-class footballers. I marvelled at the way they could be so pig headed, focused and competitive on the football field and once the game was over they were back to their friendly, casual, happy selves. It was as if they had a switch they could turn on once they walked onto the football field. They needed that switch on to help them win, because they knew that their competition had the same switch turned on and the fight was going to be hard, but they were up to the challenge, they embraced it.

Business owners should use their competitive switch. It's a good thing, and people appreciate good, honest competition. In the sporting world they get cheers and accolades for it.

In recent years I have approached my competition to ask if they would like to combine and work together on some projects. For example, I offered gym managers the opportunity for me to come along and give a talk to their clients on 'How to run right'. The gyms took me up on it and it has been very successful. I talk about running and I get to sell my books on the day or the gym also stocks my books; the gym is offering something new to their clients or attracting new clients by offering a running component to their business. It is a win/win for both parties.

Don't be afraid of any new business; embrace it as a chance to work together or for your business to be stronger and more competitive.

Lazy Bottom Line

If you really want to be successful, you will be. It doesn't happen by just wanting it, but it will happen if you are prepared to work hard and not give up on it. However, before you start on any business venture or new opportunity that comes along, make sure you define what *success* is for you.

I have told you what mine is, and I have achieved it by just doing these two things—working hard and not giving up on it.

What is your success?

Sit down and ask yourself what that word means to you. Don't be afraid to say it means 'bucket loads of money' if that is what it is for you. Once you know what it is you have to find a way to achieve your success.

Success for you could mean health and happiness, this success will take a whole new set of rules and strategies, but it will still come if that is what you focus on and work towards.

Chasing success is far easier if you know exactly what you want as then you can set goals and work towards it. If you don't know yet, stick with following your passions and dreams, they are the two things that will lead you to finding that wonderful and sometimes elusive thing that we call success.

Marie Bean

Marie Bean is a successful Australian business woman who started her first Lazy Runner club in Noosa Heads (Queensland, Australia) ten years ago. She is also the author of two very successful books on running and fitness titled Lazy Runner and Lazy Loser. Over the past few years Marie has been a sought after public speaker in the corporate and health and fitness sectors, speaking on business success and topics involving health, fitness and weight loss. After twenty-six years of running she still chases her passion. Her latest mission: to run a marathon on every continent. Six down, one to go—the biggie, Antarctica! Marie's success comes from living her dream on a daily basis; her loves are running, travelling and writing. She does each of those things daily and calls it work—now that is success!

What To Do ... When Your Get Up And Go Has Got Up And Gone!

What does your Get Up and Go look like? Are you full of vim and vigour, bouncy, excited and looking forward to the day like Tigger? Are you peaceful, contained and quietly optimistic? And when it has gone, what then? Are you droopy and gloomy like Eeyore? What's the point?", "I can't be bothered". We all have that feeling once in a while life feels like we are wading through treacle, everything is too much effort .

This is not the four o'clock sugar dip that has us wanting to curl up under our desks for a quick nap. We are not talking about medically diagnosed depression. We are, perhaps, feeling just a bit grumpy, moody, in a rut, fed-up, lethargic, stuck, miserable - see how many words there are for it? And I am sure you have your own.

The Dip, as we shall call it, can last from a few moments to a few weeks. As a coach I meet this with clients all the time and use a comprehensive repertoire of skills and techniques to support them through, what we shall call, The Dip.

Success is consciously setting off on the road to a life of balance and fulfilment whist enjoying the journey. I work with Passionate People with a Mission. Sometimes to help them reignite their passion and sometimes to support them in finding a new mission. We all, along the way, face challenges, moments of doubt or even fear when our "Get Up and Go has Got Up and Gone" and this is what we will tackle here.

In this chapter you are going to create an individual action plan to get you through the next time you lose your Get up and Go and enter The Dip. First, let's be clear, this is a Dip: not a pit. Like mortgage rates it goes up as well as down! We just want to reduce the time spent in the down side. Here's a bit of science for you: Neuroscience tells us that we can learn emotional states, just the same way we learn anything – a musical instrument or even how to drive. The first time is slow and as we practice we become faster and find it easier. Unfortunately if you've been in a dip before it gets easier and easier to go into it again. And neuroscience is increasingly supporting the techniques that coaching offers. Interrupting a pattern can divert the neural pathways and change the experience –

translated, this means recognising you're entering a dip and distracting yourself and planning ahead to avoid going into the dip in the first place!

There are three elements influencing your Get Up and Go: physical, mental and spiritual. In each element we will start by tackling the immediate dip and then go on to dip prevention.

The Physical Element

Quick Tips
First I am going to share with you just a couple of the physical techniques which are simple, fast and fun

So, we are in The Dip. When you start to go into brain fog and the blues (good name for a band) it can often be because you are in a sedentary position and so focused or numbed by what you are doing (you know that experience, mesmerized by a spreadsheet) that you forget to breathe properly. When your brain is starved of oxygen it can affect not only your concentration but your whole mood.

So jump up and ...

1. MOVE

Preferably go for a **walk** - walk really fast for as long as it takes to get you out of breath – it may only take you ten minutes.

Or if you can't get outside then run up and down the **stairs** until you get out of breath. Movement is vital to get the blood and oxygen pumping round your system and it will lift your energy and your mood.

Or, my personal favourite, put on your favourite piece of music, **sing** out full pelt.

Dance - you may be a swishy waltzy sort or maybe a salsa star - me I love "walking on sunshine" by Katrina and the Waves. If you can go wild, go mad, leap around for what , all of three and a half minutes and you'll feel like a new person or perhaps David Brent.
If you can't, because you're in an open plan office or on the shop floor, then sneak on your **ipod** and take yourself for a rhythmic

walk to the photocopier or bathroom whilst having a secret smile about what you WOULD be doing, if you could.

Another tip is to get **outside**, feel the sun on your face, stand barefoot on the grass, touch something green and breathe, I know it's sounds bit tree huggy but it does work.

Mix all of these up and you have a useful structure to remember:
Sing
Walk
Outside
Run up and down stairs
Dance

When you sense yourself going into The Dip, grab your sword and venture forth!

2.   "Put a Shape On Yourself: McCulloch"

Another physical tip we have borrowed from the armed forces. When noticing someone falling into the dip, the Sergeant Major might bark: "Put a **Shape on Yourself,** (insert your surname here!)" and this is actually a very good idea. What is the shape of the dip? Head down, shoulders rounded forward. With some clients they are almost completely doubled up, chin in neck - so we want to find another, more positive shape.

Method Actors spend years exploring their individual and unique physical representation of emotion. This allows them to differentiate their own from their character's response, get into role and authentically portray the emotional responses the role demands. This involves exploring themselves to find the physical position they use to express the emotion they are wishing to portray. Just by creating that shape they can illicit the emotion from within themselves. With self-discipline and practice they, on stage, create the physical shape and subsequently create in themselves the emotion they wish to portray. And so can we!

So in order to fool your emotions into feeling better we look for a new shape. Let's find a new shape to put on ourselves. Here's an exercise for you, if you fancy it?

Grab some paper and a pen. Once you've read and understood the exercise, close your eyes and think of a peak experience in your life, an event, a moment or time when you were in flow, when everything felt just right - your get up and go was all present and correct. What were you doing? Who were you with? What was so important about this moment?

*Then just **notice** what your body is doing. What you can feel inside your stomach and chest, where your hands and feet are, where is your chin? You may feel you want to stand up...really get a sense of how this feels.*

Once you open your eyes write down as much as you can,. it'll come in useful later.

Go on, have a go, you've nothing to lose!

This is YOUR shape of Get up and Go. It is unique to you.

So the next time you can feel yourself slipping into The Dip, and yes it can be a struggle to think clearly, you now know you can get yourself into that shape fast. Close your eyes and remember. It may well lift you clean out of The Dip, or at least long enough to slip on your ipod and wobble over to the photocopier.

Physical Maintenance of Dip Prevention:

Now to maintain your physical get up and go, (please forgive me if I sound like your mother) Long term of course, diet is important.

We know all about **healthy eating,**
1. not overloading on empty calories,
2. five to nine portions of fruit and vegetables a day
3. taking vitamins (did you know that our fruit and vegetables have lost up to 60% of their nutritional value in the last fifty years?)
4. drinking lots of water.

But it is so easy to forget, particularly when you are working from home. Either we forget to eat altogether because we are so absorbed in what we are doing or the fridge is altogether too accessible.

Hot tip

1. *Before you start work on a sedentary project put a jug or bottle of water between you and the fridge – whenever you feel tempted: take a drink.*
2. *Put an alarm on your mobile for lunch time to remind you to eat - take a ten minute walk first. If you forget and eat later you may be so hungry by then that you may end up eating more than you'd planned.*
3. *Then after lunch fill up the water and put a bowl of fruit next to it for the afternoon.*

Forty minutes of exercise three times a week is what the experts recommend and most importantly get enough sleep. Apparently for longevity they have worked out that 7.5 hours is the optimum time to sleep. Many of my clients get really obsessed with getting enough sleep - must have my nine hours - and yes, sleep is vitally important. Losing sleep is a sure fire way to trip into the dip. It is your choice - you can choose to be grumpy and tired or bright and bouncy and in a state of flow. (Do we really need to see that re-run of Sex in the City, again?) The quality of sleep is probably more important than the quantity. More exercise throughout the day will help with that, as will drinking more water and less alcohol (yup, I know, kills me to say it but it is true, alcohol is a depressant – just notice how you feel 48 hours after a "good night out" to see if you are becoming more sensitive to alcohol).

> Another structure to help you remember?
> **W**ater
> **A**lcohol
> **V**itals and vitamins
> **E**xercise
> **S**leep

I suspect you're all sucking on eggs here, but thought I'd include it, just in case you forgot.

The Mental Element:

Gremlin Perspectives

A great way to find yourself in the dip is Fear - fear of failure or overwhelm. When you have got so much to do you are like a rabbit in the headlights, paralysed into doing nothing at all because there is just too much or not enough.

Those voices in your head say "who did I think I was kidding?" "I can't do this".

This comes up a lot, particularly when we are in business for ourselves or have taken on a big promotion. We are making great headway and it might be that we do something outside of our comfort zone which is brilliant and scary or perhaps something goes slightly wrong or we don't get a contract we have pitched for and our Gremlins go bananas ...

Yes, Gremlins, saboteurs, the inner critic, your self-limiting beliefs: That sound track running inside our heads. Often they are the voice of a well-meaning parent or teacher who wanted to keep you safe, safe from harm, safe from discomfort, safe from disappointment but those are the fears for a child, not a robust and resourceful adult. I hope these ideas can go some way in supporting you.

Quick Tips

1 Three taming methods:
   a. Notice them: this is where the neuroscience piece kicks in again. When we are in fear our limbic system is activated which floods our body with adrenaline, our heart pounds, breath shortens and we go into Flight, Fight or Freeze mode. Now this is all very well when faced with a Saber-toothed tiger but not so good when we've had a snotty email or the kids are screaming in the back of the car. Just by *noticing* we pull our consciousness from our limbic state into the higher brain, which releases a substance called GOM to sooth and calm our limbic system. We are then in a better position to *choose* our response which may still be to yell at the children! And it might prevent us from being poleaxed by the email and heading into The Dip.
   b. Once we begin to recognize characteristics of our gremlin(s), give them a name and physical description - as recommended by Rick Carson in "Taming Your Gremlin". I have several. One, named **Bertha** is a forty stone gremlin whose favourite phrase is "you've done enough, take a break, have a biscuit". Keep your sense of humour –

recognise them and **laugh at them** "here she goes again Bertha - pah". I may still choose the Jaffa cake now and then but my productivity is so much higher!

c. **Ignore** them, as Suzanne Jefferson recommends in "Feel the Fear and Do it Anyway". This is tough and the most effective. It allows us to consistently push our boundaries enabling consistent personal growth and keeping us out of The Dip.

By noticing our Gremlins we recognise a negative, self-limiting perspective on a situation. If we can allow ourselves to see it as just that: a perspective, then we can of course *choose* a different perspective, or at least try some out!

The key phrase here is we can choose and when we choose we take back control and the responsibility is ours. Our lives have been created by us and when circumstances do get in the way things happen outside of our control – people leave us, people die, we get sick, the career takes a dive. We can choose the perspective **we** take on it and choose what **we** do about it.

The responsibility can weigh heavy sometimes but it is also very liberating – we stop blaming and stop waiting for help from anyone else, or God, or the Universe and just get on with it.

Now we are often really good at doing this in our workplace but we don't always apply that principle across our whole lives.

2. More Perspectives

a. So, here are some more perspectives for you to explore when you find yourself in the dip First of all *move* - if you have been cogitating, listening to your gremlins, feeling lost or blue or stuck, get up from where you are sitting and move to another room or stand and look out of the window. What feels different here?

b. Alternatively take on a perspective from another character. "What would Superman do in this situation?" or "What would Madonna's take on it be? How would it be to tackle the dip in four inch heels and a conical bra?"

Mental Maintenance of Dip Prevention:

The Polly-Anna perspective of Gratitude - it sounds trite but it really works. Make a note,– either mentally or in your journal, about what you are grateful for in your life. It might feel a bit awkward at first but keep going. For example: "I am grateful for this opportunity to create the life I want" or "I am grateful for my brilliant training" or "I am grateful for my extraordinary talent" Hey, there's no place for false modesty here, this can pull you out of a dip in a second, even if it just laughing at yourself.

In the long term, make this a habit, make a note of three different things for which you are grateful every day.

> **Hot Tip:** *To make something a habit you need to do it every day for three months. Have a structure to remind you. Put a sticky note on your bathroom mirror, write it in your journal, time-manage your Blackberry or wear jewellery the other way round - to remind you to notice.*

Sometimes it will show up how important certain people are in your life. Other times you will be grateful for aspects of *you* – your body, mind or character traits which help support you in your life. This will provide a number of positive results:

1. You actively notice the positive in your life and acknowledge its existence leaving you feeling more positive.

2. Gratitude has us notice our nearest and dearest more fully. Our attitude towards them begins to change from expectation to appreciation. *They* frequently notice the difference and the relationship strengthens as a result.

3. It changes your perspective from constantly seeking more to appreciating what you have which removes a good deal of self-imposed stress.

4. Gratitude brings you fully into the present – not the past or future – gratitude for what you have right now rather than taking it for

granted. Not dwelling on the past which you can do nothing about or worrying about the future – which may never happen.

5. Gratitude brings to light what you most value – this is a great clue to where you should be spending most of your time. Obvious when it's a person, but when it's a character trait spend time developing that character trait – read, take a course, notice how and when you use it most successfully.

Gratitude, by bringing our attention to our strengths, by strengthening our relationships and by grounding us in the present, gives us a powerful platform from which to pursue our goals. Once you are aware of the things for which you are most grateful, you can make sure your goals support them and have them support your goals - a win: win situation and one more certain to bring us real and lasting success.

Which in the long term brings us to forward planning and -

Goals

Of course goals are important, but most important is the vision from which we devise our goals. What is your vision?

Do you have a clear idea of what you want your future to look like? Is it written down? Not just a business/career plan: I mean every aspect of your life What are you doing it all for? What will it give you to achieve that goal?

1. If you are inclined, then create a **collage** of images which portray the end goal or end game. The latest thing is to create a power-point which you can play to yourself, with images, inspirational words with a bed of music. You could create it as a screen saver for a moment by moment top up. Looking at the Big Picture is a great way to lift yourself out of the doldrums and the dip.
2. Or, as Napoleon Hill states in his still brilliant tome, "Think and grow Rich", write down your goal and how you will achieve it in three sentences and say it aloud every morning and evening.
3. Go to the wheel of life and score each aspect out of ten. What would it look like if it were a 10? What would you be doing? How can you get there?

4. What challenges could you set for yourself daily to put the excitement back in your job/relationship. Set SMART goals (specific, measurable, aspirational, realistic and time bound) and keep checking on your progress.
5. Raise the bar on what you do, for your own satisfaction - the positive spin-offs are obvious but self-esteem is priceless.

Break each element down into bite-sized pieces and time-manage them backwards into your planner, diary, Outlook Blackberry, whatever that looks like. THEN DO IT!

The Spiritual Element

And so we come to the **Spiritual** - the force that gives life to the body of all living things, the fundamental, emotional and activating principle of a person.

> "There is a vitality, a life force, an energy, a quickening that is translated through you into action, and because there is only one of you in all of time, this expression is unique. And if you block it, it will never exist through any other medium and it will be lost. The world will not have it. It is not your business to determine how good it is nor how valuable nor how it compares with other expressions. It is your business to keep it yours clearly and directly, to keep the channel open." Martha Graham

Now when you come into coaching we will spend quite some time mining for your values – not your morals or ethics, hopefully you have them sorted. Your values are unique and special to you: without which your life would not be fulfilled. Values are the elements in your life which give you a sense of deep satisfaction. You may, for example, have a value called "Independence" which means financial independence, freedom to manage your own time, being in control. Another person's "Independence" value might mean taking risks, adventure and freedom. Neither is right or wrong and the combination will be unique to you.

Extracting those building blocks of personality is fascinating and incredibly enlightening and takes a great deal of time, many tools including intuition on the part of the coach. You may realise how your last job trampled on half your values and that is why you were so uncomfortable, if not down right miserable. For a ridiculous example - there are very few vegetarians who would be happy working in an abattoir. Once you know what your values are, making decisions becomes easy: from what holiday to book, to which career path to take and even as far as choosing a spouse!

Your values are unchanging through-out your life but may alter in priority at different times. Living according to your values can be hard work but will bring enormous clarity and fulfilment. Seeking fulfilment is a radical act. It takes courage, commitment and hard work. This is one of the most important things a coach will help us to discover. The building blocks of who we are, are our values. When we live according to our values, we are being true to ourselves living a life of **passion**.

So, knowing our values helps us to makes choices and to live our life and not one impressed upon us by other people or indeed by gremlins.

Whilst you may have many we focus on your top ten, here today let's try this exercise and pick out your top three:

> Go back to your Peak Experience notes and circle the things that were really important ... was it the people? Perhaps you were deep in nature? Were you organising a big event? Had you just achieved a major goal, if so what was it, what did it take for you to achieve it? Circle the key words and then expand them out to say what those words mean for you.

For example, I have a value called "Empowerment" which, for me, means to inspire, confidence, just do it, action, integrity, owning it, being responsible, being brave. I had a client once with a value of Red Knickers which for her meant feminine, subtle power, elegance, womanly sophistication. It's not one of mine but I am rather jealous of this value! What are yours? Test them out by examining how much your current role plays into your values. Are there any values that you are stepping on at the moment (like the vegetarian in an abattoir)?

These are small steps you can take yourself and working with a coach can help you deepen your understanding of yourself and the values that will bring you fulfilment more fully.

In summary then success is being able to choose and be 100% responsible for our actions AND our thoughts. We can choose to be fit, healthy, holding a perspective of gratitude and having our values as a blue-print to help us choose. We'll spend less time in the dip and more having the fulfilling life we so richly deserve.

Jill McCulloch

Coaching is a powerful human relationship where a fully qualified coach supports the client to design the future not get over the past. Jill McCulloch has been a qualified Co-Active Coach for over ten years working with Passionate People with a Mission all over the world. Sometimes reigniting their passion and otherwise supporting them to discover a new mission. Co-Active Coaching is a highly respected coaching model which has fulfilment and balance at its centre whilst ensuring the client is also mindful of the journey.

Jill is passionate about people discovering and using their unique and authentic personality, talents and experience to make a difference in the world. Whether it is one to one coaching, training or facilitating workshops or speaking to groups clients describe her as "professional, energetic, positive, fun, intuitive and powerfully challenging".

Her previous experience has been predominantly in sales and marketing for a broad range of organisations including radio, executive recruitment and engineering culminating in running a furniture manufacturing organisation. Jill enjoys working with highly successful business owners and organisational leaders who are looking for their next move.

Jill spent time at college in the United States and teaching in Canada and is based near Cambridge in England. She lives with her husband, son and daughters (when they are home from University). Most of her spare time is spent rowing with her local club. Having taken up rowing only two years ago, Jill has caught the bug and rows up to four times a week. Her steep learning curve has given her insights into facing new challenges which has given rise to a number of blogs.

For more information please see her website at www.coachyou.co.uk.

Impact

'Why fit in when you were born to stand out?' Dr Seuss

Impact in action

When we were at school we were told to work hard and we would achieve great things – the world would be our oyster. Few would dispute that hard work is a necessary part in achieving our goals; however, for true success it is not enough. There are many people who technically excel, that have all the necessary qualifications and more; they are brilliant in their field but don't ever make it to the 'top spot'. In a world where everyone is expected to work hard, it's really about finding a way to stand out. Lakshmi Mittal, Indian steel magnate and one of the world's most successful business men is quoted as saying: 'Hard work certainly goes a long way. These days a lot of people work hard, so you have to make sure you work harder and really dedicate yourself to what you are doing and setting out to achieve'.

Research has shown that to truly succeed – to get the ultimate job, seal the winning bid or be a great leader - we need something else that is harder to define. We all know someone who seems to 'own the room' from the moment they walk in. We recognise those who have that certain 'it' but often struggle to break it down in to attributes and behaviours. Barak Obama has it, Bill Clinton is a master, Oprah, and our own Queen Elizabeth all exude this quality: impact. Whatever your walk of life, impact is crucial to success. Why? Because the cliché is true: people buy people. Impact is the key to connecting and influencing: drawing your audience in, earning their trust and compelling them to be a part of whatever you are offering. Be it a product, a service or an idea; if people buy into you, chances are they will also take what you are 'selling'.

Impact closes the gap between merit and success. Those who do it successfully seem to exude impact and presence as if it were second nature, hence the common misconception that those who have it, are born with it; we even describe people as 'born leaders'. Yes, some are dealt a better hand from the start, but the great news for the rest of us is that it can be learned. And it's not just for those extroverts, or those that are larger than life – consider David Attenborough or Bill Gates – neither the most gregarious personalities but both highly influential and with an ability to communicate with passion, display gravitas with equal measures of strength and warmth and crucially, with authenticity – always being true to themselves.

True impact and presence requires alignment between your mind, body and words. It's how you show up, the energy you bring to a room and how you communicate your message. Throughout the rest of this chapter we will explore these three areas, breaking Impact down into key behaviours with practical tips and techniques that can be used immediately by everyone. We will consider:

- Visual Impact – our personal packaging
- Energy – a positive mental state
- Non –verbal communication and body language
- Gravitas and communicating with confidence
- Authenticity – being true to self
- Consistency – walking the walk and talking the talk!

Jeff Bezos of Amazon is reported to have said: 'your personal brand is what people say about you when you're not in the room'. By definition, everyone has a personal brand, and everyone makes an impact. The question is, what type of impact are you making, and are you managing it?

First impressions

Before we explore these areas in detail, it is important to mention first impressions, as they form a crucial part in the impact we make on others.

The first impression 'sets the scene' for what is to follow. Whether we like it or not, as humans we are hard-wired to make a snap judgement, in a matter of seconds, about those we meet. According to a study by Harvard Business School, the assumptions we make in this brief period are astounding, including: how successful people are, their social status, sexuality, level of education, trustworthiness and likeability. This goes back to primeval times when such a snap decision may be the difference between life and death. Based primarily on visual impact, our ancestors' thoughts would be: what tribe are they from, and more importantly, who will win in a fight?

People are often uncomfortable about 'judging a book by its cover'. The truth is, you would hope most people will stick around long enough to scratch a little deeper – but in this commercially competitive world, not everyone will. Before a workshop or presentation, I'll often watch delegates as they arrive at the venue, taking in how they communicate on arrival, their energy and all round presence. It's no secret that when interviewing candidates many companies will ask the opinion of the receptionist. It's crucial to remember that your first impression isn't always when you formally say 'hello'.

When I set off into the big wide world my Dad gave me three pieces of advice – and two of the three have taken me a long way. His words of wisdom were to have 'an impressive handshake, be able to talk sport', and the third, 'to change a tyre' – at which point I phone the breakdown people. Sport may not be your thing, but an ability to make small talk with strangers is a skill worth practicing if it doesn't come naturally to you. However, an impressive handshake is crucial when it comes to first impressions and making an impact. Have you ever had feedback on your handshake? It's interesting that everyone thinks they shake hands well, but from personal experience I know this is absolutely not the case. From sweaty hands to bone crushers, my personal bête noire is the offering of the fingers rather than the whole hand – and I'm loathed to say it tends to be a female thing.

Our first impressions are based on all our senses – the visual: how someone looks; the auditory: a person's voice and tone; how they smell - too much fragrance can be as bad as body odour; and kinesthetic - the sense of touch – when we shake hands and it 'feels' right, we get that 'gut' reaction that 'I like this person'.

So how do you perform the 'perfect handshake'? Firstly, it should be done with confidence – not an afterthought. Be ready to offer your hand on meeting someone – have your right hand free of baggage, and your glass or cup (a cold glass can leave your hand feeling clammy!). Your hand should be held out and thumb straight upwards – if your palm turns upwards – it is too submissive; a hand on top is dominant and can be perceived as aggressive. Shake hands with as much palm contact as possible, with the fleshy bit between thumb and finger touching, and meet their level of pressure. And finally, make eye contact.

Research also show that it can take a further ten interactions to right a wrong impression. A client of mine always asks to 'try again' if the first handshake doesn't go quite right – he uses humour but would rather be slightly uncomfortable than risk a poor first impression. There are many instances in business when we are thrown a curve ball and we have little control of the situation. Our personal brand, reputation and image are ours to manage. How often do we get the opportunity for a second 'shot'– why would you leave it to chance?

Visual Impact

I mention visual impact first because although it is not the most important factor in creating a positive impact, studies show that it is a critical first filter. Posture, dress, grooming, and overall appearance are the first clues about ourselves that we offer to the outside world. So although it is not the most important factor, it still requires effort and attention.

How we present ourselves often mirrors how we feel inside – if we have a positive body image, eat healthily and exercise, our appearance and the way we dress reflect that. We have to wear clothes – it is a requirement of the law – but how we dress is a social choice. We can make choices that will make us appear professional, creative and impressive. This influences others and impacts on our own mindset and performance, so an understanding of how to present ourselves well is a great tool.

When considering your personal brand and the impact you make, in the same way a marketing consultant would identify brand messages before designing the packaging of a product, it is important to know what you want to communicate and the expectations of your audience.

To illustrate this I often tell a story from my early career in the legal profession. I was serving my first trainee 'seat' with the senior partner of a firm of solicitors. He was a criminal law specialist and this particular weekend he was on the rota as duty solicitor – a service provided for those who are arrested and don't already have legal representation. On the Saturday morning I had a call from the senior partner to meet him at the police cells, as we had someone who needed a solicitor. I changed in to my suit and made my way to the police station. When we arrived the senior partner was in his jeans, anorak and trainers, as he'd been called during his son's football match and hadn't had chance to change. For the first few moments it was clear that our client thought I was the 'lawyer' because I was the one wearing a suit and met his expectations of what a lawyer should look like.

Dress codes have become more relaxed in recent years – a suit and tie are no longer obligatory in many business settings - but this introduces further challenges with a blurring of the boundaries of what is and is not appropriate.

There are the obvious contenders for what doesn't 'fit the bill' in a business environment, including low cut tops, scruffy, emblazoned t-shirts and short skirts. However, phrases such as 'smart casual' can cause much confusion. I advise clients who are presenting or pitching to a new client to err on the side of caution – it is always better to be slightly overdressed than under-dressed/appearing as if you 'don't care'. A quick phone call to a company will give you an insight into what they consider to be their accepted code of dress, especially when attending an interview or important meeting.

We know pulling on a great suit for an interview or a fabulous outfit for a date has an impact on others, but a recent study has gone a step further – suggesting the way we dress affects our own thoughts and as a result impacts on our performance.

The researchers named this concept 'enclothed cognition' and studied how the state of our bodies affects our thoughts, and that our clothing plays a huge part on that state. In the study, participants were asked to wear a white lab coat. Those who were told it was a scientist's lab coat performed better in tests than those wearing their ordinary clothes. In comparison, when the white coat was presented as an artist's overall the participants performed less well and made more mistakes.

Following this theory, if you impress your brain by selecting an outfit you would wear when you want to make a great impression, this will have a positive impact on how you think, your mental state and what you can achieve.

This may explain the apparent backlash in some companies to 'dress down Friday'. A client recently reported he had stopped 'casual dress' on a Friday as figures indicated this had a direct impact on the productivity of staff. He believed that their casual attire meant they were in a more 'relaxed' state of mind, winding down at the end of the week with performance dropping as a result.

Of course, visual impact goes further than how we dress. Grooming and general appearance are equally important when it comes to other people's perceptions. From personal experience of hosting workshops; facial hair, tattoos and piercings are divisive topics that are hotly debated. Depending on the industry and situation, one has to make a decision between creative expression and expectation – often influenced by social stereo-typing.

Impact is about building relationships and being likeable. A widely reported study from 2013 in the US said women who wear make-up can earn more than 30 percent more pay than non-makeup wearing workers. A further study claimed that subtle makeup increases people's perceptions of a woman's likability, her competence and (provided she does not overdo it) her trustworthiness. This was backed up by research by BusinessInsider.com, which reported in a survey of UK companies, 64 percent of directors said that 'women who wore make-up looked more professional.' Again the choice is personal, however if it gives you the edge, why not give it a try? A word of caution for those inexperienced at applying makeup – a light hand is required - badly worn make-up is worse than none at all.

Positive Energy

We all know people who are 'radiators' – those friends who we come away from a meeting feeling inspired and happy, grateful for their company and friendship. In contrast, the 'drains' sap us of our energy and positivity – these naysayers are always poised to put a dampener on your enthusiasm. It only takes one person to change the whole dynamics of a group, changing the mood in seconds and having a negative impact on the rest of the meeting.

The trait that differentiates humans from all other creatures is that of choice. If we don't get the results we want from a certain behaviour or course of action we can review the situation and select a different approach. We can also choose our mental state. As Henry Ford famously said: 'If you think you can, or you think you can't, you are probably right'. When you believe you can do something, you create a positive image, one of success; when you believe you can't, you create a negative image, one of defeat.

Bringing positive energy into a room is a gift to share with others. Enthusiasm is a marvelous quality. It is infectious and gives confidence to those around you as well as yourself. Let your enthusiasm – a positive belief in the absolute achievability of your goals – shine through – because when you do, success will begin to become a reality.

We will examine presence and the importance of being authentic in more detail shortly, but it is relevant here to point out the incredible appeal and magnetism of someone who shows up with a positive mindset, and who is truly at ease and relaxed in their own skin.

Non–verbal communication and body language

Our body language accounts for over 50 percent of the perceived impact of all face-to-face communications, so underestimate its power and influence at your peril! To interpret body language correctly, gestures have to be considered in the appropriate context. When communicating verbally we consider the words in the context of a sentence, gestures are the same – our 'non-verbal' sentence is formed by the 'full picture' of our posture and all our movements and signals.

When your words are at odds with your gestures your body language will be seen as the truth. If you have ever been in a situation when you have felt someone is lying to you, the chances are their body language does not match what they are saying. They appear incongruent and as a result we get that 'gut' feeling that something isn't right.

There are whole books and studies dedicated to body language and non-verbal communication, and this chapter won't even scratch the surface – however, even a small amount of awareness can have a huge impact on how you are perceived and can enhance your effectiveness and image.

We will consider some core areas where identifying and managing some common physical cues and gestures will allow you to communicate more effectively – expressing your true message rather than one left to assumption.

Posture and deportment are critical factors in first impressions. How you stand and carry yourself will have a huge impact on your audience: communicating your levels of confidence and connectivity. A slouched or laid back posture may indicate a lack of confidence and interest and will reduce gravitas and impact. In contrast, someone who appears tense and rigid can appear nervous and edgy and will struggle to put their audience at ease. If your shoulders are tense, your whole body will appear awkward.

Many people I coach have never actively looked at how they stand or sit. I advise everyone to take a full length mirror and stand in front of it and examine their posture critically. Think of yourself like a tree, with your core muscles strong like a trunk. Your feet should be rooted to the ground and you want to grow up tall from them. Ideally you are aiming for a 'relaxed' alertness, avoiding tension in the shoulders and jawline. Women have a tendency to break their stance at the hip and tilt their head to one side – both gestures undermine gravitas and authority.

If you are someone who spends much of your time seated around a meeting table, again have a look at how you appear to those around you. Do you sit upright and alert, leaning in slightly to show interest? Or do you find yourself slouching in the chair and leaning back? Alpha males may sit with their hands behind their head, elbows out to the side – a gesture that again goes back to primal instincts and ape like behaviour. In lifting the arms he is making himself bigger, taking up more space and displaying dominant (in some cases, aggressive) body language. A good way to counteract such a display is to stand up. By standing you are making yourself bigger, reducing the dominance of the display.

Hand gestures are a common clue to how people are feeling. Most of us are familiar with a 'closed' pose of arms crossed. This is a great example of reading the cue in context, as the person may be cold, or feel comfortable folding their arms. Arms across the body form a barrier, and barriers make it difficult to build rapport. In a meeting, if someone displays closed gestures, offer them a piece of paper to look at – they have to break their barrier to take it from you, giving the opportunity to build rapport again.

Often people ask me what they should do with their hands when presenting, as they feel uncomfortable. It is down to personal preference and finding an open stance that you can practice until it becomes second nature. Hands in pockets or behind the back can give the impression you are hiding something – not an ideal message when you are looking to build trust in your audience.

Politicians are often masters of the powerful hand gesture. Obama uses the 'Obama hug' to great effect when addressing a large audience – he opens his arms as he is delivering his message and 'draws' his audience to him. Former President, Bill Clinton is a master of nonverbal communication. There are numerous anecdotes describing his legendary 'presence' and his ability to make whoever he is speaking to feel incredibly special, like the only person in the room. However, even this 'expert' had help during his election campaign, as he had a tendency to point when delivering a speech. On the scale of hand gestures, where palms up is submissive, and hands down displays control; pointing is perceived as aggressive and directive. Clinton's advisers recognised the power in his hand gesture, but closed the pointing finger inwards, making it less confrontational.

When studying body language it is impossible to ignore the mind and body connection. We have been told to 'stand up straight' since we were small – if you have good posture you will feel better about yourself and appear more confident. Physically change your posture now, as you are sat reading. Make yourself feel small, drop you head, slump your shoulders.

How do you feel – it's hard to feel good when displaying negative body language.

Our body doesn't know the difference between the imagined and reality – I touched on this earlier in positive energy. We cannot possibly control the hundreds of micro expressions that flit across our face during a conversation, yet people subconsciously notice them and will interpret the expressions as being directed at them. If you've ever been in a conversation and said something you wish you hadn't - we enter an internal dialogue which goes along the lines of 'why did you say that, you idiot?' In that moment a negative expression matching that thought will flit across your face and be interpreted by the person you are talking to.

It is impossible to control these fleeting expressions, but what we can do is change our mindset and thoughts. Showing up to a conversation in a positive frame of mind – looking for the good in the situation – will help you come across as more personable and receptive. People will feel good in your company and build a more trusting relationship with you.

I've mentioned Bill Clinton's infamous presence and charisma and his ability to make people feel like the only person in the room. The secret to true presence is to listen. Listening is one of the most underrated skills in business today. How often do you truly listen to someone, giving one hundred percent attention? More often we are waiting for our turn to speak in the conversation. The impact of listening, pausing to acknowledge someone's point of view and then responding, is incredibly powerful and takes practice and confidence. As Maya Angelou said: 'People will forget what you said, people will forget what you did, but people will never forget how you made them feel.'

The Power Pose

Fans of TED talks may well be familiar with the work of social psychologist Amy Cuddy. Her research at Harvard has taken the impact of body language a step further. Her work has shown that beyond the mind, body connection "power posing" — standing in a posture of confidence, even when we don't feel confident, can affect testosterone and cortisol levels in the brain, and might even have an impact on our chances for success.

I highly recommend Amy's TED Talk – the most viewed of 2013 – as she has a fascinating personal story which puts into context her work. However, in summary if we adopt a power pose, think Wonder Woman with her hands on her hips, for just two minutes there will be a direct impact on our hormones. In the findings, cortisol (the hormone associated with stress) decreased by about 25 percent and the results showed increased testosterone (confidence and risk-taking) by about 19 percent for both men and women. In contrast, low-power poses increased cortisol by about 17 percent and decreased testosterone by about 10 percent.

The statistics implied the effect would last for around 20 minutes – no one is suggesting you conduct meetings in a power pose, but two minutes practice before an important presentation or interview could make a huge difference. With reference to my early comments on positive energy, Cuddy also comments: 'there is established research showing that while it's true that facial expressions reflect how you feel, you can also 'fake it until you make it.' In other words, you can smile long enough that it makes you feel happy.

Gravitas

One of my favourite definitions of gravitas is: Dignity, impressiveness, seriousness, influence, weight and presence. Who wouldn't want some of that?

When it comes to impact and success, gravitas is key. It is the element of communication that gives you influence and authority and allows you to communicate your message with passion and charisma. In short, when you speak, people listen and you command their respect and trust.

To achieve gravitas, one must communicate with equal strength, or status; and warmth, or connection. Status and connection are at either ends of a scale with gravitas in the middle. To make an impact we need to connect effectively with our various audiences – be it one-to-one in a meeting or presenting to a group. It is a skill to learn to adapt your style to fit the situation. When we need to connect with someone and show empathy it is useful to turn the 'dial' towards the warmth end of the scale. Conversely, there are times when a more impactful message is appropriate. However for true gravitas, to truly influence, you need strength and warmth in equal measures.

We all tend to have a default style and have a natural preference to either status or connection. There are different techniques that can be used to increase your gravitas, for example, through body language and voice tone. A great example of this, shared by Gravitas expert Caroline Goyder, is the comparison between the pilot of a plane and the cabin crew. Imagine the deep, authoritative voice of the pilot – full of gravitas – and as a result you trust him to get you from A to B safely. Then bring to mind the cabin crew – a more 'sing-songy' friendly tone, full of warmth communicating that you will be well looked after on your flight.

Those who have a tendency to displaying more 'strength' in their default style are perceived as more authoritative and are usually task-focused. They tend to know their own mind, be competitive and value status and respect. They will appear more formal and tend to have a directive style. If this sounds familiar, to find your gravitas you need to work on your connection side. Try and focus on the relationship and the people involved rather than just completing the task – take into account people's feelings and show empathy towards them and their situation. It helps to imagine people as old friends or family and truly listen to what they have to say – show interest, ask open questions and allow them to share their stories. Often those with a status style can appear quite serious because of their formal body language. To appear warmer, relax your stance, soften your facial expression and use a softer tone. Tilting the head fractionally to one side will communicate empathy, helping to soften the delivery of a difficult message. A formal voice is lower pitched and those with a status style will often be more economic with their words. To add passion and warmth, introduce some 'colour' to your conversation using different tones, a slightly faster pace and expression.

If connection and warmth are your default style there may be situations when you feel you are not being listened to or taken seriously. Connection is vitally important, especially in more caring and creative roles, but the introduction of some strength will improve gravitas. Traits of those with a connection style tend to be animated –informal and chatty in their conversation and delivery. They may nod their head and gesticulate with their hands. People, their feelings and relationships are the main focus and they want to be liked. You will tend to find them as team players and inclusive in their manner.

To counteract these traits and introduce more strength to your communication style, focus on the task not the relationship. Consider your posture and stance – stand strong and tall, exuding confidence. In a business environment look to take a more strategic viewpoint; be objective and analytical and be succinct in your conversation. Calmer body language with fewer gestures and less nodding will improve your gravitas. Use your smile more sparingly – when appropriate, but don't overdo it! Stay authentic, passionate and human.

Authentic

Oscar Wilde famously said: 'Be yourself, everyone else is taken'. Authenticity has become a buzz word in modern psychology and business, and rightly so. We can all spot a phoney and they are rarely the people we want to spend time with, never mind develop a business relationship.

When I'm coaching or presenting, one of the first and last things I stress is the need to be yourself – impact is not about churning out 'clones' who perform in exactly the same way. The tools and techniques I share here are used to help develop areas where you may recognise weaknesses – to continue growing and unlock true potential – being the best version of YOU you can be. To make a great impact and have true executive presence it's crucial to let your personality shine through – that's what makes us memorable.

Consistency

To maximise your impact it is important to develop and manage a strong personal brand and reputation. As with a product for the supermarket shelves, a necessary part of the process is to hone your message – explore your values, recognise your own Unique Selling Point (USP), what makes you special and then communicate it to the outside world consistently.

The impact of any brand is dependent on its consistency. When you buy a Coca Cola or walk into a McDonald's anywhere in the world you know exactly what you are going to get, every time. If you are talking the talk, you need to walk the walk!

I urge you to look at your public profile and what it really says about you. Always remember that it isn't how you think you come across – it is people's perceptions of you. Consider all platforms: social media – are you consistent across Twitter, LinkedIn and Facebook? If you post on Pinterest, is it consistent with your brand? How you're your telephone manner compare to your conversations in person? And when did you last listen to your answerphone message? That might be the first impression someone has of you. If you write a regular blog, is the tone and content consistent with other platforms? How do you look in your photographs? However suntanned and gorgeous you looked out in Ibiza this summer, it is not an appropriate, professional shot for LinkedIn! And if you've made initial contact with someone - perhaps via Twitter or LinkedIn - will they recognise the person in front of them when you meet face-to-face? Be brutally honest with yourself and if you are unsure, ask the opinion of an objective colleague or friend.

Summary

In the present day, where technology has opened the whole world up to be our audience, everybody is more and more visible. To succeed it is crucial to stand out from the crowd, influence and communicate with clarity – be the person people want to do business with – and when they do, be outstanding.

Impact closes the gap between merit and success. It helps you fulfil your potential, gets you to where you want to be; and when you are there – perform to your very best.

Deborah Ogden

A nationally respected performance coach and speaker on personal branding and making a positive impact, Deborah Ogden consistently delivers exceptional results.

Whether it's building better relationships, winning more contracts or pitching and presenting with confidence, Deborah's expertise has delivered breakthrough results time after time for businesses and individuals across the UK.

She has 15 years of extensive experience working on the PR and image of some high profile names including Andrew (Freddie) Flintoff and Old Trafford Cricket Ground, the British Heart Foundation, Co-operative Insurance (CIS) and CragRats. Deborah currently works with Standard Fireworks and Polypipe and knows how powerful personal branding can be, both on a corporate and individual level.

Her approach centres around increasing personal impact and how to make an impression - from body language and visual impact to communication skills - and understanding how these impact on the people around you.

Deborah works with leadership teams and individuals who are often technically excellent, yet lack 'executive presence' and gravitas. The ability to connect with the people they are meeting and leading is crucial - 21st century leaders need to be the complete package and their personal brand and profile must reflect that. Deborah ensures that they are fully equipped to win the backing of their team and the people around them to guide companies to success.

Her ability to connect with her participants and clients at an individual level enables her to quickly gain trust and be an insightful coach for them. Having trained as a solicitor, Deborah has a strong background in professional services giving her an in-depth and real world understanding of the importance of backing up content with strong presentation.

Deborah delivers her work through tailored one-to-one training sessions or group workshops to help business people stand out from the crowd and perform to the very best of their ability. Her clients include CEOs, finance directors and solicitors as well as business start-ups.

Deborah is a regular commentator on BBC Radio Leeds and is frequently booked as an motivational speaker for both businesses and educational institutions to advise on positive impact and personal brand in business.

Visit www.deborahogden.com for further information.

The Science of an 'Inner Practice' to Transform

'Success into Fulfilment'

WARNING: This chapter may contain unconventional concepts and perspectives that may challenge your understanding about your inner and outer reality. Proceed ONLY if you have a curious and open mind interested in the science behind these ideas as well as their practical benefits and applications for a successful life NOW!

This is one of the first things I mention my audiences when sharing this kind of information. I say this in a 'tongue-in-check' kind of way, to keep things a little light, but there is a shred of seriousness here as well. It is true that this chapter is going to cover some ideas and concepts that may truly be a bit of a stretch for some to connect with and that's totally fine. If the title has grabbed your attention I'm going to assume that you're open to some 'out there' concepts of success, reality and consciousness. If that's you, please keep reading, I'm pretty sure you won't be disappointed.

Having said that, here's the interesting thing. Even though what you're going to read might seem a little mystical and esoteric, let me assure you that these concepts are actually based and grounded in the most cutting edge Unified Field Physics that we have today. Some of which I'm going to share with you here in a basic understandable way. You see, I don't know about you, but I'm very open to alternative ideas and concepts of reality and metaphysics, topics that some might label as 'woo woo'. However, for me to REALLY connect with a mystical idea it has to have at least some sort of scientific evidence that supports it. Otherwise it's just a dogma. If a concept has no way of being scientifically verified, then it's a little harder for me to incorporate it into my personal belief system. I'll add to that by going one step further. When you think about it, what might seem like a 'miracle' is often just science and physics we just don't understand yet. I mean, imagine telling a person 200 or even 100 years ago, that someday you'll be able to communicate with another person anywhere in the world with a wireless device smaller than your hand. Imagine how that person would have reacted? It's worth keeping that in mind if you read something here that might make you want to LOL.

For the purposes of this chapter, I'm going to go out on a limb here and assume that you're a little like me in that sense, interested in the point where science and mysticism intersect for the improvement of your life.

When I was asked to write a chapter on 'Success' I almost instantly heard the word 'fulfilment', because for me THIS is true success. We all know someone (that someone could even be you), who on the outside seems to have achieved great 'success'. This (in a western society) may include a great job or career, financial stability, a beautiful home and car, a family, wife and kids etc. Now don't get me wrong, I'm NOT saying that these things would not contribute to your happiness as I'm sure it would for all of us. However, all of these things don't necessarily lead to fulfilment and I've always been curious as to why.

For many years now I've wanted to know why it is that sometimes when we get what we say we want, it doesn't always give us a sustained pleasant feeling that we thought it would.

There could be a number of reasons for this; some of these may include the fact that every one of those things mentioned above are external 'things', none of which originate from within yourself. Not like confidence, compassion, integrity, authenticity which are qualities that are within an individual which I'm sure you would agree are more likely to lead to fulfilment than the possessions. Also, all of those mentioned things are completely transient. Even a family could potentially be here one day and gone the next. As oppose to 'internal' qualities which once developed are far more foundational and longer lasting. Another reason could be that many us are 'programmed' to WANT and achieve those things.

What do I mean by 'programed'?

By programming I'm referring to absolutely any external factors that have in any way shaped who we are, what we do, how we think, our beliefs and so on. Believe it or not these influences started from the moment we were born and include our parents, siblings, peer group, childhood experiences, the media (in all its forms) as well as institutions such as the education system, political system, financial sector, medical institution, religious dogma and judicial system. Whether you believe it or not, all of these have influenced you in one way or another consciously or subconsciously.

I don't know about you, but for me, success doesn't so much relate to what I have, what I do, how many kids I have, the suburb I live in, the car I drive, the money in the bank etc. Yes, these are great things and I want all of this great stuff. But I have come to understand and more clearly define what success REALLY is for me. Here is a short breakdown of the elements that I define as success in my life. See if they resonate with you. The below points are going to act as the back drop and context for the rest of this chapter.

- Being a success equates to a sense of fulfilment, a state of BEING that you have which emanates from the inside out which isn't necessarily there because of some external pleasing factor but more from a world view which you have mindfully created for yourself.

- The ability to be psychologically adaptable and flexible to what life may throw at you from time to time. This includes the ability to RESPOND from a place of presence rather than REACT from your emotional wounds from a past trauma.

- The capacity to have and express the human traits we all say we want to see more of in the world like compassion, understanding, tolerance, consideration, empathy, integrity, appreciation, gratitude and most importantly LOVE, even when it might not be easy in the moment.

- Having a deeeeeeeeeep feeling of 'connectedness' not only with people but with nature and your environment. Creating an experience within you where you actually feel very much a part of this amazing planet we are on, our home.

- Being inspired by something, ANYTHING, that really excites you. Perhaps something that is in some way of service to others. We've all heard that saying that the best way to be happy is to make someone else happy. But even if you're working on making yourself happy – GREAT! The world can't be a joyful place unless its inhabitants are joyful. So don't feel bad if you don't have aspirations to 'save the world' and become a Mother Teresa. Creating love and joy within your self is the best thing anyone could do to inspire others to seek the same for themselves.

- Having an understanding of your purpose and mission, living from this place and getting PAID TO DO THAT! But at the same time, doing something that you would continue to do even if it wasn't for the money.

- Being PAID to do what you LOVE to do. And by this I don't just mean 'liking your job'. I mean doing something that you would continue to do tomorrow if you won a $50 million lottery today! If you think that you couldn't possibly make a VERY GOOD living doing what you LOVE then you simply have a limiting belief, or mental programing that DOES NOT BELONG TO YOU but is something that you picked up somewhere along your life journey. It probably came from your childhood and probably from your parents, which would have come from their parents and so on. No matter what it is that you would absolutely LOVE to do and get paid for it, there are a BUNCH of people out there at this very moment doing exactly that thing that you would love to do. Ask yourself what internal resources did that individual need to achieve that and then ask yourself how YOU could develop those same resources and let universal synchronistic forces (or what some may call 'luck') do the rest.

- An ability to be present in the moment and content for no other reason than just for the gift of being alive! This may seem pretty obvious, but it's a good thing to remember that this present moment, right here and now, is ALL THERE IS! But how often are we really IN the moment? 99% of the time we are either thinking of the past or the future both of which were, or are going to be, NOW moments. So many people are doing doing doing things in the NOW that they don't like or would rather not be doing, in the hope that there will be some NOW moment in the future that will be better than the NOW they are in. The funny thing is that for so many people, no matter what happens in the future, they will always be on this very same mental hamster running wheel.

There are probably more aspects of success and fulfilment I could add to this list, but I'm sure you've got an idea of where I'm coming from here. I think you would agree that if you were experiencing just some of the above, you wouldn't only feel more successful but more importantly – fulfilled!

So now that we've set the back, I'm going to lay out for you the scientific basis for an internal practice to help you actually achieve all of the above in your life. I don't call it 'meditation', because as you'll see, it goes WAY deeper than that. It is a scientific foundation for an inner process that I teach to individuals and to groups of people with AMAZING transformations. It's super quick, simple and can take as little as 4 minutes to do. Yep, that's right 4 minutes. But if I just told it to you in a few lines (which I will soon enough), you probably wouldn't appreciate what you're ACTUALLY doing. That's why I'm going to take my time to give you the science behind the process.

Although I'm not going to make myself out to be some sort of guru living in a fantasy of perpetual bliss, believe me, I'm not. But what I can honestly say, hand on heart, is that from the list above, I am VERY pleased with where I'm at with each one of them and excited about my future while being totally ok with what IS here and now in my life.

Even though there is some seriously complicated physics at the foundation of all this, I intend to lay out the science of this simple practice. I'll explain exactly how to do this for you to try for yourself. I'm going to take you on a step by step journey that may at times seem a little 'off track', but if you can hang in there with me, you might just have an 'ah-ha' moment (or two) that might spark something within you. My hope is that this information will inspire you to simply try this out for yourself, do some further research or maybe even get in touch with someone who can teach or guide you more personally. Or, if you're still reading this, if nothing else, I'm sure you'll find this chapter an interesting read at the very least.

Ok, the first and most obvious question is; 'What is this inner practice about?'

Well, it's basically a type of meditative, heart-mind-body, visualisation process. Through following some simple relaxation instructions, (or through self-guidance), the brain enters into the Alpha state. From here you can then energetically connect with the reality of what you want while simultaneously dissolving any blocks standing in the way of manifesting the feelings that you want. Notice I said the 'feelings' you want, not the 'stuff' you want because at the end of the day, as I kind of hinted at above you only want the things you say you want because of the FEELING or STATE OF BEING you think you'll have when you get that. So the logic here is, why not 'leap frog' the 'stuff' and connect with the feeling DIRECTLY and then be open to how the universe delivers it to you? After all if you can create the feeling without being dependant on the 'thing' first, then if that 'thing' were to disappear, you'll still feel more whole than completely empty, shattered or ruined.

Now if you're still reading this chapter I'm going to assume that even though this stuff might seem a little 'out there', I have at least stirred your curiosity. Awesome! That's a good start. Maybe you're thinking *'yeah right, what a load of crap'*. You can understand why I started with that 'warning' at the beginning right? Your reaction is neither 'good', 'bad', 'right', or 'wrong'. It's simply an indicator of where you're at on the circle of life. One point on a circle is no 'better' or 'worse' than any other, it just 'IS'.

Even though this might all sound like fluff let's start with the foundational science and physics that will hopefully build a level of belief within you that there is actually something to this. So much so, that it might inspire you to take some sort of action. Whatever that may be. Building a level belief in a self-transformation technique like the one I'm going to share with you is probably the most powerful thing you can do to create change, success and fulfilment in your life. Beliefs are an EXTREMELY powerful human phenomena. Henry Ford said

'Whether you believe you can or you can't, either way you're right'.

The power of belief is linked to the VERY well documented 'Placebo Effect' in that if you BELIEVE a pill will do X for the body, in 1/3 of cases X will occur in the body even though the pill was nothing but a sugar pill. Just think about how many wars past and present have been fought simply because of a difference in beliefs.

But why are they so important? Why am I going to point to science to help raise your level of belief? Well, because it's linked to a very powerful question that I'd like you think about for just a moment, and that question is:

'Are your beliefs shaped by your experience, or do you experience what you believe?'

Just take a moment to consider that.

Perhaps you think it's a bit of both and you're probably right. It's kind of like a loop where one effects the other isn't it? Kind of like the connection between thoughts and feelings where if you shift one thing, the other will follow. But you see the fact is that you have more control over what you chose to believe than the experience you are having in any moment. If you change your belief, you can change your experience. Maybe that's why they are such powerful things that we continue to fight over. Your conscious and unconscious belief structure will determine what you perceive, notice and hence, experience. It's like that phenomenon where you suddenly notice all the red cars on the road as soon as you buy a red car. This is also the reason why two people can recall two TOTALLY different experiences from the same event they both attended. Why? Because they have different beliefs which influence what and how they perceive the same external stimuli.

So why the science to explain this inner practice? Because it is the best and most fundamental tool we have for justifying most of our collective beliefs about ourselves and the world around us. As a society we believe things to be true about 'the world out there', because the scientific method tells us it is so.

Ok, so having said that let's start from a place as foundational as possible.

At the basis of everything is energy. This is pretty undisputable. We know that absolutely everything, when you break it down to its smallest essence, is just energy. Now if you look at the scientific definition of 'energy', as it applies to physics, interestingly enough it's actually impossible to observe energy directly. All we can observe is the EFFECT of one system on another. So in a way, you could say that 'energy' is simply the 'communication' part between two systems or things. So more practically speaking you could say that the energy we use to power our planet, be it electricity, nuclear power, the fuel for our machinery etc, is created by combining certain chemicals which create a chemical reaction and then we attempt to control the resulting EFFECT. This effect is often an explosion which produces a chain reaction often resulting in some sort of propulsion. This is exactly how anything that uses any type of oil-based fuel works be it your car or a rocket to the moon. Combining highly explosive material with some sort of spark produces an explosion that pushes a piston that turns a cog which typically powers a wheel etc.

In relation to the human body, in one way, it's not so different. We do in fact have an electrical system in the body that produces a firing of neural activity that our nervous system manages. Have you ever had an 'electric shock' when touching your car door or rubbing your feet on the carpet? This would be IMPOSSIBLE if we did not have some sort of energy surging through our body. We are in fact emitters and receivers of energy in the form of frequency vibrations. Have you ever walked into a room or met a person and experienced a distinct 'vibe' that made your hair stand on end? Well, there have been many experiments that have discovered that we have two main organs that have this inherent ability to emit and receive electro-magnetic energy, frequencies or vibrations and they are the heart and the brain.

The Chinese have known about the energy of the body for thousands of years and have integrated this knowledge into healing and health. Traditional Chinese Medicine (TCM) calls the energy, or 'life force' of the body 'Chi' and by stimulating the flow of Chi, it facilitates the body's natural ability to heal itself. This energy is a very real thing that can easily be observed by scientific devices. This is basically the science behind many healing modalities such as Acupuncture, Acupressure Massage, Reflexology, Chiropractic Medicine and Kinesiology.

Why is this stuff about energy important?

Because if it really is 'all there is' and if it is the building blocks of reality as we know it, then it makes total sense to have an understanding of what it is and how it behaves. Once we know this, we can use this knowledge CONSCIOULSY in a practical way rather than unconsciously like most people do.

Running side by side this theme of energy is the idea of the unconscious mind. It's SO important to get a better understanding of what the unconscious mind is, its role in our lives and how to work with it. Why is it so important? Well, the famous Psychologist Carl Jung had this to say about the unconscious mind:

'Until you make the unconscious conscious it will continue to run your life and you will call it fate'

Hm . . . powerful stuff I think. More about the conscious and unconscious mind shortly.

In high school we all learned two simple laws about energy that still apply today and they are: *'for every action there is an equal and opposite reaction'* and then there's The Law of The Conservation of Energy which states: *'Energy can be neither created or destroyed just transformed from one form to another'*. As I said, some of this may seem a little 'off track', but stay with me here because it will all come together and make logical sense in the end.

As for the first law, it relates to what I mentioned earlier about energy. If for every action there is an equal and opposite reaction, then that means that whatever is happening 'over here' in one system, is going to have some sort of effect on whatever is happening 'over there' in another system. Having said that lets now bring in another characteristic about the dynamics of energy. It can only ever go in one of two directions, it can either expand or contract but it cannot do both at the same time. Another way of saying this is that energy (or systems) can only ever be repelled from one another or attracted to one another depending on the energy dynamics that's happening between them.

Hm . . . ok. For some you wheels may already be turning here. Every heard of 'The Law of Attraction'? Or seen the movie or read the book 'The Secret'? There was a lot of information left out of the book and movie which explains why so many people who followed the instructions were left scratching their heads asking themselves 'where's my stuff?' They did however mention one thing about this law that is actually scientifically true. And that is 'like energy attracts like energy'. In other words, to attract what you want to experience in your life, you have to create a resonance with that energy within YOURSELF FIRST and by doing this you will emit an 'attracting force', vibration or frequency that connects to the energy/frequency/vibration of what you want and by doing this it will start to draw in the synchronistic situations, circumstances, events and people, that will allow that energy to manifest into your physical experience. This is just ONE aspect of the The Law of Attraction, which can also be defined as 'what you put out is what you get back'. But don't be fooled by the speakers and authors who are making squillions teaching this stuff because even though it may be a simple law of the universe, that doesn't mean it's easy to implement in our daily lives. Why? Because there are a multitude of other factors involved in using the Law of Attraction effectively such as the power of aligned action, your beliefs, perceptions, the unconscious mind etc. All of which are topics beyond the scope of this chapter.

Ok, so as far as explaining the process of this inner practice is concerned, trust me we are getting there but let's just check in and summarise what we have discussed so far.

Everything is energy.

Energy is simply a type of communication between 'stuff' (or systems).

All the energy that exists always has existed and always will and can only be transformed from one form to another.

Energy can only ever go in one of two directions. It's either expanding (or radiating) or contracting.

What happens 'here' has an effect on what happens 'there'.

The human body, particularly through the heart and brain, is an emitter and receiver of electro-magnetic bio-energy frequency vibrations (three words that are basically describing the same thing).

I hope this is all making some sort of sense.

It's beyond the scope of this chapter to share the examples of the scientific experiments that have been done to verify all of the above aspects of energy, but they are most definitely out there. However, having said that and keeping in mind what we have mentioned so far about energy in the context of the inner practice I'm going to teach you, let's consider this extremely relevant quote from Albert Einstein:

'Everything is energy and that's all there is to it. Match the frequency of the reality you want
and you cannot help but get that reality. It can be no other way.
This is not philosophy. This is physics'.

Hm . . perhaps more wheels are turning for you at this point? But now let's consider this idea of 'frequency' and 'vibration'. It seems to be an important element here.

But what does it really mean? WHY is it important?

It's important because all energy, everything from the subatomic world to the cosmological world is moving, or vibrating, at a particular frequency for its form to change from something that our 5 senses CANNOT detect, to something that our 5 senses CAN detect. We all know that each one of our senses are limited to the energy frequency they can actually detect. Did you know that we are only able to see and hear less than 1% of the light and sound spectrum? We know that there are certain sounds, tastes, smells etc that our ears, tongue and nose simply cannot detect. Why is this? This is simply because our senses are designed to capture certain energetic frequency vibrations which our sensory apparatus then translates into electrical impulses which are then interpreted by our brains as a smell, a sound or an image etc. If the frequency is beyond what our senses can detect then we simply have no experience of that image, smell, sound, etc. To go one step further, in a way, you could say that we are NOT experiencing 'the world out there' as it actually IS, we are simply experiencing a MINISCULE representation of a constantly moving FIELD OF ENERGY that is being translated into an electrical phenomenon within our brain and THAT is in fact what we are experiencing.

So what does this all mean?

Well it means that if everything in the universe is moving at different speeds, then to experience or 'detect' a phenomena, it needs to be moving within a particular frequency range. Otherwise to us and our senses it will seem like it doesn't exist. A simple example to explain this idea more practically is the idea of a spinning ceiling fan. When it's turning slowly (or it's energetic 'FREQUENCY' is low) you can clearly see each blade. But as it speeds up (or raises its frequency) the blades seem to become less and less visible to us. If they were to spin even faster, to our eyes it would appear that the blades disappear. However, if you now introduce the idea of resonance, there is a way that you could see the blades appear without having to reduce the speed of the fan. If you spun your head around fast enough in the same direction of the fan, you would soon start to see the blades again wouldn't you? What have you done? Apart from giving yourself a massive head spin, you've created a RESONANCE between your eyes and the fan. To relate this back to energy, it's no different with regards to a TV or a Radio. You know that you can only watch one channel or station at a time depending on what resonant frequency your device is tuned into. The more resonance between the emitting and receiving devices, the clearer your reception.

So how does all this information about energy relate to the inner practice I'm about to share?

Well let's investigate whether there is any scientific basis (or even evidence) to support the idea about how we could connect with and manifest success and fulfilment in our lives (whatever that may mean for you). Even though I touched on this earlier it deserves another mention here and now. Let's start by asking ourselves; 'what is it that I REALLY want?' If you look at the things you say you want most you'll realise that it is NOT the thing you want, but the FEELING you THINK that thing will give you. Isn't that right? Think about it. No matter what you say you want in life, you only want it because you believe that if you had that you will feel better. So you could say, that what you're really wanting is an emotion. What is an emotion? The name kind of gives it away, E-MOTION. It's the physical experience of Energy in Motion. Or said another way, it's the experience of the movement of energy within your body.

So let me map out this idea a little further with some simple logic. Energy is the basis of the entire physical (material) and non-physical (spiritual) world. Everything everywhere is energy and like energy attracts like energy. All the energy that ever is, was and shall be already exists here and now. EVERYTHING is made of energy. So therefore everything in the universe must be connected to each other. I'm sure you've heard this concept before, perhaps in more spiritual circles, this idea that 'we are all connected', 'we're all one'. Even though I deeply believe this, if you cannot show me HOW this is the case, then to me, it's just another dogma or concept.

Now let's take a more scientific approach to this idea of 'oneness' shall we? There is a field of scientific investigation called Unified Field Theory. Why does it have the word 'UNIFIED' in it? Because at present, we have two theories we use to describe the inner and outer world. We use Einstein Field Equations to explain and predict what we see in the outer world. This includes very large things in our universe like stars, planets and galaxies. Then we have a type of physics to explain the very tiny aspects of existence called Quantum Theory. This is the science used to describe our inner world and the world of the very tiny. Now since big stuff is made out of small stuff, you would think that the two of these theories would complement each other, or 'unite' in some way, but they don't. One of the ways we are trying to unify these two seemingly opposed theories of reality is by asking ourselves: 'What is it that TRULY connects all things?'

The answer is SPACE, or to use a more 'scientific' term; 'The Vacuum'.

Space is absolutely EVERYWHERE. It's between stars, planets, galaxies. And believe it or not, everything you see around you, which you think is so 'solid' (including your very own body), on an atomic level is actually 99.99999999% SPACE! To paint a clearer picture for you, the densest material we have on this planet is a diamond. However on a molecular level if you grew one of the atoms to the size of a peach, the next closest atom would be about 200 meters away! Amazing right? If you remember what I was saying earlier about energy and resonance, you'll understand that we only have an experience of the world around us as being so 'solid' because our 'human energy' and the energy of the physical matter around us is resonating within a similar range enabling us to detect it with one of our five senses. When this happens we call it 'real'. However if the energy in that same thing were to shift it's energetic frequency beyond our ability to perceive it, then it seems to disappear to us and all of a sudden it becomes 'unreal'.

So what I'm saying here is that we are comprised of mostly space.

Your next question may be, 'So what? Why is it important to know that I'm made of mostly empty space?'

It's important because of something that science discovered over 100 years ago but swept under the carpet because it was an unexpected discovery, too overwhelming for them to deal with at the time. And that is that 'SPACE' is not empty at all, but INFINETELY DENSE with energy. It might seem like it's 'empty' to our five senses, but it's actually infinitely full of energy which is in such perfect equilibrium that it all cancels itself out and seems like nothing to us. It's almost like a fish swimming in water never realising what the concept of 'water' or 'being wet' actually is.

But do we have any proof that the energy density of the vacuum is infinite? Actually we do. All we have to do is quote one of the most influential physics text books we have called 'Gravitation'. It was written by some of the most respected physicists who ever lived including Charles Misner, Kip Thorne, and John Wheeler. On page 426 it states:

"...present day quantum field theory _gets rid by a renormalization process_ of an energy density in the vacuum that would formerly be **infinite** if not removed by this renormalization."

You see 'renormalisation' is what physicists do to equation outcomes that end in infinities. Since they try to avoid using infinities in equations, they basically make the number 'more manageable' and turn it into a finite number so it becomes easier to use in their equations.

Ok, now we're getting somewhere. So if Space is infinitely FULL of energy and we are made up of 99.9999999% space which is everywhere in the universe, then perhaps we have the capacity to communicate with the entire universe. How do we do this? By doing EXACTLY what every ancient master has told us to do: by going within ourselves and connecting with the space within us, specifically our heart space, that is literally and energetically connected to everything in the universe.

Perhaps you can now see the deeper distinction and between a simple meditation to de-stress and relax and the inner practice I'm about to share with you.

Perhaps Jesus wasn't speaking metaphorically when he said 'the kingdom of heaven is within'.

So to bring it back to our topic a little, this practice is simply a process of connecting with the energy of the emotions within yourself and creating a resonate field with that reality so you can draw it into your life and experience it. If that's so, the next logical question is: 'How do you create a resonant field?'

There are 3 powerful ways to create a resonant field with whatever emotion, feeling or 'thing' you're wanting to attract into your life:

1) Set an intention just before you do the following inner practice.

2) Create the emotions within yourself as if you already HAVE that desired reality.

3) Use your unconscious mind and Alpha brain wave state.

So let's take a closer look at each one of these elements in more detail.

1) The Power of Intent. This might sound like a simple thing, but it's SO important. Why? Because energy, which has been explained above, RESPONDS to intent. How do we know this? We know this through many different experiments, the most compelling coming from the work of Dr Masaro Emoto who has analysed the effects of exposing water to different intentions. He did this by putting water in containers with different words written on them. These words included: 'LOVE', 'GRATITUDE', 'THANK YOU', positive words as well as negative words such as 'I HATE YOU', 'I WILL KILL YOU'. 'YOU'RE AN IDIOT'. He not only exposed the jars to labels but even to other stimulus such as different types of music such as classical and heavy metal music.

To investigate the effects Dr Emoto analysed the frozen water crystals before and after exposure. What he found was amazing. When exposed to anything positive such as words, music or even to the attention of meditating monks the water crystals were beautifully formed and looked just like the little snow flake cut outs you see in shop window displays at Christmas. However when the water was exposed to negative stimulus, words or music, the crystals were more deformed and ugly looking.

We have known for a long time that water is an amazing conductor of energy, especially electricity and from the results of these experiments it's not hard to see why. And when you consider that the human body is approximately 75% water, it really gets you thinking right?

2) Create the emotions within you 'AS IF' you already have the outcome. From what has already been discussed about energy, it should seem pretty obvious why this is such an important step. If like energy attracts like energy, then it makes sense that when you are doing the following practice, you want to create the emotion and energy as if you already have that thing or feeling in your life FIRST. Doing this is like fishing for what you want in the universal sea of infinite possibilities. If you want to catch a particular fish you need to bait your hook with the right food to attract that fish. This is exactly the same thing. There is no way you can attract that shiny new car into your life if you continually bait your hook (and your thinking) with 'I don't have enough money', even if that might actually be true in your reality at this temporary moment.

3) Using your unconscious mind. This is basically a process of leading yourself into the Alpha state of the brain. This is the state that I lead my clients into when conducting hypnotherapy. Self-hypnosis is not a difficult thing to do but unless you've been coached by a therapist or done some researched on how to do it, I would recommend that you simply do this inner practice during the two times of the day when you are ALREADY in an alpha brain wave state naturally. This is first thing in the morning and last thing at night, that moment when you're half-awake half asleep. This is the perfect time to visualise EXACTLY what you want, feel EXACTLY what you want to feel and hear EXACTLY what you want to hear. This is the time to make the EXPERIENCE of what you want as real as possible.

Now here is the golden nugget, the difference that makes the difference, the element that makes this entire process even more powerful. After relaxing your body and mind, just before you start to visualise everything you want to attract and create in your life imagine taking a journey into your heart. Actually picture yourself being right in there. From there, imagine shrinking in size to the size of the cells. Imagine seeing billions of cells everywhere. Then imagine going smaller and smaller in resolution past the DNA structure and opening up into the world of the atoms. Imagine seeing billions of these. Then zoom down even further until you are face to face with the subatomic world within your heart. From here emerse yourself into the massive amount SPACE that is within you. This is the place where you are literally connected to all the energy of the universe. THIS is the place to now start your visualisations and what you wish to attract, create and experience by connecting with the pictures, images, sounds, smells and emotions that you WANT. Once complete, simply zoom back up the way you came and then open your eyes. Congratulations, you've just communicated with the infinite universe.

And that's it folks. That's the formula right there for your inner practice. Sounds simple right? That's because it is. The key is to practice it daily for at least 21.
Now you might be asking; 'So what then?' Well, the answer is simple. You just have to 'let go' of the expectation of HOW you THINK the good feelings you want should come to you and just let universal forces do the rest.

But at the same time, keep an eye out for the little signs and synchronicities in your day that will present themselves as opportunities to guide you to the right place at the right time.

Getting anything you want in your life takes action, a rather huge piece of the puzzle that the movie 'The Secret' left out, however action that is in energetic alignment (following your excitement) is 100 times more powerful than action taken out of fear or lack. It's this kind of action that will allow you to synchronistically rendezvous with people, situations and circumstances at the right time and place.

And when this happens you will start to really know yourself as the creator of your reality. I couldn't think of any better way to build extraordinary levels of self-confidence as well as TRUE, deep and powerful fulfilment and success!

Nick Terrone
www.quitwithnick.com.au
Twitter: @quitwithnick
Facebook: www.facebook.com/quitwithnick

Want to eliminate stress, anxiety, a smoking or food addiction for yourself, your employees or your clients?

Want to inject more heart and confidence into your life, your business and the world but don't know how?

Whether speaking to an audience of hundreds or working one-on-one, Nick helps create transformational change by co-creatively exploring the structures that maintain the most fundamental thing that determines your life experience: YOUR PERCEPTIONS!

Nick teaches the art and science of DEEEEEEEP behavioural change as well as practical techniques to dissolve fear, doubt and resistance. This allows you to experience more of who you REALLY are and what you REALLY want with more easy and flow. The secret, Nick says, is helping clients connect with The Heart (Emotions), The Mind (Conscious & Subconscious) and The Unified Field (everything else).

Nick can help you dissolve the subconscious programming that is keeping you 'stuck' in your limiting beliefs and behaviors while helping you create new and superior ones. This helps you do what you need to do when you need to do it with ease, grace and flow.

Lasting change can only occur when you know how to leverage the 96-98% of your mind (the subconcious) which is TRULY responsible for who we are, what we do and our automatic behaviours.

Nick is an internationally published writer and speaker with a keen focus on the Heart-Mind connection and how it relates to confident self empowerment.

His gift is the ability to explain concepts of self and reality in a fun, light-hearted, easy-to-understand way while at the same time trying to keep alive his dream of becoming a stand up comedian.

Contact Nick today at: info@quitwithnick.com.au, or on (Twitter) @quitwithnick (Facebook) facebook.com/quitwithnick, to find out how easy it can be to become a more confident and empowered YOU. (Skype Sessions Available)

Follow your passion! Ok, but is that realistic and what is it anyway?

Anyone who has ever spent some time exploring the self-development or success literature will have undoubtedly come across advice that fits within the following phrases. Follow your bliss, follow your passion, follow your dreams or some variation on this theme. Therefore we couldn't compile a volume on being successful without including a section on exactly this topic.

As you read the popularised literature around following your passions you will see that these broad statements are often a lead in to stories. These stories are ones that suggest if you do follow your passion then success is guaranteed. Indeed they will often suggest that pursuing this route will make your life and work feel effortless.

But doesn't that feel rather simplistic? Is it really that easy? What about all the challenges in life? I can't just afford to abandon what I am doing and follow some dream. I've got a mortgage, a family to support etc. Besides that I can't work out how to make a living out of my passion for jigsaw puzzles! In my role as a coach I have heard all of these things said.

Then of course there are those who will offer advice that is the total opposite of following your passion. A quick web search will find the folks who claim to be practical and realistic. Doing such a search will expose you to many "experts" saying that "follow your passion" is the worst advice you can give someone. Here the stories mentioned above are likely to be described as distorted or at the very best rare examples. I would argue that this response is also in its self rather simplistic.

So what's the reality? In this short chapter I will put to you that you can indeed follow your passion and at the same time be realistic with your expectations. I am going to have my cake and eat it. I will argue that both sides of the above debate are right. I will show you that the answer is not to find and follow this mysteriously lost passion but to create one using your internal GPS. I will also suggest to you that true success is not the accumulation of wealth or material goods but living a fulfilled, purposeful life, in harmony with your values.

Let's jump straight in to the journey!

How do you know what a passion looks like?

The intention here is not to provide a text book definition of passion. If that is what you are looking for then a few minutes on the internet should get you there. Just in case some of you are about to do just that. Check out the work of Robert Vallerand. He is recognised as the leading authority in the world on this concept of passion.

Back to our journey together. I intend to describe how our real lives are impacted by passion, about how passion can be both good and bad for you. My aim is that you can recognise the feeling of being passionate rather than being able to quote the technically correct definition.

People who have a passion in life feel energised. They wake up excited by the day ahead and can't wait to get going. They aren't struggling to feel motivated the passion provides the drive. To identify a passion therefore you need to ask yourself does it give me energy? Whatever it is, it shouldn't feel like hard work.

But before we go any further it is important to recognise that you need balance. If what you call your passion becomes all consuming then it can easily fall in to the territory of an obsession. Obsessions take over everything and ultimately lead to you feeling drained of energy rather than restored. So the first question is does it give me energy and your second question should be is this creating harmony in my life or is it taking over my life. If life feels balanced it's a passion, if it feels all consuming it is an obsession.

Robert Vallerand mentioned above describes these as two different types of passion. Obsessive and harmonious passion. But what matters for our discussion is will it make your life a better experience. Harmony will and obsession won't.

Therefore what you are looking for is something that gives you a sense of purpose and meaning but allows you to lead a life full of other things too. When you are there you will know not by the thoughts that go with the experience but by the feeling. It will feel right for you. Remember humans are an emotional animal. We experience our emotions far sooner than we process thoughts. Listen to the feeling!

But at this point some of you will be saying, well that is all very well Alex but I don't have something that I wake up feeling that excited about. This is very common. Most people wake up just intending to get through the day.

But life doesn't have to be like that. Let's look at how you can change that for yourself.

So how then do I begin to find mine?

I want to begin here by being very direct with you. Unless you are extremely lucky there is no lost passion that you are going to uncover. It didn't get stuck behind the sofa cushion or left on a train. Your job now is to create your passion. But in fact that is great news. This is going to make the journey so much more fun and it allows you decide for yourself. Your passion is not given to you by the universe, it is not something you are born with, it is a choice you are making.

What you are passionate about tells me a lot about what is important to you. In essence it tells me what you value. Knowing this is crucial in discovering or creating your own passionate experiences.

On the journey to discovering what you are passionate about, a great starting point is to ask yourself what really matters to you. Another way of describing this is to say what are your values. Values are sometimes confused with goals but they are in fact a very different beast. If you can achieve it, tick it off and say that's done, it's a goal. Think becoming a millionaire. Values are what sits behind your desire to become a millionaire. They are a little like the horizon, as you move towards them they continue to stretch out in front of you. In this instance the value behind the goal maybe something like, to be a provider for my family, that's a value.

There are some very useful tools that could help you explore your own core values. Martin Seligman and his team at the University of Pennsylvania developed a tool known as Values In Action (VIA). The VIA is a freely available questionnaire that anyone can access online. Completing the VIA helps you identify what is known as your signature strengths. In essence signature strengths are values, they sit at the heart of who you are as a person. I would strongly recommend the VIA as a starting point. It is a multiple choice questionnaire and very easy to complete. The five signature strengths are identified and provided to you upon completion of the tool and the research tells us that if your life is aligned with these signature strengths you are going to feel fulfilled.

Realise2 is another online resource developed by Alex Linley's team at the Centre for Applied Positive Psychology in England. Realise2 is a more comprehensive process and as such is not free. For a small cost it provides you with a rounded picture of your major strengths, ones you are using well and those that you could explore more fully. Realise2 also helps you identify areas in life where you have learnt to do something well but it doesn't in fact bring you energy. Finally Realise2 also points out areas where you are not strong at all, weaknesses. Unlike the VIA, Realise2 offers you some practical suggestions on what to do with this information.

Not everything necessitates you going online though. When we start to explore what really matter to us as humans the work of Mihaly Csikszentmihalyi helps greatly. He researched and assisted in our understanding of a process he calls Flow. As I describe Flow to you I am confident that you will recognise the experience. Flow is a moment where you are so deeply engaged in what you are doing that it feels like time has stood still. Flow happens when you are concentrating intently on what you are doing. But it is called Flow because this concentration and effort does not feel difficult. You feel as if you are being carried along by the "flow" . By its very nature you only experience Flow when engaging in something that is really important to you.

At this point you have two tasks. The first is to complete either the VIA or Realise2 tools. Having completed this, make a list of either your signature strengths or realised and unrealised strengths, depending upon which tool you used. The second task is to jot down five areas where you experience Flow in your life and combine the two lists.

You should now have a list that comprises of at least ten things. These things that you have compiled will all resonate with the core of who you are. They are your internal GPS pointing you in the direction of fulfilment. But we are not finished yet. I want you to look at that list and choose three that you would most like to experience in your life every day. Crucially I don't want you to think about what do I need to get better at or what am I already good at. What I am looking for is those things that will make you feel that you are engaged in a meaningful life.

Write down the three things, we are going to come back to them.

Is this it?

As you begin to discover your passion you may find it is not this great mission in life. It may not necessarily be to save the planet or to be a guiding light for humanity. In fact it is quite likely to be much more down to earth. Your passion may be connected to knitting or running a comic book store and that's ok. At present there are roughly seven billion people on earth. Your personal passion doesn't have to look like anyone else's.

It is very important to accept your passion for what it is and not to try and change to fit what you think others would feel is right.

What if it changes?

What you are passionate about is very likely to evolve and change as you move forward in life. Life has a habit of throwing us curve balls. Just as we head off in one direction something happens that we aren't expecting. So this makes it very important to recognise that we are not locking ourselves in to any particular pathway. We are trying to establish the broad direction we are heading in but not the exact detail of every step. Think about where you are now in your life compared to ten years ago. Are the things that deeply matter to you the same. Some will be, others may have changed in priority and new things will have been introduced to your life. Looking forward ten years you are likely to be able to say the same.
So let your passion grow and evolve as you do.

So now what do I do?

Ok you have got your short list of the three things that carry the most significance for you. We are going to use this information to ask what do I want more of in my life.
The science of understanding goal mechanisms for humans is very well developed. It tells us that achieving goals often leads to a paradoxical effect. People often feel deflated as they think is that it. On the other hand the science does tell us that wellbeing can be found in goal striving. Having something that I am working towards that really matters to me, increases my overall sense of wellbeing. So our passion is not a target we aim to achieve. It's something we are always striving towards.
One of the biggest mistakes people make when they decided to become more connected to what they are passionate about is as follows. They wait for the perfect moment. We all know it is never going to come. There will always be something else competing for our attention.
People also believe they need to wait until they can achieve something grand like start a business based upon this passion or write a book about it. You need to jump straight in to action. Do something, anything that will move you towards having more of this in your life.

Your new task is to spend five minutes each evening, look at your list and reflect upon the next day. I want you to ask yourself how can I more of each of these three in my life tomorrow and what am I going to do to make that happen.

Now this is where the real effort comes in to play. I am not saying that you should look at this list, visualise it and miraculously it will be provided for you. You need to take action every day to bring about more experiences of the three things. The actions don't need to be huge but I suggest that you take one small action related to each thing every day for a year. That's one thousand and ninety five steps towards what really matters to you.

Remember our two questions from earlier. As you commit to action you also need to ask yourself does this give me energy or put another way am I excited to do this. Also does this action maintain balance in my life?

What does success look like?

Sometimes we can lose perspective of what we mean by success. We look at people who have acquired vast sums of money and possessions and think if only I could have that. But that is only one very limited definition of success.

There is now an overwhelming body of evidence from the likes of the field of Positive Psychology that true contentment in life is not connected to material wealth. But you don't really have to go to the research papers to see this. We have all heard of tales of very rich and usually famous people who are very unhappy with their lives. Conversely we hear of those who possess little in terms of material goods but are absolutely at peace with life. Increasingly we are beginning to understand that true success is more closely associated with living in alignment with our core values.

Here I go back to my opening comments about having my cake and eating it. If you define success by traditional, Western, measures of wealth then following your passion may indeed not be the best advice. There is no guarantee that it will bring you a private island or a fancy car etc. But if your definition of success is leading a life full of purpose and meaning, where you feel deeply connected to your values, then it is absolutely worth following your passion.

Alex Couley

Alex Couley is a Director of the International Centre for Leadership Coaching. He is an international figure in coaching, positive psychology and has a background as a clinician in the mental health field for 35 years. alex.couley@hushmail.com

People power: the key to your success

"You can design and create, and build the most wonderful place in the world. But it takes people to make the dream a reality." – Walt Disney

In terms of entertainment industry figures, few have been more influential than Walt Disney. He drove black and white animation and was pivotal in its transformation from a novelty to a highly influential genre. There aren't many in this world who wouldn't recognise the global icons that are the likes of Mickey Mouse, Minnie Mouse and Donald Duck to name only a few.

To many, Walt Disney is the epitome of success.

And there's that word – *success.* Trying to define it is complex to say the least as this one simple word tends to take on a different meaning to everyone. Not to mention, a person's definition of success is a living thing: it changes over time.

Right now, you can probably reel off a number of people who you consider to be successful... the late Nelson Mandela and Steve Jobs, Richard Branson ... the list is endless.

Today more so than ever, success is an important part of our lives. We study it, we're fascinated by it and most of us, actively chase it. Our desire to be successful is evident in almost every action we take, particularly when it comes to business.

At HelpMeChoose.com.au, an online comparison service, we're very aware that it's our team and their loyalty to our vision that makes things happen. If you embark on your business journey void of this knowledge, you'll come to learn it soon enough.

Together, successful organisations and people create the world that they want to succeed in. Before you do anything in business, in order to work towards a united vision with your employees, you need to create the world in which you and your employees can succeed in.

Here at Help Me Choose, defining who we were and how we go about business early-on was integral to our success in the longer-term. Forget about fancy logos and pretty colours: we're not about gimmicky marketing campaigns. We very deliberately chose to focus on who we are and what we believe in. It's what drives everything that every single employee here does. It's not 'a company vision', it's *our vision* and our employees are proud of it.

Speaking of brand, there's a reason 'brand' is so widely discussed – your business' brand needs to be clearly articulated and lived by. It acts as the vehicle for transforming your company into what it's destined to become and pits your business in a unique position within your relevant marketplace.

Aside from Walt Disney's endless list of credentials, there's another reason we opted to use Disney as an example. Our vision was built after seeking inspiration from Disney Institute's renowned service philosophy.

In fact, it's rare that a day passes by when our General Manager Julie Ryburn doesn't make a reference to Disney and what she's learnt from the leadership course she attended at Disney Institute. "Disney tends to think about things differently to others – paying attention to the finer details is really honed in when attending their leadership course," she said.

So, what are the key areas that you need to focus on when creating a successful business? We've documented our experiences here, focusing on the areas that we believe to be the most critical.

Find your business' key point of difference

One of the keys to being successful in any business is being different for the right reasons. Find your point of difference, believe in it and infuse it into everything you and your staff do on a daily basis.

Help Me Choose prides itself on being different from our competitors – not for the sake of it, but because at the end of the day, it's about what matters most to our customers and going about business in the right way. "We put our customers first," says Sales and Operations Manager – Health Kieran Perkins.

Live and breathe your company's vision

Understanding what you do and why will ultimately make or break your business. This may sound like an overstatement but there are thousands of businesses out there trying to be something different to everyone instead of focusing on what makes them tick. You need a solid vision that may change and evolve over time but has a strong set of values at its heart. As soon as you've nailed it, document it and never waver from it.

Every member of our team at Help Me Choose, is aware that we're here to inform Australians about their options in terms of health insurance, life insurance, energy and home loans. Most importantly, our purpose is to do so by focusing on what's right for the customer and what really matters to them – and doing so helps us to play a part in improving people's standard of living. Regardless of what the product or service you're trying to sell is, it's the human element of what you're doing that will really appeal and speak to both your staff and customers.

Once your company's vision is locked in, you need to develop strategies that will ultimately, assess the success of your vision. We do so in two ways:

- By seeking feedback from our customers – we're keen to learn more about people's stories.
- By working to develop our team and evolve our service for the better – it's our people and their loyalty to our vision that ultimately make things happen.

Now that your company vision and measurables are under control, you need to be very clear as to how you're going to achieve whatever end goals have been put in place for your business. Usually, you'll be able to identify key components that will ultimately, lead to your company's success.

Using Help Me Choose as a model, we identified the key components that would make or break our success: our team, our values, our customer service and being different for all the right reasons. Some of these components are interchangeable between businesses and industries (your team/values for example) but once you've identified your key components, document how each will operate both alone and in unison.

Recruit a dream team

We're very transparent in our belief that it's our team who are at the core of our success. As such, we firmly believe that the only way to succeed is by building a team that's suited to your end purpose. If you undertake a quick Google search for 'things to consider when employing staff', you'll see that this is a topic that's not short of attention. And for good reason too: finding the right staff for your business isn't easy but it is vital to long-term success.

If you're a start-up company, you may be able to operate for a short while without staff. That said, there will come a point when you need to consider taking on employees – this is both an exciting and crucial time for your business. Chances are, in most circumstances, you'll know within a fairly short period of time whether you've employed the right person for the relevant job role.

Before you can go about looking for the right people, you need to fully understand what you have to offer as an employer: does the role have room for growth? Are you willing to put in place a range of appealing incentives? Additionally, you need to have a good grasp of what you're looking for in terms of both personality and skill-set. You'll often hear employers saying that personality is equally as important as ability and it certainly can be the case: as they say, you should never try to make a triangle fit into a square hole.

You need people who will contribute positively to your business – take Charvele Williams, one of our Health Insurance Agents for example – when asked why she enjoys coming to work each day, she replied: "I enjoy knowing that I'm here for a purpose that I believe in. I'm thankful that I genuinely get to help people with what is a very important and imperative part of their life."

And Charvele's not alone, when asked the same exact question, Mark Abrahams, another one of our Health Insurance Agents said: "I enjoy coming to work every day – I know I'm good at what I do and that I'm making a difference by helping people to understand and choose the correct health insurance policy for them. And as a bonus, I get to see my friends too!"

Of course, creating the environment in which your staff can really step into their own is paramount. "We've created a work hard, play hard environment," says Sales and Operations Manager – Health Kieran Perkins. "We have a lot of fun but we get a lot of work done at the same time. It's a vibrant workplace and we have lots of people from different backgrounds."

You'd be surprised at how influential mentors can be in terms of meeting your company's goals. At Help Me Choose, we've appointed a number of Team Leaders who are charged with motivating staff and driving them to succeed. "One of the keys to keeping staff motivated is the sense of really caring about them as individuals," says Team Leader Chris McEvoy. McEvoy goes onto explain that this includes, without being limited to, personal coaching sessions, highlighting successes, being flexible when required and addressing any key concerns.

Additionally, McEvoy says that clearly defining goals for staff and how each of his team members is integral to achieving them, is important. "It creates a unified team", he said. McEvoy encourages his team to contribute new ideas and is willing to implement changes when deemed appropriate. "I always say to my team, your success is a measure of my success as a leader."

And McEvoy's stance is only reiterated by fellow Team Leader Alastair Cameron who said: "Make your team your priority, because we need them more than they need us."

As you've probably gathered by now, we've been very careful in building Help Me Choose based on a certain kind of employee. In terms of incentives, implementing personal incentives will really drive your staff to get more out of every minute, of every day. No doubt you've heard about some of the best companies to work for and the incentives offered to staff. Google, Facebook and Microsoft consistently make headlines thanks to daily incentives such as offering their employees free food, having on-site gyms and doctors and providing free transport for local employees.

For most businesses, while they may like to put in place daily incentives, doing so just isn't realistic budget-wise. That said, small businesses can still offer their employees rewarding incentives that are both beneficial to the recipient and the company. At Help Me Choose, we send one employee each year to Disney Institute – while key performance indicators are considered, the employee is actually nominated by their peers.

This year, Simone Dellora, one of our key Office Administrators visited Disney Institute to complete their renowned Customer Service Course and upon her return, noted that it was very worthwhile to experience an organisation that ran so seamlessly. "Visiting Disney will really help me in terms of implementing easier, step-by-step processes for my team. I learnt a lot   it was such a great, eye-opening experience." We're great believers in the course with our General Manager Julie Ryburn and Sales and Operations Manager – Health Kieran Perkins also having completed the course in the past.

If you're not in the position to fund an overseas trip, think about offering a weekend away within your state or even interstate depending on your location. Perhaps even gift cards could be of benefit: we do also use these at Help Me Choose as smaller incentives to recognise people who achieve on a monthly basis. In a nutshell, your reward system doesn't have to be epic, it's there as a way of telling your employees that you value them. As they say, it's the small things that really count in life.

Now, let's discuss an 'f-word' that really needs to exist in today's business world: flexibility. Numerous reports are emerging that prove that finding a way to offer your staff greater flexibility (within reason of course) is a great way to keep and retain the best of the best people. Equally as important is trust. It can be a big-thing for control freak bosses to accept but you need to have faith in your team, particularly if a portion of their job role sees them off-site quite often and interacting within their local community in a hands-on sense.

At Help Me Choose, we have numerous mortgage brokers who need to dedicate a number of hours to visiting clients and engaging with people in order to attract new business. In fact, getting out and meeting people has elevated our brokers' job satisfaction to new levels. When asked about one of her career highlights, mortgage broker Natalie Savic quotes being given the unique chance to host a group information session for a number of female chiropractors looking for financial guidance as well as her monthly work with The Heart Link Network. "This kind of work is incredibly rewarding and at the end of the day, it makes me feel successful and confident in what I'm doing: it's why I get up each morning and do what I do," Savic said.

Know your values and customer service expectations inside-out

Dedicating sufficient time and care when defining your company's values will serve you well in the longer-term. After all, these are the factors that will contribute to your employees' happiness. Remember, your team is the 'face' of both your business and brand. If they're happy and have faith in your values, they're more likely to deliver consistently in terms of making your customers' experiences amazing on a daily basis. Be sure that your values are a reflection of you and your business, not based upon what you've heard and read are strong corporate values.

Make no mistake, defining your company's values is a very hard thing to do. You'll also find that a number of your key components may overlap. Here at Help Me Choose, our values feed directly into how we approach customer service and this approach doesn't apply only to consumers, but is at play within the office as well. At the end of the day, we were very careful in defining customer service expectations that our staff members could also relate to. When we eventually unveiled these customer service expectations, we found that our staff took to them straight away.

Basically, everything outlined works alongside simple notions that the majority of us would've had instilled in us since we were children. And most importantly, each allow us to deliver amazing customer service and at the end of the day, we firmly believe that it's one of the essential elements to our success. That's also why we're proud participants in the annual global initiative that is Customer Service Week hosted by the Customer Service Group.

As we said earlier, we sought inspiration from Disney Institute when developing the model that we believed would govern our business. Any worthy business model won't develop overnight: ours took quite a long time to develop and tweak to a stage where we were ready to roll it out to our staff on a widespread scale.

At the heart of any good business model are values or attitudes that you and your staff are going to live by. One of our key philosophies is treating every person like a Very Individual Person (V.I.P) –
one of the greatest gifts anyone can have is the ability to make others feel important. You'd be surprised at how this leads to great results in most cases.

A good business model will also arm your staff with clear objectives – "I like having clear objectives and being supported by all levels of staff," Rebecca Gray from our QA & Training Health team says. "Support comes via our leadership team – everyone is required to make an effort and at the end of the day, we're all on the same path to success," she added.

As you can see here, we're all about customer service. Regardless of whether your business is service or product-driven, providing people with a level of service that exceeds their expectations, is essential to your success. Think about the most recognised brands around the world: you'll find that it's the word of mouth attention driven by their customers that takes their business to the next level.

Experiment, experiment, experiment!

"Do not be embarrassed by your failures, learn from them and start again."
– Sir Richard Branson

We're living in a dynamic age where things are changing at a rapid pace and on a consistent basis. You need to be able to adapt to whatever is thrown your way and if you do find that something doesn't work, as Sir Richard Branson says: learn from failing and start again. In a nutshell, this is the real key to success.

By understanding what you're trying to achieve in business, by having clarity on what your point of difference is, by implementing standards and values that your brand can live and breathe by and by surrounding yourself with the right team, your business and team really can go places.

Arm your team with everything they need to tap into the potential that every one of us possesses. Help them to grow and improve their confidence and relationships with others so that they benefit from a career that they truly enjoy. In turn, they'll reward you with better results for having belief in them.

And finally and most importantly, never underestimate the value of a good leader – respect is not earned by titles and comes back to a leader knowing what their position within the company is. As Julie Ryburn, our General Manager says: "ultimately, people are here to work but it's my job to create the environment that enables them to succeed."

Sarah Cannata

Sarah Cannata is the Communications Manager at HelpMeChoose.com.au, one of Australia's leading online comparison services.

As Communications Manager, Sarah plays an integral role in making people aware of the many options available to them when it comes to health insurance, energy, life insurance and home loans. One of Sarah's key aims is to make people aware that Help Me Choose focuses primarily on what's right for the customer and what really matters to them.

Prior to her role as Communications Manager for HelpMeChoose.com.au, Sarah obtained a Bachelor of Journalism at La Trobe University in Melbourne, Australia. Since graduating, Sarah has held a variety of communications roles and has written as a freelance writer for Australia's Leading 'Sell Your Own Home' website, *Leader* Community

Newspapers, *The Age* and *The Big Issue*. She hopes to continue building on her freelance writing career in the future.

In her spare time, Sarah enjoys travelling and has spent time exploring the United States and Europe with her favourite places to date being Malta and New Orleans. She also loves listening to music (especially when embarking on long walks) and enjoys a range of genres and artists.

Your Psychology Becomes your Biology

"Your psychology becomes your biology"
Today I work in my new career, being of service to others. This includes my volunteer position as an Ambassador for MS Australia.

I am a MS Coach, Sports Kinesiologist and Motivational Speaker.
I love my life; I truly feel that every day I get to 'walk my talk'. I am more fulfilled than I have ever been.
I feel like I am attracting my desires in life, finally. True love, career, health, abundance and I believe that I have discovered the recipe for manifesting this into reality.
Looking back, I realise I really did spend most of my teens and 20's 'asleep'.

Life sprung a massive lesson on me that was not only going to turn my life upside down, but also it was going to be the best thing that ever happened to me. Why? Because it woke me up.
In 2004 I was 24 years old. I was enjoying life in every way possible, working in the Fashion Industry a career that I loved.
This was the year I was diagnosed with Multiple Sclerosis (MS).
I was a determined, career driven young woman, so understandably I was shocked and devastated.
I had a few minor symptoms over the next few years including numbness, balance issues, and weakness on the left hand side of my body. But they were often years apart, so this allowed me to live in denial of my diagnosis.
In 2009 I lost my ability to walk following a big MS attack that paralysed the entire left hand side of my body. I lost my career and the use of my body.

Simple little things like the ability to wash and feed myself became the most difficult tasks of the day. I lost my big fashion career and life, as I knew it.
I went from running around, enjoying my life, to standing still and paralysed. I was living life to its fullest, and suddenly found myself in turmoil and darkness.
I went from feeling in complete control of my future, to feeling totally helpless.
In less than ten days my whole world had crumbled, as my body slowly, day by day, became paralysed.

I could not feel or move the left hand side of my body.
It became dead and heavy. My sister literally had to drag me, on her back,
up and down stairs along the carpet, to see my doctor.

They checked me into hospital at the beginning of January 2009, and I
knew going in, that I wasn't going to be leaving any time soon.
They started me on the standard MS therapy, a high dose of Steroids for 3
days. I was not responding – so they continued for a total of 5 days. But I
still could not move.
I was transferred into rehabilitation at Epworth Richmond in Melbourne -
and the work began. I stayed for 2 months.

I hit rock bottom; I had to ask myself "Am I ever going to walk again"?
I was stretched to my limits emotionally and physically, beyond normal
comprehension and everything stopped.

One day, I remember sitting in my wheelchair in my rehab session, working
hard, trying to make my fingers open and close, with tears running down
my face, because it was so hard!

In that moment I just decided.
I was either going to give up now. Or I was going to tackle this head on!

So I did what I knew, I worked hard. I was first in at Physiotherapy and the
last to leave. I was a woman on a mission – 3 sessions a day 5 times a week.
I had to learn how to use my hand again. I was taught all over again how to
pick things up. I had to learn how to walk again.
You don't know what you are capable of in times like this.
This is the moment that I awakened.

A switched turned on inside of me, and I transformed my rock bottom
moment into a passionate drive to overcome this battle. I was determined
to leave hospital, not only walking, but also running!
I left there running. It wasn't the most graceful of runs. I won't win medals
for it. It definitely was an awkward looking run. But I did it.
It wasn't just me, far from it. I had an amazing team of people who helped
me. These people made me believe that I could do it. They stood by me
when I couldn't stand and helped me get to where I am today.
I was blessed. I had Physio's, Speech Therapists, Counsellors, Occupational
Therapists, Neurologists, and Kinesiologists, family and friends.

I could not have come through this with the courage and determination that I had, if it had not have been for my loving supportive family friends, in particular my twin sister Nicole.

She was there every day and night. Some nights, even sleeping next to me in my single hospital bed. I cannot begin to explain how much I appreciate her and count my lucky stars for her kindness and unconditional love, through the hardest time of my life.

Week by week I started to get movement back in my toes and fingers, then arm and leg and my face. I started to walk with a foot brace. Then I progressed to walking with my knee taped up, to walking on my own.

And those first few steps to freedom were... indescribable.

As horrific it was, the experience of paralysis, it was equally as joyful taking those first few steps to walking again. I will forever be indebted to the exceptional Neuro-Physiotherapists at Epworth Richmond, especially Gavin Williams.

It was in my sessions that I met and spent every day with other patients that were going through similar things following car accidents and strokes. So many stories, so much suffering.

I found that I had re-evaluated my life, and I was grateful to finally be getting better. This kind of experience changes you, it humbles you.

Another man that got me walking again, in conjunction with the Physiotherapists, was an Applied Kinesiologist, Dr. Michael Bay.

The Kinesiology sessions woke the nerve pathways up from my muscles back up to my brain, as they are connected via the nervous system.

At the start the Physiotherapists warned me that it would take time to learn how to walk again, pick things up, drive a car, and get back to normal life. And it was going to be work and luck if it came back at all.

I ran in 6 weeks.

One year on I now had full function back in my body.

This inspired me to go back to study. Kinesiology and addressing my nutritional needs helped me restore my mobility back so well, that I returned to College to study for a Diploma in Sports Kinesiology. This in turn helped me to unravel the complexities of Autoimmune Disease and inflammation.

I believe that a number of things, in combination, have helped keep my MS dormant for the past 6 years now. Treating the 'cause' has been the big key. Providing my body with the right nutritional requirements to restore health, eliminating toxins, learning how to be connected again in life / meditation, finding happiness in my life again after loosing so much from that big attack I had.

I followed a Nutrition Protocol, addressed my gut health and toxicity and dealt with all the emotional links that come with disease. I had to learn how to connect again to get my life back on track, physically, emotionally and biochemically.

"Loose what needs to be lost, to find what needs to be found."

I have now dedicated my life to teach others how I achieved this, through my Consulting Clinic called 'Bend Like Bamboo' and Public Speaking. I am currently writing a book about my journey to wellness.

I consult with people with all types of Autoimmune Disease, symptoms of bladder urgency and frequency, depression and anxiety, fatigue, fertility and hormone imbalances, pain, sports injuries, fascia and gait rehabilitation.

You can find me here: www.bendlikebamboo.com

The best way to describe Kinesiology is it's like physical psychology. Think of Acupuncture and Counselling in one session without the needles!

90% of our brain capacity stems from the subconscious part of the brain, which is in charge of our memories, and past experiences. It is from these memories and experiences that our core beliefs, behaviours and habits and formed, usually from age 0-6 years old.
It is this subconscious part of the brain that we access as Kinesiologists, via the integrity of the muscles when muscle testing. This allows us to connect with your entire human system, your mind and body.

Rather than someone else telling you what they think is wrong, and

what they think the solution is, a Kinesiologist will use muscle-testing to

connect with you, consulting your system for the right answers and the

right questions. This avoids a trial-and-error approach with your health and

wellness.

Your system shows us what is actually happening, and guides us in developing the best solution.

It also works because the whole of you (thoughts, emotions, muscles, organs, hormones, nutrition and energy) is considered as we find a solution.

Your muscles are connected to your brain via the Nervous System and run through multiple meridians according to Traditional Chinese Medicine. Kinesiology can help you to access blocked emotions, blocked Qi and fear-based beliefs that can limit you, ultimately causing physical symptoms and illness. As a last resort these blocks appear physically in the body if they are not addressed, dealt with and resolved. The results for me have been truly astounding.

I still have MS, but you wouldn't think so now. My journey to wellness has inspired me. I now share my knowledge to others in need.

I hope I have given you an insight about MS, what it is and how it has affected me, my life and my family. I hope that by sharing with you my story of loss and triumph, that you come away feeling inspired. I hope I have sparked some motivation, to start your own discovery of disease prevention and wellness.

I am grateful for the little things in life. Like being able to go out for dinner, and pick up my glass that I'm drinking. To feed myself with two hands and to wear heels if I so desire. Because I can!
This is the space where healing occurs and manifestation becomes possible. When your subconscious core beliefs are aligned with what you actually desire for yourself in your reality around you - then it will be so.

Find your passion, live it every day and express it to all that cross your path.

I wished for good health again and I found a way to express that desire through the roles I now have and in being of service to others. This brings me so much joy, everyday.
In doing so, I stumbled on a very valuable life lesson: that wish you truly want for yourself, weather it be love, health, money – find a way to give it out to others that cross your path - and it will come back tenfold to you.

Kinesiology helped me walk again, helped me fight my MS attack and brought me back to myself, after so much loss and change, and I cannot recommending it enough.

Having MS has not stopped me from doing things in life. I have to slow down and look after myself. But I am so glad that I discovered, that purely by slowing down, stripping it all back, and focusing on the simple pleasures, we all have the luxury to enjoy every day.... is the recipe to happiness.

Amanda Campbell

In 2004 I was diagnosed with Multiple Sclerosis (MS), which lead to a paralysis in 2009, when I lost my ability to walk, wash myself and feed myself.

After a fast paced life working in the Fashion Industry my world completely stopped and was turned upside down.

It was a time of true loss that led to a miraculous awakening.

With a 50/50 chance to walk again I ran in 6 weeks.

I have now dedicated my life to teach others how I achieved this.

With the assistance of Kinesiology Therapy and adopting Dr Terry Wahls' Nutrition Protocol, I have made a full recovery, and wish to share my journey back to wellness.

Kinesiology taught me the skills that helped me achieve this and gave me the tools to make this important transition for myself.

It is in this better state of mind, that I learned how to control it and got my life back again, and ultimately my health.

As a MS Ambassador, Motivational Speaker with a Diploma in Sports Kinesiology, I now hope to make a difference in people's lives and help others deal with managing the symptoms of MS.

I speak at various events with the hope to inspire people with my story of loss and triumph, by spreading my message of disease prevention by living a happier and healthy life. I share my lessons learned along the way and educate others about my research and my journey back to wellness.

I consult with all Autoimmune Disease cases, anxiety, depression, and transitional change at my Clinic in Prahran Bend Like Bamboo.

Work-life Balance

— Achieving Success without giving up your life in the process

I have a confession to make. If you were to ask me 15 years ago if it was possible to have a job you love and a meaningful and satisfying life, I'm sure I would have responded with explosive laughter and a look on my face that said "You must be joking." As an Expert in the field it's hard to admit it, but I wasn't always expert at my craft.

In the summer of 2001 I had just wrapped up a job as a Business Development Manager for a Start-up offering organic and locally sourced lunches to downtown business people. I had so much fun at the job I had to peel myself away from work every night and in the morning I couldn't wait to get back to it. Can anyone say workaholic?

Newly unemployed and itching for a change, I started the search to look into buying a business of my own where I could do something I thought would be both fun and challenging. My plan was to turn a business around and then sell it a year or two later (at a profit of course) and then go back to being a Business Development Consultant with another success under my belt.

Not long after my search began I found a local lunch take-out style restaurant that was losing $5,000 - $10,000 per month. I could see that they weren't operating up to their potential and I could imagine myself coming in to save the day. So, on August 13th of 2001 I took the plunge and closed escrow on my new restaurant having no clue what might be lurking just ahead.

Less than 30 days into my new career as a successful restaurant owner tragedy struck. Most people know what happened on September 11th with the World Trade Center. But can you guess what happened on September 12th? Nothing. Not one person came into the restaurant and no one placed an order to go. Our already low sales were almost non-existent and it was pretty much the same for the rest of the month.

I couldn't believe what was happening. At this new business where we were already losing money, things got worse and I started to get scared. I knew I had a choice to make and I would have to make it fast. I could either walk away from the hefty investment I had plopped down just a few weeks earlier or I could make some changes ASAP.

After weighing the options I decided to stick in there and make a go of things. I mean it wasn't too late, was it? I knew this was going to be a challenge but I felt that was still possible to come out on top if I was willing to do things differently than I originally planned. Dramatically different.

So on September 30th I called a staff meeting and put my plan in play. In one day I let go of the bookkeeper, the laundry service, the lunch delivery guys, the weekend dishwasher, the person who did payroll, the manager, and food service delivery company. And guess what I did on October 1st? And, no, it wasn't drink heavily. I took on all of these roles in addition to the responsibilities I was already handling and began working 7 days a week, 12-18 hours each day.

Well I said I had a confession to make so here it is. For the next 4 months I worked every day. My family and friends pretty much wrote me off because not only did I not have time to see them but I was too busy to even return calls. Outside the restaurant my social life was non-existent. I stopped exercising and eating well too. If I slept 6-1/2 hours consecutively it was a good night. Most of the time I felt like a cat being swung by its tail trying to grab onto something solid. There was too much to do and not enough time, money, or energy to get it done.

Then a miracle happened. In the 5th month we broke even and by the 7th month the financial bleeding had stopped and we continued to grow. There was no such thing as work-life balance because I didn't have a life to speak of. Thankfully, by the 9th month I was able to back down to working only 6 days a week and I hired an assistant manager to pick up some of the slack. As much as the business was growing more and more profitable every day, I felt like there were 1,001 things that had to be done and there was not enough of me to go around. I didn't know how to get off the hamster wheel.

Even though the business was profitable and I eventually made it down to working 5 days a week only 8-12 hours a day, the restaurant practically broke up my marriage. So, I had another choice to make. I could continue growing the business or follow my original plan to move on.

In my 23rd month I met two naïve guys, I mean two very nice guys, who wanted to buy my restaurant. I provided them with financial reports showing our steady growth over the preceding 18 month period along with documented systems so that they could step into my turnkey operation and takeover without much effort. Within 3 weeks we came to an agreement and we signed papers, and I sold my restaurant at a profit.

Success was had, but at what price? Even if you don't own a restaurant, perhaps you've been there and done that. I've shared my dirty little secret now the question is... do you have one of your own?

What is Work-life Balance?

Well before you break down and confess to all your shortcomings let's first take a look at what work-life balance really is (or isn't).

If you want to determine if you are getting work-life balance right you first need to determine what makes a life "balanced." The obvious solution might be to count the number of hours you work and compare that to the number of hours in a day and decide if the ratio is "in balance" (or at least something you can live with). Well, the answer you get might give you the solution to a math problem but I've found when it comes to work-life balance it's not the math that really matters.

I think It's fair to say that we are each unique beings. Therefore it would only make sense to say that what is meaningful to one person may hold limited or even no value to the next. In other words, it's up to each of us uniquely to determine what a rewarding life looks like and what work-life balance really is for us uniquely.

When most people talk about what makes a meaningful or even soul-satisfying life, it boils down to the relationships they have created, the joy they have experienced, and the satisfaction they have felt as a result of what they have accomplished over their lives.

As much as you could create a list of things you have accomplished and count all the times you have engaged with friends in a deep and meaningful way the truth is, the numbers aren't really what counts. Pay attention to the feelings you have on a day to day basis. If you are happy and satisfied, **then** decide if your life is in balance. And if not, what would take to get there?

Let's take a look at a few different scenarios:

Jill M.

Jill is a busy Day Spa owner. She works between 5-6 days a week on average for 2-12 hours a day. She opened her business to give women (and a few men) in her community a place they could unwind and be pampered in a relaxed setting because she wanted a place like that for herself (she's a customer too). Jill knows that her business is enhancing the lives of others and she feels really good about that. Jill knows that most of her clients feel better after visiting her Spa and that makes her feel good. Even though Jill spends many hours at work, her kids are happy she has found something she loves and her husband says he always knows where to find her. Although her social activities mainly revolve around her work (with staff and customers) she feels good about what her day to day life looks like even if she puts in more than 50 hours a week. Most days she would tell you she is having fun.

Monica W.

Monica and her husband co-own a Bakery. She has 2 school-aged children. A driving force in Monica's life is her passion about making an impact on the environment so that she can feel like she has made the earth a better place to be for her kids. She takes the early shift at the bakery so she can pick her kids up from school at 3:00 pm. Usually that means that she has already worked for more than 10 hours each workday before tending to her duties as Mom. Family life is a non-negotiable for Monica. The same goes for taking holidays and making sure that she is part of something larger, like attending church every weekend, and putting in countless hours as a volunteer for various causes. Monica would tell you that her life is full, but that she laughs a lot and feels like every day is a blessing.

So after reading Jill's and Monica's stories, who do you think is living a balanced life?

Well that was actually a trick question because if you asked them, each would tell you that their lives feel in balance. The point here is that work-life balance is personal. You get to choose what work-life balance looks like for you, uniquely.

Do you absolutely adore your work? Do you feel like you couldn't imagine anything else you'd rather be spending your life doing? Are you having so much fun that it's hard to peel yourself away from work at the end of the day? Well, it's possible you are already in balance. On the other hand, if spending time with family or friends trumps everything, then you'll be in balance when you are carving out time for family and creating meaning in your life.

Can You Have it All?

The question is... Can you have it all? A thriving business or a job you love AND a rewarding and balanced life? In a word, yes. That is yes if you are willing to invent or reinvent your life so that you are taking time, on a regular basis, for the things in life that you feel are most important, the things that create for you personally "a balanced life."

How Do You Know When You're Doing it Right?

If you are not living your version of a balanced life, or if you aren't sure if your life is in balance, where do you start? With the obvious of course.

Exercise:

Begin by asking yourself the following question:

How do I know when my life is in balance?

Then create a list outlining your answers. Perhaps your life is already somewhat in balance and you didn't even know it! After answering this question several times with all the answers you can come up with you'll want to dig a little deeper.

~~~

You know how when you want to take a vacation most of the time you don't just get into the car and then drive until you land somewhere? For most people they chose a destination. Then they determine when they'll travel, where they'll stay, who they'll vacation with, and if they are really organized they'll even have an idea of what they'll do when they are officially on holiday. Well the approach to creating a balanced and meaningful life works the same way as planning for your next vacation. If you don't know where you are going (the balanced life) you may not know when you get there.

Figure out what you want

After selling my restaurant I made a lot of promises to myself for the future. There were things that I was never going to repeat and others that I knew I wanted again down the line. As much as I may have given up most of my personal time during those 23 months, I came out of the experience with a great sense of satisfaction. We served local people delicious food all week long and on the weekends we catered weddings, corporate affairs, family reunions, and other events. Through planning, preparing, and serving at these events I knew my business was helping people enjoy the events they dreamed of while giving them positive memories they would cherish for the rest of their lives. That felt great.

When I decided to open my next business I was very clear that I wanted to know that I was making a difference in the world. For me this became one of my non-negotiables (and still is).

Now is the perfect time to start creating an outline of what it is that you want where work-life balance is concerned.

Exercise:

Dream Big and Create Your Own Vision for Personal Work-life balance

Take some time to give some thought to your life up until this point. Think about what worked for you and what didn't turn out so hot. Then, give yourself permission to Dream Big! Imagine what your ideal day to day life would look like where work-life balance is concerned. Capture your Vision for what life could be like when you have finally created a life you love.

Think about how you can reinvent the way you do business now so you can live a life you'd be proud of living. Include the aspects that will bring you joy and satisfaction. Don't hold anything back. Think of this vision as your own little secret. It's not about looking good on paper or impressing anyone. It's about living your life in a way that gives you time and energy to do what you enjoy in a balanced way.

~~~

Once you create your Vision for work-life balance, do your best to tell the story in a positive tone. Rather than saying "I'm not bothered by anyone during the day" turn the statement around and think about what you do want. Your new sentence might say something like "My office is quiet and private. I have the space I need during the day to focus and get things done."

If you have written down a vision that seems impossible, you may want to check in with a few other people to help you fine tune it so that it feels realistic and do-able. Remember, no one drops 100 pounds in a day and the same goes for changing your life where getting more in balance is concerned. Start by creating a vision that you feel is possible or just outside of the realm of possibility. The goal would be for you to be able to step into your vision in the next 1-4 months and then set a new goal to take you to the next big leap.

What Can You Do to Stay on Track?

Once you've got a good outline of what your vision for work-life balance is and what your non-negotiables are your next step is to:

Recommit Yourself Daily

When something is important to us, like a love relationship, we set the intention to make a long-term commitment to it (by getting married). If you want to transform your life into one that feels energized, empowered, and rewarding, recommitting yourself on a daily basis is a great way to help you stay on track.

Exercise:

Start by reading your vision for your ideal work-life balance every morning. Remind yourself of your non-negotiables and the role models who are "doing it right" so you can remind yourself that if others can do it, so can you. Stop and think of 3 things you are grateful for and then set an intention to stay balanced and to make this life of yours enjoyable and satisfying. You may want to create a ritual (either imagined or physical) to help ground you in this new life you are creating and practice it daily.

Adopt the Habits of Work-life balance Thrivers

So what is a Thriver?

A Thriver is someone who has integrated balance into their lives giving them more time, more energy, and more Zest for life on a daily basis. They have learned what they need to do personally so that they can show up consistently to the best of their ability and live a life they enjoy.

You've already learned the first two steps every work-life balance Thriver knows;

- Be clear about what you desire
- Commit to it daily

But what else keeps these who have mastered the process on track?

1. Know Your Whys

Your "Whys" are the fuel to help you stay on track when the going gets tough.
Whenever we take on a new habit or behavior it's not uncommon for things to start off with a bang and then over time see that your new resolve has fizzled out. If you want to stay committed to your new balanced life you need to have some very good reasons to stick with your plan. That's where your "Whys" come in.
There are two main "Whys" to consider:
First Why – **Why do you do what you do?**

Think about your work. Why are you doing this work and why are you putting in your time, energy, and for some people, money? The real question is – what's in it for you?

Second Why – **Why will Staying in balance help you achieve that goal?**

Consider your goals and identify how your new commitment to work-life balance can enhance your ability to get there.

Exercise:

Write down 3 reasons why you do what you do.

Next record 3 reasons staying in balance will support you.

~~~

Now as you move forward with your plan for work-life balance when you get derailed or find yourself just a little bit less motivated you can come back to your Whys to help you get that train back on the track.

   2.   **Master Your Mindset**

Ideally when you start a new project you want to adopt a beginner's mind. The more you can do to stay curious and open-minded the better chance you have for staying on track with your new work-life balance system.

In addition to staying open-minded remember to be patient with yourself. If you are a recovering workaholic you'll want to ease yourself in slowly and make sure you are setting yourself up for success. Be prepared mentally and emotionally for the busy time before it strikes and have a plan for what to do when stress, overwhelm, or frustration take control. The better you get at being able to quickly get out of a funk, or move beyond overwhelm the better!

   3.   **Surround Yourself with a Support Team**

If you are embarking on new behaviors, keep in mind you don't have to go it alone. In fact, you'll increase your chances for success if you move out of isolation and surround yourself with a positive and supportive team to help you stay on track. Then you'll have some allies to help you celebrate when you stick to your new plan!

Just like when you start a new exercise program or decide you are going to diet to lose those last 20 pounds, there are people who will champion you and others who simply won't be any help at all. Whether these not so helpful types (I call them Success vampires) intend to or not, their words or actions might keep you practicing you old patterns or habits making it that much harder for you to stay on track.

Let's look into the story of Jessica K.

Jessica is an Assistant Branch Manager for a large retailer that prides itself on excellent customer service and a company culture of caring. The company offers several outlets and trainings to support the well-being of their team throughout the year. Their philosophy is: We treat the customers and others on our team like respected and appreciated dear friends.

Work-life balance is something that the company has identified as being important for the management group in each location to oversee.

Knowing that the company generates over 60% of its annual gross revenue between mid-November and the middle of January, everyone on staff mentally gears up for the holiday rush knowing that 12-14 hours days and high stress will be expected.

All year long Jessica has sat in management meetings where someone from the corporate office shared how important supporting the staff was to the overall success of the company. So Jessica had an idea. This holiday season she was going to make sure that work-life balance was in full force. A more relaxed staff could mean better customer service right? And maybe that just might result in higher sales.

Jessica got approval from the corporate office to set up trainings before the busy season to help everyone on staff prepare for what they can do to stay on track all year round. Then November rolled around and the closer and closer they got to Black Friday, the biggest shopping day of the year, the more stressed out Jim, Jessica's boss became. This was the exact opposite of what she had hoped.

Jim (the store manager) said he was onboard and then Jessica learned that his actions were giving others on the team the idea that nothing had changed. Since Jim set the tone for the entire group, Jessica knew she needed to check in with him ASAP!

When Jessica talked to Jim, he agreed with her philosophy that having his team feel well-rested and well-supported was a great idea. He also acknowledged that he hadn't really changed. As much as Jim was under tremendous pressure to meet financial goals, he agreed that he would be willing to try things a little differently. Although it wasn't his intention he was sabotaging Jessica's success until he agreed to give her system a try.

The outcome? The team did their best to practice their new work-life balance system through the busy season. Some people felt it was the easiest year ever and the best part... the company exceeded its all-time sales records. Overall it was a win for all.

~~~

So like Jessica it's important to find a team of support when you decide to make changes (for yourself or everyone on staff). Make sure that you've got someone who can help you remember your Whys when you get off track. Have someone else on your support team help you make sure that you are taking time off for yourself, and another to help you celebrate your successes.

Find a coach or accountability buddy to help you stay on track and help you make keeping your life in balance a priority. And do your best to surround yourself with healthy uplifting people.

4. Have a Plan

Create systems to support you all year round.

Thrivers know that there will be good days when it feels like the whole world is conspiring for your success and bad days with challenges along the way. They are prepared and ready for whatever crosses their paths.

If you know that the high time at work, summer months, or the holiday season brings up frustrations or emotions that aren't helpful for your health or your productivity, then plan ahead for what you can do to change your state of being before the need arises. Find strategies for overwhelm and frustration before it arrives. Create a plan so you can stay focused and on track every day.

5. Declutter

Do what you can to eliminate clutter before the busy season starts. This includes your e-mail box, your home, and your car, as well as your circle of friends. Get rid of everything that isn't a good fit.

You'll be surprised by how much energy a whiny client or unreliable staff member sucks out of you. Same goes for a friend who is always on an emotional roller coaster. Or a family member who smothers you with love or one who is constantly complaining about how bad things are.

You don't have to get stuck in the same old habit or patterns. Clean your desk top, your file cabinet, and your e-mail inbox and then move on to letting go of stuff you no longer need. Don't be afraid to let go of clients you don't love and anyone on staff that isn't living up to your expectations. Learn how to control the time you spend with friends or family who don't share your commitment to a drama free life. Clear out the junk that doesn't serve you and make room for more of what you want.

6. Put Yourself First

Remember the best way to serve others is to give them the best you have to offer, not the leftovers. So, what do you need to do to make sure that you've got the best of you to give?

Know your boundaries and be willing to say, "No."

Practice saying, "No," and setting boundaries with your time. Remember, just because you <u>can</u> "do it," doesn't mean you <u>have</u> to do it. Reach out for support when you can, and be willing to walk away from anything that isn't essential. You don't get extra points for trying to be a superhero and doing it all. Reinvent your life so that you can be at your best for yourself first and then give back to the rest of the world.

Body, Mind, Spirit

Pay attention to your body, mind, and spirit and honor what works for you and your health. Take time out for meditation or relaxation and practice being a human being rather than a human doing for at least 10 minutes every day. Give yourself time to recharge and allow yourself to take some mental health breaks. Stay focused on what you love and decide to keep your life vibrant and interesting every day and don't forget to have fun!

7. **Celebrate Your Success**

Thrivers know how to party. They understand that when you "get it right" you need to make sure you reward yourself for what you've accomplished. Being prepared to celebrate is a part of setting yourself up for success by thinking like a winner.

Exercise:

Write down what your reward will be for mastering work-life balance for a day, a week, a month, and through your "busy season." Note: If your celebration includes someone else (ex. I'm going to take a trip to Hawaii with my best friend Susie) then reach out to them early on and let them know your plans. Then they can help motivate you to stay on track.

~~~

Work-life balance Success

So, where do you go from here? When venturing out into new behaviors and practices you'll want to give yourself time to take on new ways of doing things. Take each idea on one at a time until you start to get a feel for how it works before you challenge yourself with something new.

Although I'm a master at taking vacations (4-5 per year) and getting massage (almost weekly), I'm still not perfect where work-life balance is concerned. In fact, I'm far from it. My tendency even after years of practice is to lose myself in my work (which I love) and forget to take lunch or even go outside. But every day I keep trying, and like a fine wine, it seems like I'm getting a little better and better with age (and practice).

I know I've already said this, but I'll say it again. Be patient with yourself. Don't expect life to change dramatically overnight. Lean into your coach, accountability buddy, or people on your support team so you don't feel like you are going it alone. Try teaching what you are learning (even if you haven't quite mastered it) and be creative to help yourself stay on track.

When I was having trouble exercising on a regular basis I asked a neighbor if she could take me for walk when she went out with her dogs in the morning.

Whatever you do try to reward yourself often, maintain your sense of humor, and most of all, have fun.

Work-life balance is no longer a Mythical Unicorn. It is a real white horse that you can pet and saddle and ride into the magical life of your dreams.

Jennifer Martin

Jennifer Martin is a published Author, Speaker, Business Coach, and the founder of Zest Business Consulting. For more than 15 years she has helped Small Business Owners, Managers, and Executives get out of overwhelm and build thriving businesses while enjoying balanced, meaningful and soul-satisfying lives.

Jennifer works with clients all over the world offering one on one and group coaching programs as well as onsite presentations, workshops, and leadership trainings. She lives in Ojai, California with her sweetheart of 18 years.
Sign up here: **bit.ly/ZestBizNewsletter** to receive your copy of **10 Fast & Easy Ways to Get Out of Overwhelm and Feel More Balanced at Work**

To learn more visit: http://www.ZestBusinessConsulting.com

4 Strategical Steps To Overcoming Obstacles

I have always been someone who - most of the time - I knew where I was heading and what I wanted to achieve in life. Again, this was the case most of the time as of course, at times I did lose my direction when I got my eyes off what mattered most to me.

So because having goals and achieving them came natural to me, I thought that writing them down or having a defined structure to overcome obstacles is not something that I would ever need... that is until I had to do it first time myself. You see, an important factor in becoming a good coach is to be able to walk the talk, which means that I can only help other people through a transformation when I have gone through it myself. In other words, I can only work with someone in order to overcome their obstacles and achieve their goals by using a specific structure, a proven model, if I have experienced and used it myself.

So here I was in that seminar room thinking to myself "Yeah, whatever, I will do it, but it's not like is going to help ME much... I'll just do it for the purpose of this exercise." However, I was not prepared for what I have experienced then.

If you think similar to the way I used to think, and/or if you have overcome many obstacles in your life, you might ask yourself "Why do I need it? What's the point? Since I have overcome obstacles before and have achieved what I wanted, I do not need to know this." The truth is though that in a world of information overload and overstimulation of the nervous system, what people lack most is clarity. What structures and proven models do, is giving people such a crystal clear view that overcoming obstacles in order to achieve what you want becomes very easy no matter the circumstance. Think about it, how many times have you been in a situation where you wanted to achieve or obtain something, a specific outcome, and you wasted so much time and energy dwelling over the actual obstacles? Didn't you wish you had a step by step structure, which by simply following it you could have gained the clarity you needed to move towards your goal fast and steady?

Well, here is your answer, here's how it works, a system known by the acronym GROW, which stands for

Goal
Reality
Options
Way Forward

In this chapter I will be guiding you through this strategical step-by-step model, so that by simply following it you will be able to gain the clarity necessary to overcome any obstacles in your life as well.

Goal

So much has been said and so many books have been written about goal setting that I am sure you have at least heard about how important it is to have goals.

As Earl Nightingale put it:

"People with goals succeed because they know where they are going... It's as simple as that."

Imagine you want to drive somewhere you haven't been before and instead of setting your navigation system, you just drive off without being clear of how exactly you want to get there. You might get somewhere, but is it where you actually want to get to?

"It's common sense" you might say, but you will be surprised to find out that majority of people actually don't set goals, at least the important ones. They might spend more time planning their next holiday than setting important goals for their life.

Following are the findings of a Harvard Business study, which revealed remarkable statistics relating to goal setting:

83% of the population does not have goals

14% have a plan in mind, but are unwritten goals

3% have goals written down

The study found that the 14% who have goals are 10 times more successful than those without goals. The 3% with written goals are 3 times more successful than the 14% with unwritten goals.

So the reason why it is important to be clear about your goals is because knowing exactly what you want to achieve is the first step to gaining clarity of the overall situation.

Let's take an example. Your goal might be to achieve a senior management level in your career. You will need to be specific in regard to what role you want to be in – is it a CEO, Managing Director or CFO, the timeframe you want to achieve it in, how much do you want to earn in that position and why do you want to reach that level. By defining your reason, the big WHY behind your goal, you become clearer about your motivation and what achieving your desired outcome will mean for you.

Now is your turn. Describe your goal in the space provided below and in a specific and concise way. Remember, only when you can define exactly what you want, you can achieve it. So start with the end in mind. It may be something related to your private life, career or your business.

_____

_____

_____

_____

_____

_____

Reality

An objective reality check is what sometimes people struggle with. Some people are their own worst critic and do not believe in their talents and abilities to reach goals and as a result they don't go for what they truly want. The real cause is mostly a fear of failure, which means that if they try to reach their goal they may not be able to achieve it and hence they will not even give it a go.

The fact is – and this is what most of us do not realise - if we keep on trying then there is no such a thing as failure. It's just feedback on how it doesn't work. As long as we keep on trying, adapt and change our approach, our endeavour will not be a failure. Think of the inventor of the light bulb, Thomas Edison who tried thousands of times until he got the right filament material to work, glow well and be long-lasting for the end product that we use to have in our houses until it was replaced by the energy saving version.

Another example here is Oprah Winfrey, most iconic woman on TV, who – back at the beginning of her television career - was told that she was unsuitable for the screen. Or Michael Jordan, often praised as the best basketball player of all time, was not accepted into his high school's basketball team.

Imagine if these people – and so many others for that matter – would have stopped trying, would have succumbed to their fear of failure. The truth is, fear of failure is a universal fear, as we all experience it to various extents at some point in time in our lives. The key to success is to overcome this fear.

"There is no failure except in no longer trying" Elbert Hubbard

So an objective reality check would be – compared to your goal – where are you right now?

Taking the example given in the **Goal** section, where would you be right now? You may be let's say, at the medium management level. In this context a reality check will include an analysis of your resources (skills, capabilities, knowledge, emotional intelligence) - which you require in order to be able to achieve your goal.

To continue with our example, questions you would ask yourself would be:
Who do I need to be in order to achieve my goal? What attributes do I need to have for that?

What attributes does a CEO, Managing Director or CFO have that I need to embody?

Where am I right now compared to all the above? What do I need to learn in order to achieve the required level for that position? Is it a course? Is it a practical skill? Do I need a coach or a mentor?

These days it is common practice for leaders to be honed into their new role with the help or coach and/or mentor. Organisations learned from the past mistakes when people were promoted into leadership roles just because they were good performers in their technical profession, so they were expected to perform as just good in a leading position. The reality is that these are two completely different types of roles. The consequence was that so many people were seriously struggling in their leadership roles. It was learning the hard way that being a leader requires far more than technical skills.

Now is your turn to describe where you are at the moment compared to where you want to be. The above example may not be relevant to you, but the structure is cross contextual.

So ask yourself these questions:

Where do I want to be?
Compared to that, where am I right now?
Paraphrasing the above questions – What attributes does a person who already achieved your goal need to have in order to achieve it? Or imagine you have achieved your goal already – what attributes did you need to tap into, what skills did you need to use in order to achieve your goal?

What am I missing, what do I need to acquire (skills, capabilities, knowledge, attributes) in order to achieve my goal?

What supportive relationships / alliances do I need to build in order to move towards my goal?

The answer here is not supposed to be something like "I need to win the lottery in order to achieve my goal". As much as we are interdependent to our environment, your outcome must be self-initiated and maintained and not entirely dependent on other people or external circumstances on which you have no influence.

_____

_____

_____

_____

_____

_____

Options

If the reality check was somehow focussed on the gaps or problems arising from your current situation, the options section is focussed on the solution, because this is all about identifying all possibilities lying in front of you.

This is a step that is often forgotten because many people focus so much on the problems, gaps or road blocks that they forget that there are always more than one option to overcome that situation.

When I say 'possibilities' I refer to them with no judgement about their quality – good or bad, which means that both opportunities and traps should be taken into account.

There are two reasons for this.

Firstly, to gain a clear overview all options should be assessed. Secondly, when people perceive that they have only one option, they feel stuck. Having just two options is not real freedom either. Only when people see multiple possibilities they feel empowered because they feel like there are choices available, that they have the power of decision and influence over their situation.

So what this means in practical terms will become clear as we continue exploring the previous example.

Since you discovered where you are at right now compared to your goal, what are your options?

To start with, one possible option is to do nothing, which means to stay where you are and not achieve your goal. This may not make you happy, but whether you like this option or not, it is still a possibility, that is in case you listen to your fear of failure, which, remember, we all have to a certain extent. Looking at this possibility may even give you that extra motivation to take action and achieve your goal because it highlights an outcome that you most probably do not want to have.

To continue with the example of achieving a senior management level in your career, another option here would be to express your desire with the respective decision makers in your current organisation. If this is welcomed there might be a mutual plan set up in order to get you where you want to be, which might include KPIs from your side and support for you to develop into that role, such as courses and coaching.

Another scenario could be that in your current organisation there is no place for you to move up in the hierarchy or there could be just a mismatch between your aspirations and values to the ones of your current organisation. In this case a third option would be to look elsewhere for an opportunity and to find an organisation for which your ideas and values are a fit.

A good example here is Steve Jobs, who left Apple in 1985 after a power struggle with the board of directors. In 1996 he returned to an almost bankrupt Apple Inc. By 1998 he was able to bring Apple to profitability. The rest is history.

Now is your turn again. Describe here ALL your options you see lying in front of you. As you write them down, just notice your feelings about each one of them. What feeling do you notice when you think of the possibility of doing nothing and staying the same? Most probably "No way!" is your answer.

_____

_____

_____

_____

_____

_____

Way Forward

After assessing all your options, the one that stands out most for you is going to be your way forward, your opportunity to achieve your goal by following and implementing it.

The way you recognise your best option as thus: as you think of your chosen option, what feelings do you notice? Is it excitement and empowerment? What are you telling yourself? Is it something along the lines: "This is great! I can definitely see myself doing it!"? If you can connect with the image of yourself taking that particular path and achieving your goal by doing so, then you chose the right way forward for your situation. In other words, you need to *believe* that you can achieve your goal by taking that option in order to be able to follow with the required actions.

"But what if the option I took doesn't work or turns out to be a bad idea?" you may say. You are right, this can happen, but at the same time what also happens is that – as long as you set your mind to look for *other* options in such cases - as soon as one door closes, another one opens for you. As Sean Stephenson said "Until you *believe* you have options, you'll continue to feel stuck."

I remember coaching Mark S., an aspiring Managing Director of a medium size company in Sydney. He had a few options that he could take up at that time, but he found it hard to decide which one would get him closer to his goal. The strategy that I taught him and that helped him to move forward is amazingly simple. I got him to ask himself one question:

If I make a choice and it doesn't turn out to be the right one, can I handle the worst case scenario/ consequence?

If the answer is yes, then it becomes clear that from the perspective of that particular point in time you are making the right decision, you are taking the right option.

This strategy helped Mark S. and many other clients, therefore it can help you as well. It's simple, but powerful.

To conclude the example of achieving a senior management level in your career by following the four steps, a way forward could be to look at your opportunities and discuss them with the decision makers within you current organisation. If this turns out not to be a good idea, in the sense that you realise that there is no suitable role for you there, what is the worst case scenario? Your manager will find out about your aspiration of taking the next step up your career ladder. He will either not care, encourage you or feel threatened by you, right? As there is no suitable role for you within your current organisation, would you still want to continue putting your energy and ideas into that place anyway? Probably not. So what it was thought to be a bad idea, it turned out to be an opportunity for you to find out earlier in the processes about the right way to go. This is a great example of how, by asking yourself a simple question like "What is the worst case scenario?", not only you realise that you can easily handle it, but you can even turn it into something positive, because in every adverse situation, there is a positive learning.

After having assessed all your options, write down the one that you want to move forward with.

_____

_____

_____

_____

_____

_____

Final Thoughts

There is more than one way to achieve your goal and each one will unfold in front of you as you step forward, because with every step you take you will be able to see further and learn new things about yourself, others and the world, about the capabilities that you never thought you have.

In contrast, if someone doesn't trust themselves to take any of their options because they may not feel like they are able to handle the unknown of the next step, then they will not be able to grow and learn how to overcome obstacles in life.

The truth is that there is no growth in staying within your comfort zone, which means that only by stepping out of it, by doing something new and challenging, you will be able to grow.

Once you have mastered a new challenge it means that you can do it again, and again, and again. It is like a muscle that you train and by doing so it becomes bigger and stronger every time. Slowly you will see that you can lift weights that are heavier and heavier, which means you can solve problems that are more and more difficult.

With time, facing new challenges will become an easy task for you. Imagine how confident this will make you feel, knowing that you can now deal with any kind of problems. You have just created a new belief about yourself, that you can solve any kind of challenges you may face along the way.

This is the mechanics – if you like – of creating new beliefs. It starts with just one step, with a decision to step outside of your comfort zone and take one of the options presented to you at that time. And then you take another step and another one, as you realised that handling the uncertainty, the unknown of whether it is going to work out or not, is not as difficult as you thought. The more steps you take the more evidence you see that your new beliefs about yourself and your capabilities are true.

This is when you realise that by following this step by step logical thought process presented in this chapter, every obstacle can be overcome. It is a proven and replicable process, which means that you can use it over and over again, regardless of the circumstance.

Since the first time I used the GROW model during that seminar, it has helped me to overcome many obstacles I faced while achieving my goals. I then realised something that I was not prepared for. I realised that by having a step-by-step structure or model, such as the GROW model, enabled me to reach a level of clarity and focus which I have never experienced before, and that it increased my overall performance.

Ever since I have started using it with my clients, the GROW model has helped them immensely in overcoming their obstacles. Now that you have worked through this chapter you have the evidence that it can work for you as well. So go ahead and use it, love it, share it!

To your success!

Corina Lorenzi

Corina Lorenzi started her career in Foreign Trade in 1996 in Germany and successfully climbed the corporate ladder thanks to her natural ability to achieve and perform at the highest standards. During this time Corina was able to observe many executives and identified the need of helping them to perform at their full potential as a way to make the organisations thrive as a whole. At the same time she developed strong relationships with her stakeholders, allowing her to identify opportunities and growth potential for these companies.

At that point, her next career step into the area of Business & Executive Coaching was only natural.

After undertaking further studies with internationally acclaimed coaches and mentors, Corina became a sought-after Business & Executive Coach recognised by the International Coach Federation and a certified Neuro-Linguistic Programing (NLP) Practitioner.

Using her extensive international experience and strong background in Sales and Foreign Trade, Corina then founded Elite Success Strategies, which focuses on helping business owners and leaders to create the thriving and profitable organisations they desire.

A major part of Corina's work is to develop Executives by preparing them to achieve and most importantly to sustain high performance. The globalization is facing Executives with new and ever changing challenges and Corina helps them to develop the necessary adaptive thinking ability to overcome them.

Today Corina lives in Melbourne, Australia, from where she conducts her business internationally, which is based on the idea of Constant And Never-Ending Improvement (CANI).

The study of human potential and behaviour, personal development and neuroscience are Corina's main areas of interest.

OUT NOW: HOW TO START A BUSINESS WITH LITTLE OR NO CASH

Available from Mithra Publishing

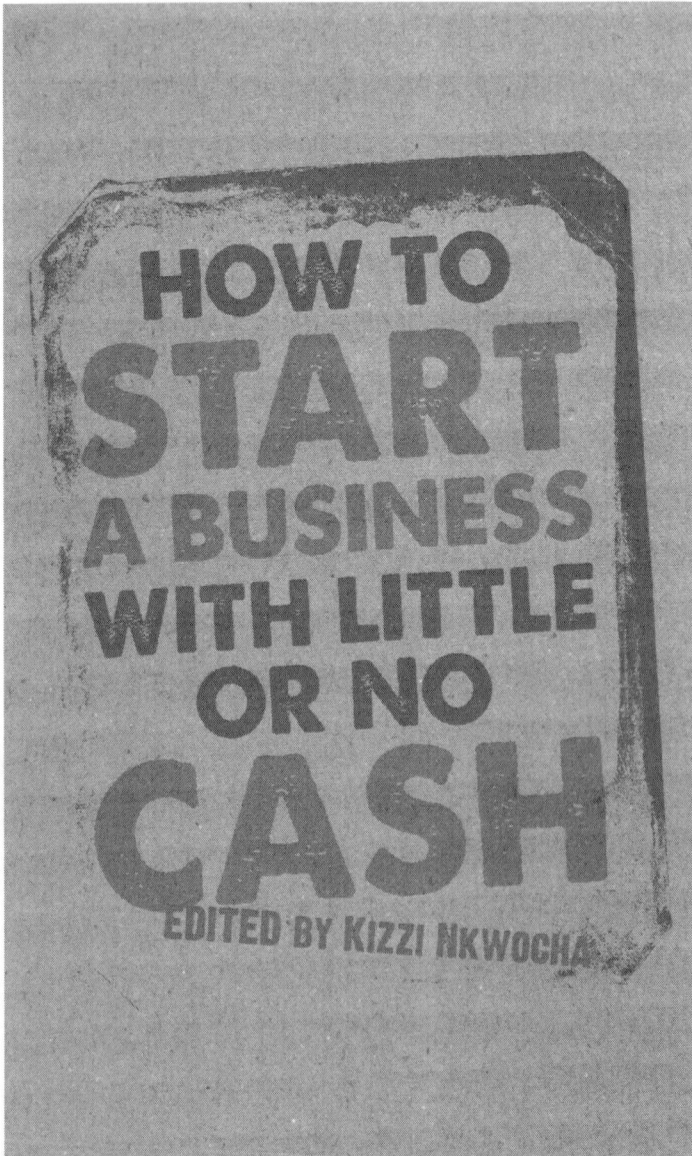

Printed in Great Britain
by Amazon.co.uk, Ltd.,
Marston Gate.

9298812R00158